Irons in the Fire

A HISTORY OF COOKING EQUIPMENT

RACHAEL FEILD

THE CROWOOD PRESS

First published in 1984 by
THE CROWOOD PRESS
Crowood House,
Ramsbury, Marlborough,
Wiltshire SN8 2HE

British Library Cataloguing in Publication Data

Feild, Rachael
Irons in the fire.
1. Kitchen utensils-History
I. Title
638′8   TX656

ISBN 0-946284-55-5

Designed by Wendy Bann

Set in 11 on 14 point Ehrhardt by
Alan Sutton Publishing Ltd, Gloucester

Printed in Great Britain by
The Pitman Press, Bath

Contents

-*Acknowledgements*-

Acknowledgements are due to the following for their help in supplying material for this book: to John Davis and Graham Hood, Directors of the Colonial Williamsburg Museum, Virginia; Dr Frank Sommer and Don Fennimore of the Winterthur Museum, the Henry Francis du Pont Winterthur Foundation, Winterthur, Delaware, for their valuable time and help; Ian Taylor, Director of the Castle Museum, York; Hugh Roberts for the freedom of his fascinating private collection; Tony and Elinor Foster; Michael Wakelin; Christopher Clarke; Derek Green of Cedar Antiques; Mac Humble; Belinda Gentle; Jeremy le Grice for his help and encouragement; Mrs Pam Walker for information on the Kenrick family; Mr A.V. Nichols for his help in explaining the mysteries of iron and steel; Martin Northey for his practical demonstration of the same mysteries at Birdbrook Forge, Berkshire; Blantern & Davis, Studio Wreford, Coverdale & Fisher, Barnes & Bradforth, Aubrey Mills and Nick Alloway for photography; and to the BBC Hulton Picture Library, the Mansell Collection, the Trustees of the British Museum, the Victoria & Albert Museum, the Museum of London, the Castle Museum, York, the National Trust for Scotland and the Colonial Williamsburg Museum, Virginia, for permission to reproduce photographs from their collections and archives.

My special thanks are due to Christopher Bankes for lending me his unpublished manuscript of receipts and recipes; to Christopher Bangs for editing out some of the worst errors, and for his general advice and knowledge of the subject; and, in the USA, to Tim and Betsy Trace for their very special help.

Rachael Feild

—1 The Kitchen:—
Outside and Inside

1 Spit-roasting fowl and piglet – from an illumination in the Louterell Psalter, 1340. *Mansell Collection.*

IT IS A PROVOCATIVE THOUGHT that the art of cooking developed because of a shortage of wood for burning. Cooking – the actual physical business of making raw food edible by roasting, boiling, grilling and frying – depends more on the materials available than it does on the creative imagination of great chefs. Indeed, it is generally accepted that it was this aspect of French cuisine which brought cooking out of the Dark Age. But, contrary to what that great nation of gastronomes would have us believe, the origins of *haute cuisine* lie not in France but in Italy. And the Italians owed little of their culinary expertise to their Roman forbears and a great deal to the Arab civilisations of the Mediterranean.

It was the Arabs who introduced the subtleties of flavouring with spices, and they who invented conserves and jellies made with sugar. It was the Arabs too who introduced the almond tree to Italy, and used the milky extract of almonds to thicken and flavour sauces. It was the people of the southern shores of the Mediterranean who discovered 'stone honey' by drying steeped sugar-cane in the sun until it formed crystallised sugar. In their sparsely wooded lands they cooked on charcoal braziers to conserve fuel, and their traders returned from India and China with the basic inner truths of culinary art – that of the five flavours and the four humours – and restored to Europe a hygienic, balanced and scientific approach to food which had been lost in the over-rich, ostentatious tables of Rome's old empire.

The Crusades took European warlords and their households into new territory, with new customs and traditions. When the conquerors returned, with sodomy and syphilis, cinnamon and mace, they marched up the long leg of ancient Rome, from ships which had brought them to Amalfi and Naples. Between these two trading ports lay Salerno. It was in Salerno that Galen the Greek physician practised his *nouvelle cuisine,* in a pocket of ancient Rome hemmed in by Byzantium and Islam, under the auspices of the Benedictine monks of Monte Cassino. An eclectic background indeed, from which came a whole new delight of sugared confits and jellies, scented with rosewater and orangewater, little braziers filled with charcoal for more intense, controlled heat, frying pans, small saucepans for reducing broths to basic sauces, the use of sheep's milk and goat's milk, and new cheese-making processes. Hygiene too was part of Galen's Graeco-Roman-Italian health regimen, though this seems to have had more effect on the knights crusaders' eating habits than their cooks' culinary practices. Finger bowls and napkins proliferated – and none too soon, for everyone from Constantinople to Carlisle ate with their fingers, which they dipped into the common dish.

It was not too difficult for the Greeks and Romans to achieve the culinary heights they are reputed to have reached, for their knowledge of ventilation, air ducts, hygiene and architecture was highly civilised. They paid a great deal of attention to the pleasures of life, as well as to expanding their empire and opening up trade with the rest of the world. But it was not so easy for the people variously described as Britons, Celts or Anglo-Saxons, who inhabited the damp and foggy islands on the other side of the water from the Franks and Gauls. Even though the Romans penetrated far to the north of Britain and built themselves beautiful villas and bath-houses, in which they lived almost as comfortably as they did at home under the blue Mediterranean sky, their influence was only temporary. When the Romans left, they took with them their skills of brick-making, metal-working, road building, architecture and design, and Britain sank back into its smoky, foggy, unhygienic way of life without a murmur. The Romans had used the fertile wheat-growing expanses of England as a granary for their empire and introduced olive oil and spices into the kitchens of the conquered barbarian kings, but there was neither olive oil nor cinnamon to be found in the dark chaos which followed their departure.

Between the going of the Romans and the coming of the Normans, the barons and earls of England maintained their households in draughty keeps and moated manor houses, choked with smoke summer and winter from the central fires which burned without benefit of any chimney in their Great Halls. Around these central fires stood a quaint variety of iron supports on which great sides of meat were spitted and roasted, designed to feed the entire complement of their households from the lowest to the highest. The numbers to be fed were seldom less than fifty and often exceeded two hundred when feudal knights rallied to their barons' support. Early cooking in an Englishman's home was more akin to an army field kitchen than to a cosy dinner for a few well-chosen guests. Since there was no shortage of wood to encourage more delicate methods of cooking, fires were large and fierce and prevented the cooks from approaching close enough to do more than haul out the meat from seething pot or turning spit. And because of their dangerous unruliness, cooking fires were often removed from the main hall to an outside building, which could always be rebuilt if it burned down.

However, fires for light and heat blazed in the centre of keeps and castles for the first ten centuries of the Christian calendar. In poor houses they were built on the beaten earth of the ground floor, but noblemen would not countenance the idea of wading ankle-deep through the mess of mud, rushes and general dirt, compounded with other most unsavoury things, which constituted the ground floor. Their entrance, straight into the Great Hall, was up a flight of stone stairs outside the building, so that they arrived relatively clean and dry-shod. Because of the necessity for a central fire, the floor of the Great Hall was built of stone and was supported below by piers and arches of stone, which formed the 'undercroft'. In the centre of the undercroft was a vaulted chamber, reached only by a trap door inside the Great Hall, in which the lord kept his treasure, his arms and all his precious possessions – a personal bank vault secure from besieging armies, who could not break in and plunder except over the dead bodies of the defending household.

English castles tended to be square, squat and rambling. The Normans, when they came, brought their own way of life and built tall castles to symbolise their power which towered over the surrounding landscape. There was room in these high towers for a separate chamber on the second floor, where the lord and lady could retire from the noisy household in the Great Hall. The idea of a separate chamber greatly appealed to the English, but instead of copying the high round towers of the Normans, they extended the Great Hall over the bake house or 'pain-try' (adopting the French word for bread) and the 'bouteillery' or

2 The medieval kitchen at Stanton Harcourt, Oxfordshire, in the seventeenth century, unchanged except for the bread ovens, which have been bricked up to make smaller openings and fitted with oven doors. *Mansell Collection.*

buttery, where bread, wine, ale and provisions were kept, and turned the outhouses into a proper kitchen leading out of these closely-guarded store rooms. The kitchens were built on the same pattern as monastery kitchens, with great open hearths and vents in the ceiling to let out the smoke, though there were some with huge hooded chimneys in the side walls in areas where stone was quarried locally.

3 A seventeenth century kitchen with a woman scouring pewter dishes: a pot-hook hangs on the wall and a gridiron is propped against the dishes. *BBC Hulton Picture Library.*

By the thirteenth century life in England had become more settled and there was less need for the massive security of stone keeps and defensive buildings. Moreover, the great feudal barons were no longer prepared to leave the Great Hall and go down the outer stairs into the cold and damp in order to climb more outside stairs up to their private inner chamber. So the main entrance came down to ground level and stairs were built inside the main building to take the lord and his servants up to the inner chamber. The vaulted undercroft became cellars and store rooms, and the kitchen was properly attached to the main building, separated only by a screened passage leading out to the kitchen yard and the kitchen itself, built against the outer wall.

The Black Death brought prosperity and bricks to medieval England. With so few men and women left to till and plough the land, acre upon acre was turned over to sheep, which could be managed by a man and a dog. The wool trade made England rich and the ships which took the staple trade across the Channel returned from Flanders with their holds full of Flemish bricks for building. But many other facets of life suffered from lack of able-bodied men. There was less milk, butter, cheese and beef, because cattle were troublesome and had to be milked and driven to and from the impoverished pasture. Land which had grown pulses – peas and beans – and vegetables went back to the wild. Grain crops deteriorated in an inevitable chain of consequence: no cattle dung, no fertilising of the soil, poor harvests, no grain, no cattle. But at least there were bricks for Tudor mansions and fireplaces.

The most striking feature of the few Tudor mansions which have survived untouched is the forest of chimneys swirling and sprouting out of the roof, one to every fireplace in the house. The main ground plan was still much the same as the medieval castle, with the undercroft changed to a semi-basement which contained vaults to support the building, a central Great Hall and a single wing like the cross-stroke of a 'T' housing the pantry and buttery below and the inner chamber above. But the idea of balance and elevation was seeping in from the great 'surveyors', or classical architects, of Italy. Builders added a second wing to the house to make it H-shaped, with a winter parlour with a great bow window filled with coloured glass for the ladies to sit in and take their ease. No matter that the window in the other wing was wasted on the pantry or the buttery – symmetry was all. As time went on there was some rearrangement, and the pantry and buttery were moved to the back of the winter parlour, the Great Hall shrank in importance in favour of a dining parlour which ran the whole length of the second wing. The

4 An eighteenth century kitchen, behind the winter parlour which can be seen through the open door. A grand fireplace has been built into the old open hearth and the fire more or less contained behind clumsy bars. *Mansell Collection.*

kitchen yard was reached from the pantry and buttery and eventually, with plenty of bricks for chimneys, it was not long before it was incorporated into the house itself, often between the two wings at the back of the house. When this was the case, the kitchen chimney was quite often built back to back with the fireplace in the Great Hall and provided extra support for the walls of the house itself.

There were yeomen farmers by the fifteenth century, grown fat on wool, with money for manor houses instead of cold and uncomfortable farmhouses where they shared their living space with the animals. Their houses were based on grander ones, but in many cases their Great Halls served as kitchens too, and one hearth and one chimney was all they had. The store rooms were built behind the central chimney where they would be kept dry, and the chamber was above them, making the most possible use of the one source of warmth in the house. When, after the Reformation, the prohibition on baking bread was lifted, they built their bake ovens into the side of the central chimney and often added a bacon loft above it for smoking.

The day of reckoning had to come. By the sixteenth century there was no timber to spare in many parts of the country and the huge log fires sputtered and died. On the Continent charcoal had been used for centuries for cooking fires but England had had no need to economise – and now it was too late. Charcoal was desperately needed for making iron, glass, brass and copper. Timber was needed for building ships to fight the Spaniards and there was none to spare for domestic hearths in many areas of England. There was coal, though, and where it could be transported by water, it began to be used. Coal meant smaller fireplaces and thick iron firebacks to prevent the more intense heat from cracking and damaging the brickwork of the chimneys. Coal changed the shape of houses, inside and out. Iron baskets were needed to burn it in, grates were needed to make it manageable for cooking. The yeoman separated his kitchen from his parlour, the owners of the great houses cropped their forests of chimneys and built flues inside to carry the smoke from several fireplaces up and out of wider, lower chimneys hidden behind the smooth façades of the classical architecture which mathematician Sir Christopher Wren had made so fashionable. A different sort of fire changed the face of London in 1666 and when it was rebuilt every house had a coal-burning fireplace and a stout brick chimney.

Outside the cities, where there was no coal, continental cooking methods were imported and well-built country kitchens had brick-topped charcoal-burning cooking fires. Where there was still timber nothing changed – neither the design nor the shape of houses, nor the old habits of blazing log fires, spits, hanging cast iron cauldrons and down-hearth roasters and toasters. In old Tudor and Jacobean houses the kitchen court was enclosed by new additions to the building, or smoothed into the elevations of classical façades.

Living was infinitely more gracious by the end of the seventeenth century, and kitchens intruded an unwelcome, earthy flavour of smells and smoke. They were also a considerable fire hazard still. An occasional experiment by far-sighted Italian-influenced architects had taken them down into the old undercroft or cellar in coal-burning districts of England as early as the sixteenth century. But by and large the English preferred to set them apart, where they could not damage the air of gracious living. Robert Adam, that great classical architect, was entertained by the grandest in the land, at tables piled with fine dishes and *haute cuisine*, but he had little sympathy for those who sweated to

5 The kitchens of the Georgian House, Charlotte Square, Edinburgh, restored and equipped to their original condition. The square was built from a design by Robert Adam and building began in 1792. The kitchen is typical of a late eighteenth century house, with mechanical spit, separate cast iron oven, and smoking chamber above the fireplace for smoking hams or kippers. *National Trust for Scotland.*

6 The Great Kitchen in the Upper Ward of Windsor Castle as it was in 1800 (from Pyne's drawing in the Royal Library). The old louvres in the roof have been replaced by windows, but the butcher still carved up whole carcases and weighed the joints on steleyard scales. The baker stands by his bread ovens close to the dresser. *BBC Hulton Picture Library.*

produce them. One of his designs for a country villa shows that he sited the kitchens in a pit, sunk a considerable distance from the house, connected to the basement by an underground tunnel.

In Georgian towns, where houses were part of the grand design of sweeping crescent and street, kitchens sank below ground, reached by 'area steps', as though it were a place apart. Kitchen staff slept under the table or curled up on the floor by the fire. There was no access for them to the upstairs part of the house where those they served lived. The door through which the food must somehow come was padded with leather or baize to keep out the smell which rose from below, and it was carried up by a different, cleaner class of servant altogether. In the country, though the eighteenth century lady of the house was inordinately proud of her store rooms, still rooms and preserving rooms, she never ventured near the kitchens where the cooking took place. Her doors, too, were sealed with green baize to prevent any whiff or hint of food in preparation from penetrating into her elegant airy rooms.

The walls of every kitchen, be they high or lowly, were limewashed two or three times a year, the floors sluiced and scrubbed weekly, if not daily, and the dairy in particular was kept immaculate, for the least dirt would sour the cream and turn butter to cheese. Flies buzzed and bred and, if not somehow controlled, laid their eggs in the sides of hams hanging from the rafters, putrefying a whole winter's provisions. Switches of elder hung from every cottage dairy to discourage them, and kitchens of larger houses were painted blue to keep the flies away. The pigment that was mixed with the limewash was most probably made from woad, the weed that ancient British Kings made their own and gave England its Royal blue.

The conservative habits of the English changed very little from the first yeomen's houses in the fourteenth and fifteenth centuries to the turn of the nineteenth century. Samuel Bamford, nephew of a wealthy weaver, described his uncle's house at that time:

7 The Great Kitchen after modernisation in the 1850s. The open cooking fires have been bricked up and a single enclosed oven has been installed. Victorian Gothic beams have been added to the roof, and the working areas are lit with gas jets. *Mansell Collection.*

'My uncle's domicile, like all the others, consisted of one principal room called "the house"; on the same floor with this was a loom shop containing four looms, and in the rear of the house on the same floor were a small kitchen and scullery and a buttery. Over the house and loom shop were chambers; and over the kitchen and buttery was another small apartment and a flight of stairs.'[1]

Substitute 'the Hall' for 'the house' and the winter parlour for the loom shop and the pattern is virtually the same as it was in Tudor days.

It was probably plumbing which finally changed the place of the kitchen to the famous 'upstairs, downstairs' way of life at the beginning of the nineteenth century. The first roaring, greedy cast iron 'kitcheners' or kitchen ranges were installed, smoke-belching monsters which consumed scuttle-loads of coal, heating the water at the same time. At first, hot water was drawn off into brass or enamel jugs and carried by below-stairs maids to bedrooms and bathrooms, but soon nineteenth century plumbing technology embraced the idea of water rising by natural convection and conduction. The kitchen, as far as the rest of the household was concerned, was thankfully banished below stairs, with its dirty water-heating ranges and smutty chutes for coal in the pavement which debouched into the coal cellars in 'the area'. Alone, a miracle of science, clanking pipes carried the water up to huge brass taps and vast cast iron baths.

Today the kitchen has reverted to its proper place, as the warm centre of the household, the informal social gathering place for coffee and gossip, scented with mouth-watering cooking smells, decorated with old-fashioned crocks and copper pans, jars of herbs and spices and libraries of cookery books. Inquisitive cooks read about foreign cuisine and adventurous ones try it out for themselves. The odd piece of antique cooking equipment sits on the dresser, and perhaps fires the cook's imagination to start a collection of butter stamps or jelly moulds. The more we live with high technology, the more we seem to look over our shoulders at old customs and a way of life which, from this distance, is hazed with comfortable myth. The truth is all there, in the kitchen. The threads of every civilisation – its politics, wars, industry, agriculture, sport, law and custom, religious belief and pagan tradition, social customs, house-building and architecture, are nowhere more tightly woven together than in the tammy cloth, the hair sieve and the pudding bags of yesterday's kitchens.

——2 Preparation——

8 Sixteenth century kitchen from *Calendarium Romanum*, showing round-bellied cooking pot on a three-legged iron brandreth standing over an open-hearth fire. On the left the butcher deals with a whole carcase. *BBC Hulton Picture Library.*

THE EARLY, UNCOUTH INHABITANTS of pre-Roman Britain used whatever came to hand to prepare the raw materials for their food. They scraped meat from the hides of animals with flints or sharpened deer-antlers, crushed dried grain between stones, and used crude wooden mallets to crack open bones for marrow or to pound dried meat to an edible consistency. Their mortars were hollowed-out logs, their pestles rounded stones, and with these they pounded up roots and hedgerow herbs to add to the basic brew. With great ingenuity, they discovered that coarse sand added to clay produced a bowl with a surface rough enough to crush grains. They made apple corers out of sheep-shank bones and, once they had iron for knives, they carved rough wooden spoons and ladles.

By the time the Norman overlords imposed their foreign ways on the populace, the people of the British Isles had a basic form of cookery consisting mainly of roast meat and various brews of pounded grain mixed with blood or ground chicken, pork or veal flesh, known as pottages, mortrews and mawmeny. They knew how to prepare liquamen, amulum and verjuice, and how to make vinegar and alegar (beer vinegar), all legacies of Roman occupation. They had discovered the secret of rennet for making cheese, and as far back as Celtic days they had added beer barm to ground cereal and found yeast to rise their coarse bread. In Lincolnshire, Norfolk, Essex and Kent they made salt by evaporating sea water in great flat pans.

The tools they needed for such preparations were few. Liquamen, which formed the basic seasoning for many of their dishes and continued to do so for centuries, was made by taking oily fish such as mackerel, anchovies, sprats or whitebait and adding them to the entrails of larger fish. The whole unappetising mixture was steeped in water, then left to evaporate. The putrefying, concentrated juice which remained at the end of this operation was strained through a coarse cloth and stored in earthenware jars.

Verjuice, the univeral cook's friend, was simply the juice of unripened fruit, such as grapes, crab-apples or gooseberries, fermented to produce a sour-tasting liquor not unlike vinegar. It was added to pottages and, with its ferocious acidity, helped to break down the toughness of stringy, sinewy meat. Amulum, which thickened sauce, was prepared by soaking hard wheat-grains in successive changes of water for ten days, after which it was squeezed through a new linen cloth and left to dry. The resulting paste, when pounded, resembled cornflour.

Norman cookery must have seemed outlandishly exotic to the plain cooks of Britain, for the Normans traded with the Venetians and the Genoese, whose fleets sailed as far as southern China, the Moluccas, Malaya and India. Cinnamon, ginger, saffron, cardamom, nutmeg and mace, cloves, grains of paradise, zedoary, galingale, sander and cubebs all crossed the Channel with the Conqueror. Without doubt the basic standing and running pottages – thick and thin – benefited greatly by the addition of these spices, for before long the dull dish of cullis, made from pounded chicken flesh amalgamated with broth was transformed into 'blanc dessore' with the addition of breadcrumbs, egg yolk, ground almonds and spices. Sometimes it was coloured gold with saffron, which the Knights of St John of Jerusalem cultivated in their English castle gardens in Cambridgeshire and Saffron Walden in Essex.

Colour was all-important in medieval cuisine, for with the exception of the meat itself, the side-dishes, sauces and desserts were all uncooked and cold. Saffron and sander (sandalwood) coloured winter foods fiery gold and heart-warming red. In spring, parsley juice and spinach juice made all things green and new, and there were ground almonds and almond milk for white sauces, violets for rich purple, and dried blood for black.

There were no ready-made colourings to dash with a light hand into sweets and meats, and one of the main tasks of preparation was to distill

9 A pair of iron-bound oak coopered jugs and an elm dipper or scoop, probably turned on a primitive lathe. It was the custom for turners to leave a small piece of bark on the rim of the bowl to prove they had not wasted any wood. Late seventeenth century. Jugs: height 12inches. Dipper: diameter 8¾ inches. *Private collection.*

essences from flowers, herbs, fruits and vegetables as they came into season, so that they could be stored away for later use. Presumably the following recipe was handed down from generation to generation, for although it appears in what seems to be an eighteenth century cookery book, the method goes back long before Tudor England.

'To make syrrop of Violetts: Take a pound of Picked Violetts and put them into an earthen pipkin then pour upon them a quart of scalding water and lett them stand warm nearly four hours then Strain the liquor and put to it 4 pounds and 3 ounces of loaf sugar when you have done soo put a Skillett of Water on the fire and the pipkin into it and so lett it difsolve gently takeing off the Skum as it doth arise when it is Cold put it into glasses for use.'[2]

White mortrews and blanc dessore were served with a bright sauce of red wine, vinegar, sugar, saffron and sander. Fish was garnished with green sauce made from pounded parsley thickened with breadcrumbs and seasoned with vinegar or verjuice. Mawmeny royal was made from pounded pheasant, partridge or capon flesh, mixed with pine-nuts and spices and amalgamated with almond milk. Then it was doused with aqua vitae, set alight and brought flaming to the table.[3]

The Norman barons loved hunting, and game appeared to a profligate degree on noble tables, while the peasants were denied the occasional pleasure of civey (hare) or coney (rabbit), or any wild bird whatsoever. So jealous were their overlords of feathered game that the Guild of Poulters was established in the eleventh century for the only lawful sale of birds of any kind. The list was comprehensive: swan, cygnet, crane, heron, bustard, pheasant, partridge, quail, blackbird, lark, sparrow, finches, green birds, stockdoves, thrushes, bittern, brewe (snipe), egret, gull, lapwing, mallard, plover, ruff, shoveller, and woodcock. All that remained outside the royal deer parks, hare parks and hunting preserves were rabbits reintroduced by the Normans from France, where they were bred in monastery courtyards. With a perverse idea of fair play, the English preferred to catch them in a semi-wild state from artificially established warrens. Taken from anywhere else the penalty was death.

Chopping, pounding and pulping were the three basic methods of preparation, and refinements to the tools with which these endless chores were accomplished began to creep into medieval kitchens. There were punched iron discs with handles for 'scumming' which were far more efficient than curled wood chips or shellfish shells. There were perforated pottery and earthenware bowls for straining, and horsehair sieves made on the same principles as a drum. Ridged wooden rollers crushed stale bread to make breadcrumbs, the only sauce thickener available, and also rolled softened oat grains to make oatmeal. Wooden mortars were still used for pounding cereals, grains and small quantities of meat and fish for pottages, but now there were brass and bell metal mortars from the Continent for pounding dried herbs and spices, and alabaster and marble for amulum and sugar. Stone mortars also doubled as mixing bowls for a long time to come.

There is a popular misconception that sugar was not introduced into England until the sixteenth century, but as far back as the seventh century the Arabs were growing sugar-cane all along the southern Mediterranean coast and spice traders brought it into Europe in small quantities which were reserved for the Court and the barons. The first time the ordinary English citizen came across sugar was during the Crusades, when the soldiery 'beheld with astonishment and tasted with delight as a thing unknown, the cane growing in the plains of Tripoli.'[4] The Arabs too must take the credit for discovering 'stone honey' made by soaking sugar-cane in water, then evaporating the syrup till it crystallised.

Refining and clarifying sugar was one of the many regular tasks of preparation, for even when sugar came into England in quantity it was often only half-refined, and the loaves of sugar were black with molasses

10 Beechwood pestle and mortar, probably late seventeenth century. Beechwood is hard and close-grained and was often pickled in brine to increase its durability. Wooden mortars were mainly used for pounding cereals and small quantities of meat and fish. Spices and herbs would have penetrated the wood and adulterated the flavours of individual spices. Mid-seventeenth century. Height 11 inches. *Rupert Gentle Antiques.*

inside their white hats. It was a tedious, time-consuming business which continued well into the eighteenth century.

'To clarify four pounds of Sugar you must take the white of one Egg and a quart of Water att the least you may ufe 3 pints or more of water if you please but lesse than a quart cannot serve. The lesse water it is done with the better it will keep. With a Whifk beat the Egg to a froth then put a little water to it and beat it again then take the Sugar and put it in. You must have as much water as will make itt indifferently thin. Stirr it well and sett it over a pritty quick fire when it begins to boyle again put in so much water as to keep it from boyling over So you must do every time that it is ready to boyle over till the Scum be hardened and the Sugar appear clear. Scum it as clean as you can and lett it boyle Still putting in Water as you see occafien till you have Skimd it clean. Lett it stand off the fire for a while to settle then if it needs Straining Strain it. Boyle it again till it is ready to Draw with a Small Hair behind your Thumb and finger and then a pint will weigh a pound but if it will fully Draw with a Small hair lesse than a pint will be a pound but the surest way to know a pound will be first to weigh the thing you put it in and then in that to Weigh your sugar.'[5]

11 An extremely rare pair of cast brass measures, dated 1601. The Company of Founders persistently tried to wrest the monopoly of making official weights and measures from the Pewterers, but although they gained the privilege of making weights, they could not break the Pewterers' hold on measures. These are pint measures, measuring the old pint before the introduction of the Imperial measure: Height $5\frac{1}{8}$ inches. *Michael Wakelin.*

And it still had to be pounded to a fine powder in a mortar after all that.

Cooking in England changed with the return of the Crusaders, for the knights and their depleted armies brought back innovations from the Middle East and Italy which they had learned during their unholy wars. They brought home sauces and dishes with strange new tastes which they had begun to appreciate. Dishes made by cooking meat in a previously-prepared sweet-sour sauce became very popular. Egerdouce was a favourite: a sweet-sour pottage in which goat meat, coney or sliced brawn was cooked in a sauce of young red wine or vinegar, honey or sugar, and dried fruits. Chicken, eels and oysters were cooked in 'gravey' made from ground almonds and broth seasoned with sugar and ginger. And there was charlet, a dish which sounds Chinese in origin: boiled shredded pork was mixed well with cows' milk, eggs and saffron, and seasoned with powdered ginger and sugar. There was 'blanc manger' too, which bears no relation at all, except for its whiteness, to the blancmange of today. A fat capon was cooked and its flesh teased out to fine shreds with a pin and added to boiled rice, almond milk and sugar, after which it was decorated with red and white aniseed comfits.

With the increasing richness of the Court and the nobility, food became more flamboyant. New ingredients were needed to make the ostentatious banqueting set-pieces so characteristic of the age and so reminiscent of Roman feasts in their ingenuity and invention. Not that the English palate was dulled with too much high living and rich food. It was rather that lavish banquets brought warmth and entertainment to an otherwise grim and chilly existence, enlivened only by occasional skirmishes with rival barons who had stolen their cattle or burned their crops. The set-piece of medieval banquets was the 'remove' or 'soteltie', which often depicted the conquests or virtues of an honoured guest or portrayed a great hunt or battle. The architecture of these amazing confections depended entirely on strong jelly.

To make a really hard-setting jelly, the swim-bladders of fishes were boiled until the liquid became glutinous. Calves' feet were boiled separately and the two liquors were combined, coloured with dye and poured in layers to set. Then different colours were cut into suitable shapes and laid in a shallow bowl over which transparent jelly was poured. Sun, moon and stars were suspended in a quivering firmament, fish swam in a motionless sea. Down the ages the process of making jelly was brought to a fine art, and by the reign of Queen Anne it was far less disgusting, though no less tedious to make:

'Take two Calves' Feet, slitt them in halves then cutt all the fatt and black pieces out of them then steep them in water for an hour, boyl 'em in three quarts of water over a gentle fire 'till 'twill jelly in a Spoon and skimm it well while tis boyleing, let it stand all night. Scrape the fatt off the topp then break it into your preserving Pann, then putt in a half a Pint of White wine, the Whites of five Eggs beaten, about half a quarter Pound of Loafe sugar, the juice of six lemons and a little piece of the Peel, then boyle it over a charcoal fire 'till the Eggs are hard at ye topp, take the Eggs off and putt 'em into the bottom of your Jilly-bagg, then run it slowly thro your Jilly-bagg three or four times, till it is perfectly clear in your glass.'[6]

12 A brass-bowled spoon riveted on to a wrought iron handle which has been decorated down the shaft and finished with a heart-shaped device, a recurring decoration in kitchen ware. It probably dates from the end of the eighteenth century. Overall length 15 inches. *Rupert Gentle Antiques.*

Orangeflower water and rosewater were essentials in a seventeenth century kitchen – not innocent, flowery essences as they are today, but strong distillations of fruit and spirit. Orange peel, lemon peel or rose petals were steeped three days and three nights in three pints of brandy and added to a syrup of spring water and sugar, left to settle, skimmed, strained and bottled for the store cupboard. The essence of herbs had to be extracted and preserved too. The herbs were crushed or bruised so that the juice ran from them, then 'cast into a Galleypott and the pott put into a Skillett of Water on the fire till it hath cast all the skum'.[7] Then it was skimmed, the pot removed from the skillet and allowed to settle when the liquor was strained off and boiled into a syrup.

By the eighteenth century fragrances and perfumes were regularly distilled for many purposes, from sweetening the foul air of bedchambers and parlours to sprinkling over meats and dishes as they were served up at the table, One of the quicker ways of preserving roses without distilling them runs as follows:

'Pick Damask Roses and Sift them bruise them in a mortar no more than to make them lye close in the Pott take such a pott well Glazed as people putt butter in. Cover the bottom of the Pott with Bay Salt beaten cover it thicker than a straw put upon it some roses presse them Downe with all the Strength that is possible lett them be about an Inch thick when they are hard prest then lay upon them a Row of Salt almost as much as att the Bottom. Over that lay another Row of Roses pressing them as hard down as is pofsible soo doo till you have filled your pott the upper and the under rows must be very thick. Lye the pott up very clofe with a Bladder and a Brown paper upon it. If you would perfume a Room att any time in the Winter carry the Pott and sett it in the Room when you need no longer the perfume lye it up again and open it as you have occafion. If you would Still it you must not open it till you goo to Still it. Still itt att any time in the Winter as you doo in Sumer this is so much sweeter than the Sumer Water or that one Spoonfull shall goo as farr as three of that.'[8]

A great deal of activity took place in the dairy or 'milk room', for the other main task of preparation lay in making butter and cheese. Like so many culinary discoveries, the properties of rennet were probably found by accident, when a suckling calf was killed. Young milkfed animals were eaten as a delicacy, and their stomachs would certainly have contained milk curd. Natural curiosity being what it is, and milkfed animals being precious and scarce, the possibility occurred to some adventurous milkmaid that perhaps the stomach bag alone might produce the same result. Accordingly the stomach bag was refilled with fresh milk and the miracle occurred.

More experiments followed, using the 'dead' stomach bag, devoid of stomach juices. In order to prevent the delicate membrane from cracking or splitting, it was filled with milk and floated in a pail of water. Soon the contents curdled in quite a different way from milk which is soured naturally, and produced more curds. Though they certainly did not know it, they had set up a system of osmosis between the water outside the bag and the milk inside, making curds without the natural enzymes in the stomach bag. Soon it was discovered that all kinds of acid juices produced the same result, and sorrel, bedstraw, nettles and many other hedgerow herbs were used to make cheese at almost any time of the year, without the sacrifice of calf, lamb or piglet.[9]

Before the Normans, butter was made from whole milk and cheese from the buttermilk which was left. These 'cream' cheeses were

13 Coopered elm chessel for pressing soft cheeses, sycamore butter scoop and iron-bound butter mould in three pieces. Wooden utensils for the dairy were usually made by the 'white' or 'wet' cooper, though such items as butter scoops were often carved by woodmen and sold at local fairs. The chessel and butter mould are probably late eighteenth century. The butter scoop with butter-print handle may be considerably earlier. Chessel: diameter 12½ inches. Butter mould: length 10 inches. Butter scoop: length 10¼ inches. *Private collection.*

coloured and flavoured more or less at whim, varying from region to region, with herbs, smoked bacon, garlic and in particular sage, which, when doused with vinegar, seemed to increase the keeping properties of cheese. In France, Holland and Northern Europe, however, cheese was made from skimmed milk, and all their butter was made of cream only. Whey cheeses kept much better, and were harder in consistency, and soon the practice of making whey cheeses was adopted with great success in England.

Big flat wooden and pottery bowls stood in milk rooms and dairies and the cream was skimmed off and beaten by hand to butter. Deep wooden barrel churns and plungers came into use to improve and hasten the butter-making process. As the keeping properties of salt were better understood, it was added in accurate proportions: an ounce to a pound of butter, after which the butter was laid to drain on a mat of rushes or fine osier. Then it was 'flung down into the barrels', knuckled and kneaded to break down the air holes, which encouraged it to go rancid, and patted up or pressed into wooden bowls.

Naturally there was a surplus of butter and cheese during the summer, when cows grazed the rich wild pastures of common land, and in country towns fairs and butter markets became a regular feature of seasonal country life. Butter crosses still stand in many market towns, where the fair dealings of buyer and seller came under scrutiny. Large quantities of salted butter were sold off to the merchant fleets to be eaten in an increasingly rancid condition aboard ship. Smaller producers pressed their pounds and half pounds into wooden bowls and marked them with their individual identifying stamp, many of them beautifully carved and later adopted purely for decoration in Victorian England. To each region its own eccentricities: in East Anglia butter was forced through ring gauges and sold by the yard. In Norfolk it was sold by the pint in wooden measures like tankards.

14 A pair of simply-made butter scales with sycamore bowls suspended by three cords from an ash balance arm. Some butter scales are more elegant, with turned wooden columns and arms, and carved pedestals, but the accuracy of the 'weigh bogey' was more important than its decorativeness. Height 18 inches; length of arm 24 inches. *Private collection.*

England was making so much cheese by the middle of the seventeenth century that 'great store of cheeses were exported to France and Spain and probably went to the Navy.'[10] Cheese presses were a common sight in the major cheese-making districts such as Gloucester, Cheddar, Cheshire and Wensleydale. They were similar to linen presses or block printing presses, with a cylindrical cavity in the base and a channel for the whey to drip through as the press was tightened on a wooden screw. Stone, marble and alabaster bowls without lips caught the liquid which ran out and were standard equipment in dairies up to the nineteenth century. They can still be found, often described as 'mortars' by the less well-informed.

The different properties of woods began to be taken into account. The little butter bowls were probably sycamore because it is quick-growing, tasteless and odourless. Elm lasts well in damp conditions and

15 Three nineteenth century butter-prints. The basic shape was usually turned on a lathe before being carved on the end-grain. The wood was generally sycamore, though some are found in beechwood and fruitwood. There seems to be no definite regional motifs to these designs beyond the obvious Scottish thistle. By the nineteenth century individual farms had their own individual stamps. Oval print: 9 inches.   *Peter Nelson.*

16 Continental kitchen at the end of the eighteenth century. The only women employed in kitchens until the middle of the nineteenth century were those who fetched and carried and helped in the preparation of vegetables. *BBC Hulton Picture Library.*

was used for making chessels – small cheese presses which were simple circular wooden cylinders, fairly shallow, with holes punched in base and lid for drainage, mainly used for pressing soft cheeses. Lime wood, alder and sycamore were used by coopers for butter-tubs and churns, willow for beating paddles and plungers, and rush, osier and willow were all plaited into mats and baskets for draining and packing butter and cheese.

By the eighteenth century butter and cheese-making was a regular part of the routine of any household of any size. Butter churns had improved in design: there were churns with paddles turned by handles and small barrel-like churns which revolved, turned by a handle at the side. But in cottages and isolated farmhouses the old plunger-type churn remained in use for nearly two more centuries. The cooling properties of slate and marble had been noted, and most surfaces in the dairy were polished stone at the very least, though slate was now available almost everywhere. In Wales and the north Midlands lead-lined sinks were often used to set cream, and elsewhere brass and copper pans stood in the cool shadowy dairy, with a switch of elderflower hung above them to keep off the flies.

An increasing number of implements, containers and equipment was in use, as this extract from an inventory of the contents of the Manor House, Houghton Regis, dated May 23rd 1740 shows:

'. . . two trussells, and two slabs, four wooden bottles, a cheese press, and three batts, two butter boards, two forms, one pair butter scales, one pound lead weight, a strainer, sciming dish, one round baskett, one stone bottle, thirteen pieces earthenware, fourteen quart glass bottles, a cheese curd rack, a pair milk tongs, one sheet'.[11]

All this was for the household's private use, for the lady of the house sold none of her dairy products.

The 'trussells' or trestles might have been made of elm, ash or lime. Elm was never used in the kitchen itself, for though it lasts well in damp conditions it warps and cracks in changes of temperature and humidity. The 'batts' and 'forms' may have been beech, soaked in brine to season it, for butter stamps, bats and clamps had to last a long time. Beech is one of the finest hardwoods for domestic use, but it was valuable and expensive, and was usually reserved for making serving bowls and platters for the parlour and dining room. As always, so much depended on what materials were available locally, and which part of the country had timber in any quantity. Many smaller domestic items were made from fruitwoods, where an apple or pear tree had outlived its productive usefulness. Burrwood or the roots of trees may first have been used by turners as free pickings from the great private forests and acres of woodland, once the standing timber had been cut.

Straining cloths had been used for many purposes from the earliest days of food preparation, but the ones used in the dairy were only horsehair or linen. No woollen or coarse cotton cloth was allowed for straining or cleaning any of the utensils, since the threads might catch on the wooden surface and trap minute amounts of waste which would curdle or sour the next batch. The only exception were floor-cloths, which were used to mop up spilt milk and then rubbed over the floorboards to give them a shine. Nothing except metal, stone and slate was scoured, for it would roughen the smooth wooden surfaces. Metal utensils were scoured with horse-tail *(equisetum)*, a primeval plant which contains a lot of silicate and was later known as pewterwort, as it still is today.

Apart from yeast, which had to be renewed and kept in a constant state of fermentation, the only raising agent for flour-based dishes such

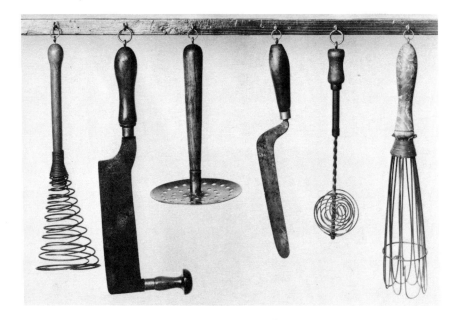

17 Choppers, whisks and spinach presser. *Left to right:* iron wire egg whisk; cast steel chopper with turned handles; perforated steel spinach presser with wooden handle; chopping knife; spiral-thread and iron wire whisk which revolves as the handle is pushed down; early iron wire balloon whisk with turned handle. All these items were manufactured over a span of fifty years from 1880 to 1930. Spiral whisk: 12 inches. The rest to scale. *Jeremy Le Grice.*

as puddings and cakes was egg white, beaten till it stood in peaks, and added at the last minute to aerate the mixture. This state of affairs lasted into the middle of the nineteenth century and explains the apparent prodigality of all those early recipes which begin 'Take eighteen eggs . . .' The only way of whisking eggs until the late seventeenth century was in a bowl with a bunch of birch or willow twigs bound to the shape of a small besom brush. When copper bowls began to be made in any quantity around the turn of the seventeenth century, cooks and scullions discovered that eggs beaten in copper bowls attained a far thicker, more enduring stiffness than when beaten in an earthenware or stoneware bowl.

In 1656, when England took the island of Jamaica, cocoa-beans became a regular trading commodity. It became fashionable to drink chocolate, which was first made with wine and then, by the eighteenth century, with milk and eggs. More important to the preparers of food, the chocolate mill or 'moliquet' was introduced into England. This late seventeenth century recipe goes into some detail over the 'moliquet'

18 A rare and handsome turned lignum vitae pestle and mortar. Lignum vitae is an extremely dense living wood, as cool as stone. It is rare to find such a large object made in lignum vitae, for the trees, which grow in the West Indies, rarely attain any size. It first came into Europe in the late sixteenth century. The fine turning on the mortar indicates that this is probably early seventeenth century. Height $7\frac{1}{2}$ inches; diameter $6\frac{1}{4}$ inches. *A. & E. Foster.*

which was still very much a novelty. 'Then mill it with a mill for that purpose till it becomes thick and proper for drinking; this mill is a stick with an head at the end full of notches which you must, at the little end, hold in your hand and hastily twirl about.'[12] The effect was to produce such a frothing, foaming drink that the 'moliquet' was instantly seized upon and used to beat egg whites with great success. By the mid-eighteenth century tinned wire whisks were on sale and in great demand. But it was not until 1873 that the first mechanical egg-beaters were introduced from America.

The West Indies were the source of another material which was totally unknown in the western world: lignum vitae. This is not, as some suppose, petrified wood but a living, growing tree whose wood is 75 per cent denser and heavier than oak and which has remarkable self-lubricating properties because of the resin it contains. It is used today for making parts of ships' propellers, which gives an idea of its strength under extreme stress. When it was first brought into Europe it was principally used for making spice mills and pepper mills, and occasionally for mortars. But since the tree seldom attains a greater height than nine foot or so, the trunks were slender and it is rare to find anything large made of this remarkable wood. The Elizabethans believed it had great healing propeties, which is why they called it 'wood of life'. It continued to be used for hand-grinders until turned steel spindles eventually replaced it in the late eighteenth century.

Inevitably, with the expansion of industry and the flood of technical developments in the iron and steel industries which began in the middle of the eighteenth century, knives and choppers improved out of all recognition. Manufacturers of spades, hoes and tools for the plantations began to improve the cumbersome cutlery of the kitchen. Makers of

19 A pair of remarkably fine herb choppers with pierced decoration and carved fruitwood handles similar to handsaw grips. The more elaborate one has a pair of doves pierced into the blade and is marked 'S. Mason'. Probably dating from the early eighteenth century when swordsmiths began to make knives and garden tools. Height 9 inches *(left)*; 10½ inches *(right)*. *A. & E. Foster.*

steel in Sheffield, craftsmen in Birmingham who had been making steel tinder-pistols and strike-a-lights, workers in armament manufactories, scissor-makers and tool-makers of all kinds began to produce a wide variety of cutting implements, varying in design from region to region, most of them sadly thrown out when their usefulness came to an end. Spice mills and pepper mills, coffee grinders with steel spindles, herb cutters and choppers were all given as much attention to design and craftsmanship as almost every article made in England in the eighteenth century.

Curiously, this great expansion was not mirrored in America, where simple oval cast iron boat-shaped bowls, reminiscent of grisset pans in England, continued to be used with disc-shaped cutting wheels for

20 Steel spice grinder. These box grinders with steel spindles gradually replaced the old 'quern type' hand-mills towards the end of the seventeenth century. Many of them were imported from the Continent during and after the Restoration. This one is probably French, dating from around 1680. Height 9 inches. *Rupert Gentle Antiques.*

21 Cast iron herb grinder and chopping wheel. These herb choppers were more common in Colonial America, though the boat-shaped troughs can be found in England and are often confused with grisset pans which are almost identical in shape. Late sixteenth to early seventeenth century. Height $7\frac{1}{2}$ inches; length $16\frac{1}{4}$ inches; wheel diameter $7\frac{3}{8}$ inches. *Colonial Williamsburg Foundation.*

22 Cast iron grisset pan with three hoofed feet, used for melting wax of all kinds for making rush lights and tapers, and very similar to herb choppers except that grisset pans have handles. Late sixteenth – early seventeenth century. Length $9\frac{3}{4}$ inches; height $3\frac{5}{8}$ inches. *Christopher Bangs.*

chopping herbs, and there were few refinements in the kitchen. Most of
their essential tools and implements were imported from England, and
even when America gained its independence, Europe remained the
main source of manufactured goods for some time to come. It was
German rather than English craftsmen, settled in and around Pennsylvania, who were responsible for the growth of the American iron and
steel industries. The great flowering of mechanical devices and mechanical domestic equipment of all sorts did not really begin until after the
end of the American Civil War in 1865.

In England, now that steel knives and choppers were being manufactured specially for the kitchen, pounding meat to a pulp gave way to
chopping it up and cooking it in small pieces in broths and stews, but
dried meat and dried fish still presented problems. For centuries large
catches of cod in the North Sea were dried and salted to form the staple
diet of England in the lean winter months, when the last of the livestock
had been slaughtered and meat of any kind, dried, salted or fresh was a
rarity. On the rugged coastline of the New World intrepid early settlers

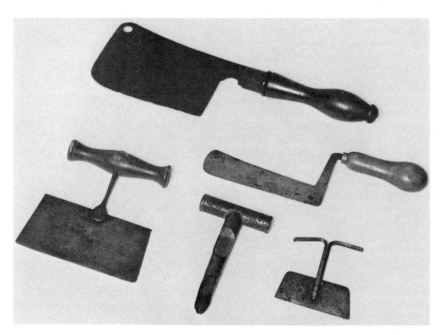

23 Meat cleaver, choppers and apple corer. Turned handles were usually of beech, ash,
sycamore or fruitwood. All these items probably date from the second half of the
nineteenth century, and have cast steel blades. The designs remained virtually
unchanged until well into the present century. The apple corer is sheet tin over a
wooden frame. Meat cleaver: length 14½ inches. Vegetable chopper *(left)*: width 8
inches. *Private Collection.*

had been drying and salting their catches on the shores of Newfound-land and Labrador and trading it for wine, cloth and manufactured goods in Europe. The spicy Portugese *'bacalao'* owes its origin to this transatlantic trade and not to the North Sea fishing fleets of the sixteenth and seventeenth centuries. Best Newfoundland cod went to Southern Europe, the middling quality was kept for the home market, and the poorest was sold off to the West Indies, where it was exchanged for brown sugar, molasses and rum.

When America began to trade with China after 1785, homesick merchants hankered so strongly for 'dunfish' that it was sent specially to Canton. 'Dunfish' was best quality salt cod, alternately dried and buried, sometimes in haymow, till it was so indestructible that even a six month sea voyage made no impression on it. Such must have been the stockfish of England, which had to be soaked in change after change of water to eliminate the salt, and then pounded repeatedly until it was reduced to an edible consistency. Instructions in an Elizabethan manuscript are specific: 'And when it is desired to eat it, it behoves to beat it with a wooden hammer for a full hour, and then set it to soak in warm water for a full two hours or more, then cook and scour it very well like beef; then eat it with mustard or soaked in butter.'[13] The blander palates of eighteenth century England liked it 'layed in water twelve hours, then lay it twelve hours on a board, and then twelve more in water'. But grooved wooden hammers, known today as 'steak hammers' were certainly used for many other purposes, as were most items of kitchen equipment, except for fish-knives which were always kept separately, along with fish-cloths used for straining and drying fish before cooking.

Many other tedious processes were involved in preparing food right up to the nineteenth century, when the proliferation of mechanical aids took much of the drudgery out of the kitchen. Most of these involved undoing the harsh effects of preservation and of rendering basic raw materials into substances suitable for cooking and eating. Rancid butter was melted down, skimmed and sweetened. Fat of all sorts was rendered down and the best was used for cooking – the rest for making rush dips and candles. Sugar was refined, fruits dried, preserved and then reconstituted. Dried beef received the same treatment as stockfish, salted meat was soaked and seasoned, boiled and pounded.

Essences of herbs and food colourings had to be made for use later in the year and even when cochineal was freely available, replacing sander or alder chips for colouring food red, it still had to be prepared for use. Cochineal came in from Cochin-China and was used as a dye by the

24 Pressers, mashers and cooking spoons. Elm, ash, and beech were the most common woods for such utensils. *Left to right:* carved stirring spoon with hooked handle; turned potato masher; carved Welsh paddle spoon; fish and meat hammer; disc-shaped spinach or cabbage pressers: lemon squeezer. Wooden kitchen implements such as these were still being made in country districts at the turn of this century, but the carved spoons probably date from a century earlier. Welsh paddle spoon: length 24 inches. Potato masher: 12 inches. Lemon squeezer: 10 inches.   *Private collection.*

25 Tinplate graters. Early punched graters usually had rolled edges round an iron wire frame. Later the joins were machine-pressed or seamed. Sometimes a simple decoration was incorporated into the stamped metal. Height of tallest: 10 inches.   *Jeremy Le Grice.*

woollen and silk industries, but in its raw state it was obviously not bright enough for kitchen use.

'To make Cutchinool Scarlett: Take the Cutchinool beat it very fine as much as will lye upon a sixpence and halfe as much Cream of Tartar finely beaten. Mix and boyle them together in 4 or 5 spoonfulls of Orange Flower Water then Straine it and to colour your Sugar plates take some in a spoon and put sugar to it till it is something thicker than a Syrrop then warm it over the fire a little and it will be of a good Scarlett you may do a greater Quantity and it will keep in a Glasse Close Stopt.'[14]

The preparation of meat is dealt with in more detail in the next chapter, but an idea of the task facing a cook about to roast a sucking pig may be glimpsed from the matter of fact directions written down by Sarah Josepha Hale in her *Ladies New Book of Cookery* for the benefit of emancipated American women.

'Take the wax out of the ears and the dirt from the nostrils by using a small skewer covered with a rag; then take out the eyes with a fork or sharp-pointed knife which you must wipe off upon a clean dishcloth, clean the tongue, gums and lips by scraping them with a clean knife and wiping them . . . and with your hand up the inside of the throat take out all the clotted blood you will find there.'[15]

That was written in 1852 and the rest of the instructions are similarly explicit. It is no surprise, therefore, that the inhabitants of the New World, as soon as they were free to do so, turned their minds towards the problems of preparing food, and produced a welter of labour-saving gadgets to save themselves from the ghastly rigours of the kitchen.

3 Roasting

26 Sixteenth century Italian kitchen, equipped with freestanding charcoal braziers. Wooden spoons with hooked handles appear to have been made to the same pattern all over Europe at that period. *BBC Hulton Picture Library.*

PRE-ROMAN BRITAIN was not just uncivilised – it was untamed. Land and people, rivers, forests, marshes, hills and valleys were wild and hostile. Scattered over the more habitable regions were lusty, ferocious, hard-living tribes, living in round houses made from the timber they felled to make clearings in the rampant woodland, or in hill forts high on the uplands. They dug firepits and feasted on sheep and cattle in part-celebration, part-sacrifice to their ancient gods, hunting game with wild enthusiasm and eating almost everything they killed, regardless of taste and with little attempt at finesse.

The thin strip of what might remotely be called civilisation in Britain ran along the south-east coast. Here the Belgae lived, Iron Age invaders from the Seine, Marne and Rhine, giving at least a good first impression to the highly cultivated Romans when they landed. The Belgae mined and smelted iron in the Weald of Kent, on the same site used by the famous Elizabethan ironmasters hundreds of years later. From the few remaining artefacts preserved from the days of the Belgae, their craftsmanship, technical abilities and sense of artistic design were unique in Britain. There is a model of a double-headed wrought iron spit with bullhead finials in the British Museum which is as fine as any made by their sixteenth century descendants.

The elegant Roman cuisine and hygienic way of life made little lasting impression on the heterogenous tribal people of Britain, but the invaders left behind a considerable increase in livestock, both wild and domestic. They brought in rabbits, native to the Mediterranean, and bred them for meat. They introduced the forerunner of the domestic fowl, descendant of the North West Indian jungle fowl which had first been domesticated in Persia and Greece. They built dovecotes and bred pigeons for the table, and enclosed parks for hares to breed in. There were guinea fowl and peacock in the courtyards of their neatly ordered houses. All this must have seemed a waste of time and effort to the Britons to whom hunting was a way of life and horses and cattle the only animals worth domesticating.

After the Romans withdrew, beaten as much by the climate and the terrain as by the fierce defence of hostile tribes, the Britons reverted to their profligate, riotous way of living. They ignored the culinary refinements of their foreign invaders and went back to roasting whole carcases, which they ate till the fat ran down their chins and into their beards. By the time the Normans came, they had raised great castle keeps with huge hearth fires in the centre of high banqueting halls. Sometimes there were louvres in the roof to draw the smoke away, sometimes there were not, and it escaped where it could, through the slit windows and down the draughty passages. Where there was stone available for building, they built their cooking hearths against the wall, with huge stone hoods to guide at least some of the smoke up cavernous chimneys. When they ate, they threw their gnawed bones onto the evil-smelling rushes which littered the floor for their dogs to fight over.

Monasteries and religious communities, probably because of their constant contact with Rome, were more refined. The Abbot's Kitchen at Glastonbury is built like a cathedral, with lantern roof and louvred vents to guide the heat and smoke out of the building. It has two great hoods, one for roasting, one for boiling, and a sluice over a running stream. But chimneys brought new hazards with them, as well as improvements in cooking methods:

'Beware of pyssunge in draughts and permyt no common pyssynge place to be about the house and let the common howse of easement be ower some water or else elongated from the howse, and beware of emptynge of pyssepottes and pyssing in chymnes so that all euvle and contagyous ayres may be expelled and clere ayre kept unputryfyed.'[16]

The impressively vast medieval kitchen at Stanton Harcourt, a medieval manor which has remained almost untouched since it was built, gives a better idea of domestic life than the Abbot's Kitchen, for it has a wall-hearth without a stone hood, and a wooden lantern roof with the original smoke-blackened timbers, protected outside by a lead octagon roof topped with a heraldic griffon. Simple A-shaped standing spits, consisting of two iron rods held together with an iron ring, were probably used on the roasting fire. These standing spits had iron hooks on the front rods to support the long iron spit on which the meat was skewered. There would also have been a shallow iron trough or dish to catch the fat which dripped from the roasting meat, which the cook basted with a wooden or iron ladle. If the household had foreign connections, the ladle would be a long-handled brass or a copper-bowled ladle on a wrought iron handle.

Cresset firedogs may have made their first appearance around this time, for descriptions of cooking mention coating or 'dredging' almost everything from whole carcases to delicate dishes such as 'pommes dorres'. These were meat balls of pork or beef mixed with currants and spices threaded onto the spit, roasted and dredged with a mixture of shredded parsley, flour and beaten egg to look like green apples or coloured gold with powdered saffron. The wrought iron baskets which top these firedogs may have been used to hold small bowls of such basting mixtures clear of flying ashes, though from their name they are generally assumed to have held flaming torches. But in medieval times, the main meal of the day was always eaten in daylight and there was probably little need to light up the hearth until it became the custom to eat a light 'supper' of broth and toasted bread cooked over a dying fire.

Wrought iron spit-dogs were made in pairs for hearths built against stone walls. In addition, smaller firedogs supported the logs of the fire itself, so that a full complement for an early down-hearth would have been a pair of spit-dogs and a pair of firedogs, chenets or creepers.

Flesh-hooks, or meat-hooks of all shapes and sizes, again made of iron, spiked out chunks of meat, and pokers were certainly being used by the fourteenth century. An inventory for 1311 for a medieval hall runs: '2 dorsars, 2 bankers, 2 pieces of ware, 2 brass lavers, 2 large pots, 1 bowl of brass, 2 andirons and 1 poker of iron, 3 boards with trestles and one fixed, 2 chairs, 3 benches and 3 stools.'[17]

Until the art of casting was mastered in England, wrought iron had a tendency to soften in the great heat of the fire, and the legs and bars of firedogs needed small supporting stems to prevent them from sagging when they became red hot. But central hearths continued to be the rule in all but the grandest manor houses, monasteries and castle keeps until well into the sixteenth century. A fireback, 'dorsar' or 'reredos' consisting of a slab of iron or granite dug into the earthen floor helped to guide some of the smoke upwards and contained the fire on one side at least.

Although metal-casting was widely practised all over Europe, England

27 A fine example of an early English cast iron fireback, reredos or dorsar, commemorating the defeat of the Spanish Armada. The rope decoration round the edge was typical of many Sussex ironfounders of the period who cast in heated sand or clay to achieve a crisp definition. Height 21 inches; width 24½ inches. *Victoria & Albert Museum.*

contented herself with importing foreign goods which came through Flanders, until Henry VIII severed England's connections with Rome, and Spain occupied the Netherlands. England, out of necessity, had to begin to manufacture her own goods. Among the first items to be cast by the ironmasters of the Weald of Kent, cradle of England's Tudor iron industry, were cannon and firebacks. The first cast iron firebacks were crudely decorated with little more than a border made by pressing rope into the sand mould and adding rough impressions of fleur-de-lys, compasses and Tudor roses. But soon the ironmasters began to produce such crisply decorated work that it is hard to believe they were still using primitive sand-casting techniques and not *cire perdue* or lost-wax. They heated the sand into which they pressed their carved wooden moulds to achieve a crisper line and later took to casting in clay, thus achieving elaborate heraldic designs and scenes from the Bible, myths and legends. In 1588 they produced a batch of commemorative firebacks to celebrate the defeat of the Spanish Armada.

Many of these firebacks were not intended for down-hearth chimneys but for central fires, for wall-hearths were by no means common, even as late as the second half of the sixteenth century. The Reverend William Harrison chronicled the change and regretted it:

'Now we have manie chimnies, and yet our tenderlings complaine of rheumes, catarhs and poses. Then we had none but reredoes and our heads did never ache. For as the smoke of those daies was supposed to be a sufficient hardning of the timber of the house, so it was reputed to be a far better medicine to keep the good man and his family.' In 1577 he noted that 'chimnies' had become general even in cottages whereas 'in the villages where I remain, old men recalled that in their young days under the two King Harrys there were not above two or three chimneys if so many, in uplandish towns . . . the religious houses and manor places of their lords always excepted, but each one made his fire against a reredoss in the hall where he dined and dressed his meat.'[18]

Two simultaneous developments hastened the proliferation of chimneys in England. Flemish workmen had settled in East Anglia, and finding no local stone available and the houses crudely built of timber and wattle-and-daub, began to make bricks. Soon after Queen Elizabeth I's accession, bricks were in great demand because there was an acute shortage of timber in many parts of the country, both for house-building and for fuel. Acres of forest had been cut down to provide wood for charcoal for smelting iron and making glass, brewing beer and to meet the demand for timber for the shipyards. Coal was being mined in the north-east and in Wales and 'sea cole' (so-called because it came coastwise into London and Bristol, Southampton and King's Lynn) became the principal cooking fuel in many parts of the country where there was no peat to cut or wood to burn. Firebacks became a necessity, for the greater heat of coal fires against the fine new brick chimneys was a hazard, especially in towns, where the houses were crowded together so closely that if one caught fire, the whole town was in danger.

At Carisbrooke Castle on the Isle of Wight there still stands evidence of that kitchen revolution, bare now to the elements, but showing clearly how new brick chimneys and flues were let into the massive stone walls. Their curving shapes are plainly visible and the method of construction can be seen in open cross-section where the wall has since crumbled away. A single flue from the cooking hearth is duplicated by another, far wider one, directly over the baking ovens, making a warm dry chamber for storing and drying meat and grain. Owing to the abysmal state of the roads in the sixteenth century, it was not possible to transport fuel from one part of the country to another, except by water. Cookshops proliferated in towns during the seventeenth century, but in the countryside hearths were cold and the outlook was bleak. Manors and monasteries had huge stone baking ovens, but they exacted tithes for cooking food brought in by the peasants who lived and worked on their estates.

'No more hare, jugged in an earthen pot, buried in hot wood ashes – a whole meaty hare, blood and bones, with a few wild plums or crab apples to give a tang to the gravy.'[19] Nor any other wild game either, for ever since the Norman barons had enclosed their forests, the progressive increase in land reserved for sheep-rearing cut the only supplies of free food to all but the rich and privileged. Peasants who used to keep a cow and a few sheep could no longer do so because there was little common land left for pasture, and they owned no land themselves except for a few strips for arable crops.

It was a very poor household indeed that did not own a pig, however, for a pig needs no special food or pasture and can forage for itself in the most unpromising landscape. By the seventeenth century too, there were scraggy farmyard fowls and geese, whose eggs were roasted in their shells in the embers or fried on flat griddle pans with collops of bacon. So there was pork and salt bacon, sausages and blood pudding to relieve the otherwise monotonous diet of cereal and bean pottages. If the pig

28 A pair of wrought iron cresset firedogs and a 'yetling' or 'Dutch oven'. Cresset firedogs are generally assumed to have held flaming torches to light up the hearth – hence their name. But it is possible that they may have had more than one function and also held small bowls of dredging mixtures, or even contained small charcoal fires so that sauces could be cooked on a bright, controlled fire. Some cresset firedogs have small metal bowls which fit inside the wrought iron baskets which would seem to bear out this theory. The lidded cast iron cooking pot was used for baking as well as for stewing. In Colonial America these heavy cooking pots are known as 'Dutch ovens'. The pot-hook is detachable. Firedogs: height 22 inches. Baking pot: depth 7½ inches; diameter 28 inches. *Private collection.*

were a boar, his head was forfeit once he had mated in autumn and it was certain that the sow would farrow. A good average weight for a 'salter' was twenty stone, and pig meat had the added advantage for poor peasants in that it needs no butter or oil to cook it in, since it has fat enough without.

Once the English had mastered the art of casting iron, they began to make spit-dogs, firedogs, andirons and creepers in reasonable quantities. Early examples were distinctly European in design, giving rise to the shrewd suspicion that they made their master-casts from foreign articles already in the country. Brass andirons and firedogs were far more rare. Some were being made in England by the middle of the seventeenth century, but they were probably the work of Dutch and German metal founders who had been brought over to teach mining, smelting and metal-working to the backward English. Iron at least was available and within the reach of most householders, and local blacksmiths and forges began to make basic articles for domestic use. Central crossbars were built into brick chimneys from which hung chains and hooks. Simple standing spit-dogs and spit-rods were to be found in the

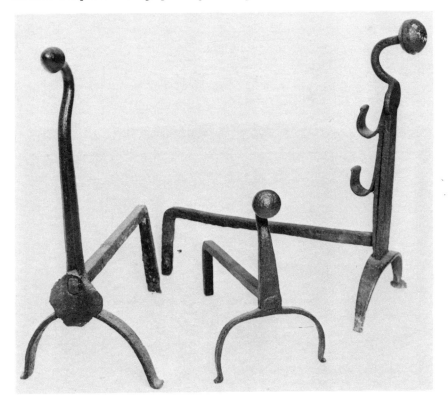

29 Andiron, creeper and spit-dog. Three wrought iron examples of sixteenth and seventeenth century firedogs of unembellished design. Andirons or brand-irons kept the logs from rolling forward in to the hearth, with the addition of chenets or creepers in the centre. Firedogs for supporting spit-dogs had hooks at the back of the uprights for that purpose. These examples come from farmhouses and are probably eighteenth century, though by this time there were far grander and more decorative fire irons being made. *Left to right:* 18½ inches × 13 inches; 11 inches × 12 inches; 17 inches × 16 inches. *Private collection.*

lowliest peasant dwellings, as well as rough grisset pans, pokers and flesh-hooks.

There were two basic methods of roasting meat: by hanging it from a hook suspended over the fire, or by skewering it and roasting it horizontally on a spit. The choice depended on the fuel, the hearth and the chimney. It is interesting that in Wales, where there was stone enough to build all the roads in England, the basic firepit construction of hearths continued in farmhouses and small cottages until the first enclosed stoves and kitchen ranges were introduced in the eighteenth century. Most households in Wales depended on peat for their fires, since timber went to make charcoal for the smelting furnaces. Miners and their masters were more fortunate and burned coal in their kitchens. So, although horizontal spits and spit-dogs were sometimes used, it was more common to find a standing roaster and a blackened iron hook hanging from a crossbar in the chimney on which the meat was spiked and roasted, often with a crude version of a dangle-spit to turn the joint. Fish and meat were also grilled or broiled on cast iron grids which fitted over the fire pit.

30 Spit-roasting over a raised brick-topped hearth in an eighteenth century Continental kitchen. The cook bastes the joint while the kitchen boy pounds spices in a mortar and in the background a man wields a meat cleaver. The cooking fire is set into a trough on top of the brick top, wood was stored beneath. *Mansell Collection.*

Iron for casting was easier to make than bar iron for forging, and, as the supplies of wood for domestic use dwindled in parts of the country, coal was used in grander houses as early as the sixteenth century. It goes without saying that this only occurred in districts where coal was near at hand or could be transported by water, for the state of the roads was so abysmal that none could go any distance overland. At this time coal was mostly used in parlours of larger houses, rooms from which all cooking activity had been removed, for coal still presented problems in the kitchen. Cast iron fire grates, known as 'chamber grates' or 'cole basketts' were installed for burning this new and noxious fuel which burned with great belches of sulphurous smoke.

In seventeenth century kitchens, the horizontal method of spit-roasting was still favoured for more creative cookery, since it was much more adaptable for complicated and decorative dishes. Iron or brass-and-iron trivets and footmen stood beside the fire in the dining hall or parlour to hold dishes and plates to keep them warm, and more sophisticated steel or steel-and-brass fire irons lay in the grate. There was an improvement in the old methods of vertical roasting too, for dangle-spits with counter weights allowed the meat to be cooked more evenly over the open kitchen hearth. The hook or dangle-spit was twisted so that the joint rotated. When it reached the end of its revolution, the impetus would wind it up again in the opposite direction so that it went on turning without assistance until all the momentum was spent.

If coal was already being used as a domestic fuel in the sixteenth and seventeenth centuries, why then was charcoal still being used to smelt iron? There is no way of avoiding confusion without going into a few technical details about the making and smelting of iron ore and the problems with which the great early ironmasters had to contend. Iron smelted with charcoal has a very high carbon content, making it easy to pour when molten and so malleable that it can be worked almost like plasticine. When it had been smelted out of the ore, the molten iron was poured into a cast consisting of a central channel which fed rectangular moulds and made brick-shaped ingots. These ingots were known as 'pigs' because the whole cast resembled piglets feeding from a sow. Hence 'pig iron'. Originally these 'pigs' were known as 'wrought iron'. In that sense the term has long since ceased to be used and is now applied to any iron which has been worked or 'wrought'. Artefacts made from charcoal-smelted iron have a bloom and silkiness which is unmistakeable to the expert, and it does not rust.

As well as being used to make wrought iron, high carbon or 'supersaturated' iron was also beaten into sheets to make armour, which is probably where the technique of making steel was first discovered. Steel is iron with some of the carbon removed, which would have happened as the iron was constantly reheated during hammering into thin sheets. Swords and cutting blades were made with a different technique known as 'case-hardening'. Bar iron was heated and beaten into blades and then thrust into powdered animal bones which added a 'skin' of carbon to the surface of the metal. The process was repeated again and again, so that the steel became immensely strong yet remained flexible. Finally, blades were tempered – heated to a very high tempera-

31 An elegantly-designed steel dangle-spit which enables the cook to vary the height of the meat from the fire. The weights are clearly defined at the end of the arms, which curve in opposite directions to increase the spin of the spit. *c.* 1790. Height 32 inches. *Rupert Gentle Antiques.*

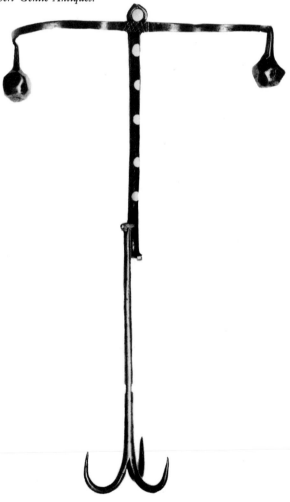

32 Transitional bar grate consisting of a pair of wrought iron firedogs joined together by three horizontal bars, with two additional tiers which hooked over the lower ones to give additional height to contain a heaped fire. Hooked on to the lower bars is a bar grate kettle-stand holding a small brass cooking pot. This type of transitional grate was first introduced during the early eighteenth century. Height of outside spit-dogs 43 inches; width 36 inches. *Private collection.*

ture which gave a hard outer surface to the steel, akin to 'blueing' on a gun barrel. Tempered steel was less liable to break and was much less susceptible to rust than untempered steel.

Iron for casting did not have to be as pure as bar iron – indeed some of the high carbon content had to be removed so that it would stand up to the high temperature of burning coal in grates, because pure iron melts at a relatively low temperature. Early spit-dogs had to be supported with additional legs so that they did not bend with the heat of the fire. Although Wales was seamed with easily-mineable coal, iron was not smelted there in any quantity until the eighteenth century when Abraham Darby discovered that coke – coal with the sulphur burned off – could be used, with some difficulty, for ironmaking. But the iron which came from the coke-fired furnaces was only suitable for casting, and not for making bar iron to be forged and wrought. So where timber for charcoal was scarce, England imported bar iron from Russia and

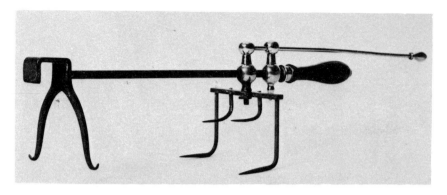

33 An elegantly-designed and exceptionally well-made steel-and-brass bar grate larkspit with adjustable cooking prongs. All manner of small birds were cooked and eaten in the eighteenth century, including sparrows and bullfinches as well as larks. *c.* 1780. Length 34 inches. *Rupert Gentle Antiques.*

34 Cast iron cheek grate from a Wiltshire farmhouse. The ratchet-operated cheeks could be wound in to contain a smaller fire. These grates may have been built so that coal could be used as an alternative fuel to wood. This type of adjustable grate was first introduced in the 1720s, probably for town houses. This example is a later design for country houses, dating from the mid-eighteenth century. Height 24 inches; width 42 inches. *Private collection.*

Sweden, whose timber supplies seemed inexhaustible. Where there was timber in England, the ironmasters continued to bury themselves in forests, moving from place to place in search of water power to drive their hammers and slitting mills. Wayland's Smithy had good reason to be hidden away in the woods, for forges needed charcoal for their hearths.

By the 1760s there were seventeen coke-fired blast furnaces in England, producing a harder, less silky metal which was used for making cast iron. England's timber supply was rapidly being eaten up at the rate of twenty-four hundredweight of charcoal to every ton of iron, and the Russians and Swedes demanded more and more exorbitant prices for their bar iron. No new charcoal-fired blast furnaces were built in England after 1775, and by 1790 there were only twenty-five left in the whole country. It was John Wilkinson or 'Iron Mad Jack' who finally solved the problems of smelting iron with coal in the 1780s. This was the song his workers sang in praise of the saviour of the iron industry:

'That the wood of old England would fail did appear
And tough iron was scarce because charcoal was dear.
By puddling and stamping he prevented that evil –
So the Swedes and the Russians can go to the Devil.'[20]

Proud as they were of their master's achievements, it is worth adding that iron from this period onwards had an increasing tendency to rust.

In Scotland, however, matters were slightly different. Coal had been mined and used as a domestic fuel long before it became common in England as 'sea cole' from Newcastle. Timber in Scotland was still plentiful, so the Scottish smiths could be profligate in using bar iron to make all manner of beautifully wrought roasters and toasters. In Edinburgh too, living conditions were unique in the whole of Europe. When the English defeated the Scots at the Battle of Flodden Field in 1513, the Scots built a great wall around their capital city to defend it. They felt so threatened by constant attack that they did not dare to live or build outside the security of its battlements. So Edinburgh grew, not outwards, like every other town and city in the rest of Europe, but upwards. Gaunt small-windowed granite towers of as many as fourteen storeys high shouldered their way into the grey skies of the north, and these tenements or 'closes' housed every class of citizen, from high-born to lowly artisan, under their high roofs.

Small hearths were built within these great stone edifices, with chimneys leading to a central flue. Since coal was the only fuel available in any quantity, Scottish smiths made bar grates to contain the fierce hot fires. So there evolved the bar grate roaster, later adopted in many other parts of the country when down-hearth cooking gave way to enclosed fires with bar grates and hob grates. Because of the cramped living conditions, all cooking in the 'closes' was done in the presence of host

35 A finely-made steel bar grate fish roaster from Scotland with a heart-shaped handle. Whole salmon could be impaled on the wicked spikes as well as collops of meat or fish steaks. *c.* 1760. Width 17 inches. *A.& E. Foster.*

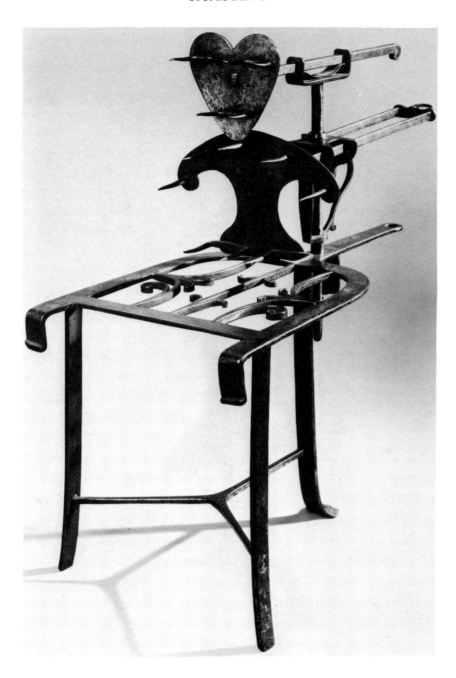

36 An exceptionally fine eighteenth century wrought iron standing roaster, which can also be hooked to the bars of a grate. The refinements in design include springs to hold the two adjustable arms, which can be moved independently backwards and forwards. The trivet top has been forged from three single pieces of bar iron, pug-welded to the frame, and it has a maker's mark under the handle. Height: approximately 22 inches. *A. & E. Foster.*

37 A wrought iron bell-shaped or helmet larkspit with an elegantly turned finial, for use with transitional fire grates. Toasted cheese and spiced buns were toasted in front of the fire in the drawing rooms and parlours of the eighteenth century. *c.* 1780. Height 35 inches.   *Rupert Gentle Antiques.*

and guest. And so the Scots made beautifully wrought roasters and toasters, many of them elaborately decorated with hearts and scrolls, showing the lasting French influence on their culture. On these roasters and toasters the Scots cooked collops of meat, barm bread, oakcakes, sourdough scones, salmon steaks and appetising concoctions of toasted

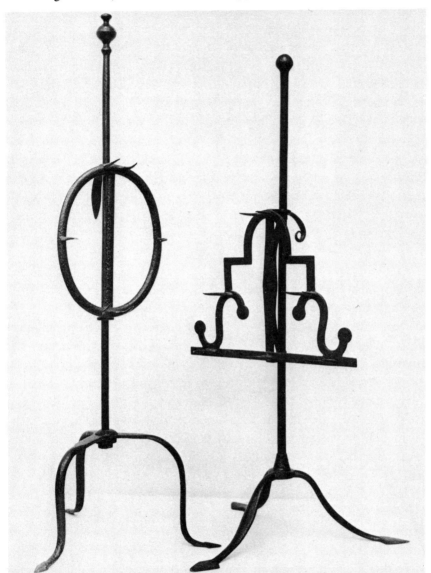

38 Two elegant wrought iron and steel standing roasters. From their height, they were intended for down-hearth cooking, although it is possible that the one on the left, with its circular frame, was used to hold a fire-screen made of plaited straw of similar shape to an archery target. *Left:* height 32¼ inches, *c.* 1780. *Right:* height 29½ inches, *c.* 1750. *A. & E.Foster.*

cheese: soft cheese melted with butter and mixed with chopped gammon, onions or anchovies.

Standing larkspits may also have developed originally from this unique pattern of living. Early three-legged meat roasters and toasters were certainly used for down-hearth cookery as their height indicates, and it is possible that they were first used in Edinburgh as early as the sixteenth century. Helmet-shaped or bell-shaped larkspits are also found in Wales, where they were suitable for cooking small birds and pieces of meat and fish over peat fires, but it is doubtful that they were in widespread use before the end of the seventeenth century. Certainly by the reign of Queen Anne, standing meat roasters and larkspits were widely used, though their elegance hints that they stood in the hearths of 'chamber grates' in parlours and dining rooms, and were not intended for the kitchen quarters. The height of these decorative eighteenth century toasters, often made of steel trimmed with brass, indicates that they were used during the transitional period when fires were partly enclosed and raised off the hearth. Perhaps they were made to toast tea-cakes for the lady of the house to offer her guests in the drawing room.

Until the end of the seventeenth century, meat was so tough and stringy that it was often parboiled before it was roasted. Sheep were bred primarily for their wool and not for the table. They were small, goat-like animals with short straight horns and long straggly fleeces – thin rangy beasts whose descendants roam the sheepwalks of Wales and the Cheviots. Beef-cattle too were small, lean, wild-looking versions of today's Black Welsh and Red Devon, or ferocious shaggy beasts like Chillingham cattle. There was no winter feed for animals until after 1650, when the practice of keeping stock alive through the winter by feeding them turnips was introduced into England from the Netherlands. Slowly, domestic animals became stronger, better-fleshed and quicker to mature.

Scotland was a prime beef producer. Cattle were the main currency of highland chiefs and as such were the subject of endless contention between clans, and the main objective of most Border raids into England. Even before Scotland was finally united with England in 1707, more than 30,000 cattle a year came from northern breeders. But the animals who plodded down the drove-roads were small and thin even before they started their long trek south. Drove-roads criss-crossed the land from the northern uplands to the fast-expanding towns and cities, bringing meat of all kinds from pasture to market. High-feeding cattle

39 Two down-hearth standing roasters. These standing roasters are excellent examples of the varying skills of country blacksmiths both in design and finish. Height 32½ inches *(left)* and 29½ inches *(right)*. *Private collection.*

travelled the drove-roads ahead of close-feeding sheep, and last to come were pigs and geese who foraged on what was left of the food. There were regular penning and watering places and at regular intervals along the roads blacksmiths made small shoes for oxen. The animals kept to a steady eight miles a day after four miles on the first day to break them in.

There were few abattoirs or slaughterhouses until ways had been found to keep meat tender in its raw state. Animals were eaten fresh-killed, before sinew and tendon toughened. If this was not possible, the carcase was hung until the right state of decomposition had been reached, in much the same way as game is hung today. Cattle were hamstrung, their heads pulled down on to a block in the ground and their tails twisted up over their backs to keep them down. Goats and sheep had their throats cut, and pigs were always slaughtered near the house where there was plenty of water. The blood was caught in bowls filled with hot boiled corn, barley, oats or pulse, and made into black

40 An ingeniously-designed bar grate roaster, which could hardly be described as elegant. It is probably an excellent example of the kind of roaster made and used by artisans in the 'closes' in Edinburgh, although this one came from Perth. *c.* 1780–1800. Base plate: width 13½ inches. *Private collection.*

41 An alehouse kitchen in the eighteenth century from a print by Rowlandson, showing a dog-spit in action. Although the roasting spit has a disc wheel at one end, there is no second wheel fixed to the chimney breast – the usual way of transferring power to turn the spit. A stockpot sits in the flames and an iron drip pan holds the basting spoon. *BBC Hulton Picture Library.*

pudding. A 'pigsticker' rode around the countryside at harvest time to peform this gory service at the back doors of houses and cottages. This grunting, rooting mainstay of the household throughout the winter was not fat, squat and smooth like today's porkers, but long-legged and tough, and more akin to a wild boar than a pig.

In the high halls of manorial kitchens, cooks were without exception male, and scantily dressed owing to the great heat. The main hearth was vast, and the strength required to turn a spit carrying a dozen or more different joints and carcases was too much for a whole brigade of little spit-boys, half-dead with heat. Taking their cue no doubt from the machinery of mill-wheels, seventeenth century blacksmiths discovered that a horizontal spit could be made to turn with a vertical drive, powered at first by the proverbial spit-dog. This poor creature trotted round the inside of a clumsy treadmill of creaking wood, suspended from the wall much as a mill-wheel hangs from the outside of a mill. But it was hardly a convenient, humane or hygienic way of cooking, and all manner of men turned their minds to the search for better sources of energy to turn their spits.

In spite of cumbersome cooking methods, a wide variety of inventive
and delightful dishes helped to detract from the poor quality of meat.
'Trayne Roste' for example, was still being served in country districts
with regional variations until the nineteenth century:

'Take dates and figges and kutte them and take grete reysoms and
almonds and prick them through with a nedel into a threde a mannys
length and one of fruit and another of another frute and then bynde the
threde with the frute arownde the spete. Take a quarte of wyne or ale
and fyne floure and batur thereof and cast thereto pouder ginger, sygur,
and saffron, poudre cloves, salt (and make the batur not fully rennynge,
nother stonding, but in the mene) that it may clove. Then reste the
trayne and caste the batur on the trayne as he turneth so longe, till the
frute be hidden in the batur. And as thou casteth the batur thereon hold
a vessell undere nothe for spilling of the batur, and when it is y rosted hit
wol some a hasselet (sausage). Then take hite uppe from the spete al
hole, and kut in fair paces a span lengthe and serue a pece or two in a
dissh al hote.'[21]

It does not take a great leap of imagination to realise that the habit of
basting with 'batur' resulted in small gobbets of uncooked batter
dropping into the dripping pan and cooking in the hot fat – the origin of
Yorkshire pudding.

As methods of cooking improved, hot 'graveys' and sauces accompa-
nied both meat and fish. It is possible that cresset firedogs had their
wrought iron baskets filled with small quantities of coals from the main
fire to make small braziers over which these hot garnishes were cooked
in small saucepans. Basket spits allowed more delicate flesh to be
cooked without disintegrating. They must have often been used for fish,
which falls apart very quickly, even when it is cooked whole. Turbot was
roasted on a spit, basted with verjuice and spices, haddock with garlic,
and skate with a sauce of fish liver and mustard. Salmon too, which
came down from the North by sea, was also cooked whole. But up to the
end of the seventeenth century, the problem of providing the power to
turn a spit remained.

Almost certainly the credit for the invention of weight-driven spit-
engines must go to the clockmakers, for the mechanics are remarkably
similar to the weights which drive the mechanism of a clock. Wheel-
spits were already in use in the early seventeenth century, turned by a
dog or cranked by hand. They operated in much the same way as a

42 Wrought iron adjustable basket spit. The two-pronged fork secured the meat, and the basket adjusted to clamp it firmly and prevent it from disintegrating. The spit-bar has a disc-wheel for use with a spit-engine. Plain four-hooked spit dogs are of the same period. Basket spit: width 25 inches. *Private collection.*

bicycle chain driven by pedals. Two iron discs were riveted together to make a grooved wheel which was attached to the end of the spit bar. A second wheel was fixed to the chimney-breast by a spindle and crank, and a rope or chain was looped round both wheels. But wheel-spits were not very efficient, and soon weight-driven spit engines began to supply the driving power. A wooden drum replaced the crank handle and a length of rope or chain was wound round it with a heavy weight attached to one end. As the weight – usually a heavy stone – dropped, the drum turned the spindle and drove the wheels of the wheel-spit. A governor wheel regulated the speed at which the drum turned, and the first mechanical gadget had been invented for the kitchen.

Some spit-engines were crudely made in iron, and some had beautifully engraved brass faces which again betray the hand of the clockmaker. A few early ones have survived, bearing the dates of the last two decades of the seventeenth century, but they are rare. By the mid-eighteenth century however, they were in common use all over England, fixed to the cross-beam of the kitchen chimney with long bolts, effortlessly turning spits in farmhouses and manor houses, coaching inns and public houses. Mechanically they were remarkably advanced in

43 Spit-engine with brass face and original wooden running chock. The face is inscribed 'Broad. Bodmin', a late eighteenth century clockmaker. The counterweights can be adjusted to control the speed of the turning drum. *c.* 1760–1800. Height 16½ inches. *Christopher Bangs.*

the principles they used, and decoratively they provide one of the finest examples of the incredibly high standards of craftsmanship devoted to so many common domestic items of the eighteenth century.

The universal use of spit-engines in eighteenth century England was not copied in Colonial America however. Horizontal spit-cooking was restricted to grand and privileged homes with labour enough and to spare, while the rest of the community relied on the most primitive ways of roasting meat. The ban on manufacture, high taxes for imports and lack of technical skills prevented any advance from the old method of suspending meat by a hook in the chimney hanging from a pole of green wood. One new arrival wrote home complaining that her roasts were very poor for they had no spit-engine. And at Valley Forge a talented Parisian chef resigned from Baron von Steuben's household because of the primitive conditions in the kitchen, saying that a waggoner could roast as well as he.[22]

These conditions lasted until the 1850s when Sarah Josepha Hale of

New York State published *The Ladies New Book of Cookery* and gave instructions for spit-cooking which have long since vanished from any manuscript in England, if indeed they were ever written down. She advocates a brisk clear fire, a clean spit, tightly trussed meat, weighted with skewers with leaden heads so that the meat would turn properly. The fire should be three to four inches longer than the joint, and the dripping pan should be removed before stirring the fire which should on no account be allowed to get dull and low. Meat should not be sprinkled with salt when first 'put down' as salt draws out the meat juices. A leg of

44 Cast brass spit-engine with steel spindle and governor wheel. More elaborate and decoratively-engraved spit-engines were being made by the middle of the eighteenth century. This example shows the mechanism clearly and its simply functional form dates it around the middle of the eighteenth century. Height 10 inches. *Rupert Gentle Antiques.*

lamb was usually hung down to the fire, and so was a sirloin of beef so that it could be turned evenly.

There were obvious difficulties in roasting meat vertically, for Sarah Josepha Hale instructs her young housewives to tie a piece of well-buttered writing paper round the meat or secure it with small skewers, particularly over the fat side. She advises covering the meat with a paste

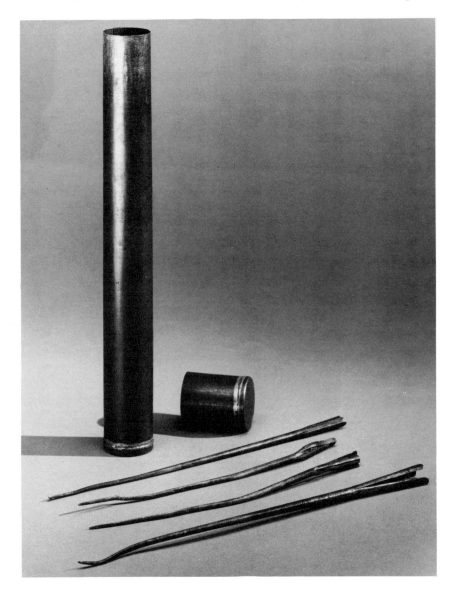

45 A set of larding needles and sheet tin case. Sets of skewers are frequently found, but it is rare to find a set of larding needles in such a good state of preservation. Case: height 10 inches. *Colonial Williamsburg Foundation.*

of flour and water over thin paper, then more paper over the paste. The 'coat' should be taken off a quarter of an hour before serving, when the meat should be dredged with flour and basted with fresh butter.[23] Small wonder that the regular way of cooking meat in Colonial America was to bake it in an iron pot buried in hot coals. Meat was 'baked'. 'Roasted' seldom entered the vocabulary of American kitchens except for cooking coffee-beans and hot chestnuts.

Some colonial farming families built ovens like small kilns, made of brick or clay, some distance from the house, frequently on the flat surface of a felled tree-stump. In these were baked bread, cakes, pies, beef, geese, turkeys, chicken pies and pork and beans. In winter, when great fires of oak and rock maple blazed indoors, they used a 'tin kitchen' or reflector oven. It is widely held that the reason that Colonial American kitchens are so often built separately from the main house was because of the fire hazard to the clapboard buildings. In the suffocating heat and humidity of summer it must also have been a practical solution to the problem of cooking without increasing the already insufferable high temperature indoors.

Kiln-type 'Dutch ovens' were relatively rare however, and the name is generally applied to a heavy cast iron pot with a lid, similar to West Country English 'yetlings' or Irish 'bastables'. These were general-purpose baking utensils made, according to eighteenth century records of the Pine Grove Furnace, Pennsylvania, in three sizes: small, middling and large. Presumably because cast iron shatters easily if it is dropped, the demand for lids greatly exceeded the demand for 'Dutch ovens'. Similar cooking pots, known as 'camp ovens' were also made in England for export to the Colonies, and in 1782 the famous firm of Carron Co., Falkirk, was making them in quantity in sizes graded from six to twenty-four inches in diameter. The term 'Dutch oven' however, is the cause of great confusion, because in England it usually means something completely different.

Towards the end of the eighteenth century many houses in England had 'kitcheners' or cooking ranges installed, made of cast iron, which contained the fire between iron cheeks and incorporated an oven. Thomas Robinson took out a patent for his kitchen range on October 21st 1780, describing it in great detail:

'One side of the fire is the oven and the other is made to wind up with a cheeck. The top bar in front is made to fall down occasionally to a level with the second bar. The moving cheeck is made with a socket in it to receive a swinging trivet. The oven is made of cast iron, nearly square in front, the door hung with hinges and fastened with a handle and a turnbuckle and the oven is provided with fillets for the shelves to rest upon. The oven must be enclosed with bricks and mortar.'[24]

In some cases horizontal spits were adapted to these new grates, but elsewhere the meat was suspended from a sophisticated version of a dangle-spit which hung inside a metal hood known as a 'hastener' or, confusingly 'Dutch oven'. This metal hood stood in front of the grate and had a door at the back, and a drip-pan which fitted into the base so that the meat could be basted without having to move the whole contraption away from the fire. In England the term 'Dutch oven' is usually applied to these 'hasteners', the equivalent of American 'tin kitchens' and not to cast iron cooking pots which the Americans call 'Dutch ovens'.

The greatest revolution brought about by hob grates and ranges was the employment of women as cooks in the kitchen. As long as cooking was done on open, down-hearth fires, women had only worked in dairies and sculleries, preparing food but not cooking it. The reason is plain, though gruesome. Up to the seventeenth century the principal cause of death among women, second only to childbirth, was hearth death. With spreading skirts and spreading fires the picture conjured up is horrendous. Raised brick-topped hearths reduced the danger to some extent, but once cooking fires were safely enclosed in cast iron grates and ranges, women began to come into their own in the kitchen. The first cookery books written by women for women were published towards the end of the eighteenth century, coinciding with the development of kitchen ranges.

Apart from Mr Robinson's patent range, enclosed cook-stoves and ranges were already being manufactured by the end of the eighteenth century, not only for kitchens, but for ships. George Oliver of No. 80, Wapping, London,[25] was selling enclosed stoves with bar grates in 1799, complete with hearth, shovel, poker, spits and spit-racks, all tinned to prevent them from rusting in the salty atmosphere. In spite of these innovations however, the Englishman remained wedded to the spit, enclosed stoves notwithstanding. This was partly due to his predeliction for meat served scorched on the outside and almost raw on the inside. But it was also because the first kitchen ranges baked and roasted very unevenly. One side of the oven, against which the fire was pressed, became red hot while the opposite side was considerably cooler. Some

46 A sheet iron 'hastener', also known in England as a 'Dutch oven'. These hoods were placed in front of the cooking fire and date from the time that the first hob grates were introduced. The hood simultaneously increased the heat in which the joint cooked and shielded the cook from the fire. They were still in use in large kitchens well within living memory. The brass bottle-jack was wound up with a key and the clockwork mechanism turned the meat without assistance. Hastener: 54 inches; width 20 inches. Brass bottle-jack: overall length 11 inches. *Private collection.*

47 A fine plain wrought steel dangle-spit dating from the middle of the eighteenth century. The two weighted arms add impetus to the turning meat. Length 18½ inches, extending to 27¾ inches. Width 13¼ inches.   *Christopher Bangs.*

enclosed ovens were fitted with dangle-spits, as were the first gas-fired ovens nearly fifty years later, and for the same reason. Others had shelves fitted on pivots so that the meat could be turned to cook evenly, but on the whole it was an unsatisfactory method of roasting.

Bottle-jacks, so-called because of their shape, had been in use since the middle of the eighteenth century. They were clockwork devices which developed from the old dangle-spit method of vertical spit-cooking, and were a neat solution to the problem of roasting meat over enclosed fires. Made in bright brass or japanned metal, they hung from jack-racks fixed to the chimney-breast, or inside a curved metal hood or 'hastener'. Though few bottle-jacks have survived, since they wore out and were thrown away, jack-racks can still be found, some plain, some grand, with a plate on one end to fix them to the wall and a hinged bracket ending in a hook so that they could be swung from side to side and folded against the chimney-breast when not in use. Some jack-racks have small wheels running down a central groove so that the joint could be moved backwards and forwards, towards or away from the fire. Bar grate trivets and freestanding trivets probably held dripping pans as well as kettles keeping warm by the fire.

Cooking ranges and kitcheners presented new problems: the early ones had no enclosed flues and consequently there were great difficulties in controlling the smoke which belched upwards from sooty coal fires. In 1795, an American-born Englishman called Benjamin Thompson of Salem, Massachusetts, came to London to investigate the problem of smoky chimneys and fireplace construction in general. Later given a title by the Holy Roman Empire, he is better-known as Count Rumford, and under that name is credited with inventing the first kitchen range with an enclosed flue.

48 A late eighteenth century working drawing of the mechanism of a 'Smoak Jack' showing how the fan in the throat of the chimney is turned by hot air currents in the chimney and powers the spit-wheel in the hearth. *Mansell Collection.*

But the new 'kitcheners' were also extremely expensive and wasteful to run. The Bodley Range of 1802 with its advanced solid cast iron cooking surface and smoke flues used a prodigious twelve to fifteen scuttles of coal a day and the nauseous pollution of such quantities of soot and smoke which poured from town chimneys plunged London into an era of 'pea-souper' fogs from which it did not emerge until the 1950s. But though a pall of smoke continued to hang in the air outside, inside, in early nineteenth century kitchens, a revolution was taking place. In 1840 Monsieur Alexis Soyer arrived in England to redesign the new kitchens of the Reform Club in Pall Mall.

What Monsieur Soyer thought about the last development in spit-cookery is not generally known, but Count Rumford was extremely outspoken when he first encountered a 'smoke-jack'. This remarkable piece of scientific engineering made use of convection currents rising from the fire to turn a paddle-wheel in the throat of the chimney. The driving shaft was at first set inside the chimney, but later models were installed with their steel and brass mechanisms outside on the chimney-

49 A magnificently-preserved smoke-jack mechanism made by Jones Brothers in brass and steel. The motive power was supplied by a giant paddle-wheel in the throat of the chimney which turned in the convection currents from the heat of the fire. These last and most sophisticated spit-engines adapted themselves to the age of locomotion with their cogged gears and milled brass wheels, though they were made first at the end of the eighteenth century. *Peter Nelson.*

breast, where they did not get clogged with grease and soot. Count Rumford declared that no human invention was so absurd, nor so wasteful. He calculated that less than one thousandth part of fuel necessary to be burned in order to provide enough power for a smoke-jack to turn a loaded spit would do the same job if it powered a small steam engine. In any case he considered that cooking meat on a spit in front of an open fire was an altogether barbarous practice.

Count Rumford's opinion was totally ignored. Although 'smoke-jacks' were far too large for domestic cooking, they were installed in stately homes and country houses, coaching inns, restaurants and hotels which now sprang up as the railway linked city to city. Monsieur Alexis Soyer was prevailed upon to install smoke-jacks both in his revolutionary new kitchens at the Reform Club and in the Royal Pavilion at Brighton. Enthusiastic as he was for all things French, the Prince Regent, like all Englishmen, insisted on having his roast beef done to a turn.

4 Boiling

50 Skimming broth – from an illumination in the Louterell Psalter, 1340. *Mansell Collection.*

'WHEN YOU COOK A CRANE, see to it that the head does not touch the water but is outside it. When the crane is cooked, wrap it in a warm cloth and pull its head; it will come off with the sinews, so that only the meat and bones remain. This is necessary because one cannot eat it with the sinews.'[26] The Romans must have learned this neat operation from bitter experience after years of cooking tough, stringy wild game. Alternative methods of cooking meats were tried simultaneously with roasting, particularly when the food available was tough and old, or was not able to be eaten fresh-killed.

Neolithic tribes, living in caves and huts in primeval Britain, made rough pottery vessels into which they put hunks of meat wrapped in bark or hide and covered with water. Then they dropped hot stones into the pot until the water 'seethed'. This word has roots in Norse, Old German and Frisian as well as Old English, from which it may be deduced that 'seething' was a fairly widespread practice in Northern Europe. 'Seethe' meant variously 'boiled sheep's flesh', 'sacrifice', 'soak', 'steep', 'stew' and 'pit' and was therefore probably also applied to boiling troughs, the other method of cooking meat. A pit was dug and divided in half. One half was lined with flat stones and made roughly waterproof with clay, and a fire was lit in the other half. Eventually the heat penetrated to the water in the trough and it began to 'seethe'.

Primitive tribes in Britain skinned animals and tied the hide by its four legs to stakes, fur side down over the fire. Into it they put gobbets of raw meat which they covered with water. The subcutaneous fat on the inner side of the skin cooked into a rich, greasy broth, and as long as the fire was kept low the hide would singe but not burn. The inhabitants of remote lands in the north of Scotland were so isolated, backward and primitive that this method of boiling beef in the hide persisted in remote parts of the country until the 1720s.

The principle had been grasped, but there were no containers which would stand up to the heat needed to boil food and broth. True, Greek traders on their courageous forays into the savage northern seas in search of gold, copper and tin, brought metal cauldrons to barter with the wild inhabitants of the West of England and Ireland as far back as the eighth or seventh century BC. But apart from rich trading colonies who had minerals to barter in exchange, it was not until travelling Irish

51 Sheet brass cauldron. The base has been riveted and may well have been an early repair for the side has also been neatly patched. The rolled rim is reinforced with iron, and the lugs and handles are also of wrought iron. This rare survival probably dates from the early seventeenth century. Height 14½ inches; diameter 24 inches. *Colonial Williamsburg Foundation.*

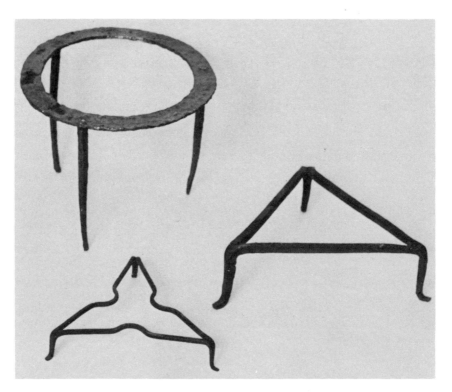

52 Three wrought iron brandreths to hold pots, baking irons, frying pans and griddle pans just off the direct heat of the fire. These humble and essential articles wore out quickly in the constant heat and few of them have survived. Triangular brandreth: height 1½ inches; length 7 inches. *Private collection.*

tinkers and smiths copied the cooking pots from the Mediterranean that metal cooking pots were used to any degree in Britain. English metal cauldrons are quite distinctive from Continental ones because of their sag-bottomed shape which persisted in both metal and pottery cooking pots at least until Tudor times.

The use of metal cooking pots was the first great leap forward in culinary art. Food could now be boiled rapidly over a high fire, or simmered slowly at the edge of the hearth in the hot ashes. If the metal pots were placed directly onto the fire, food stuck and burned, but if the pots were raised a few inches above the heat, allowing the air to circulate beneath them, the problem was minimised. At this early stage, metal pots made in England were of sheet copper or brass, and so it was impossible for the smiths to copy the grand cast-metal three-legged pots and cauldrons. Instead they fashioned rough circular, triangular or square stands called 'brandreths' to stand their pots on, and achieved the same result.

Although the Romans did not make much impression on the untamed, mist-shrouded islands of Britain, they did not leave empty-handed. They ate very little beef before they crossed the Channel, but in England they developed a taste for it, and cattle-breeding became an important activity in the Frankish lands of Northern Europe to which they retreated. Anthimus, a Greek physician, wrote at length to Theoderic, King of the Franks, on the subject of food and dietary disciplines in the sixth century AD. Anthimus predates Galen and his Salerno school of diet and medicine by nearly four hundred years, but already there is a distinct Eastern Mediterranean flavour about his instructions for cooking beef. The meat should be washed and boiled in clean water until almost cooked. Then sharp vinegar, heads of leeks, pennyroyal and roots of smallage or fennel should be added, together with honey to the quantity of half the vinegar. The stew should be simmered over a slow fire for another hour, while a seasoning should be prepared in a mortar from a little ground pepper, costmary, spikenard and cloves dissolved in wine. This should be blended into the beef broth to give aroma and delicacy to the finished pottage.

53 Reconstruction of a Roman kitchen showing the raised brick-built cooking hearth and iron griddle to hold cooking pots. The earthenware amphorae and water-carriers have been excavated from Roman sites and are original. *Museum of London.*

The importance of this recipe is Anthimus' use of leeks and the sweet-sour combination of honey and vinegar which helped to tenderise the meat. Garlic, leeks and onions all originated in Egypt and Palestine and were generally believed to be good for health, virility, eyes and throat. The Latin for leek is *'porrum'* and porrays and pottages were basic peasant diet all over medieval Northern Europe in one form or another. For a white porray 'take up the white of the leeks and seeth them in a pot and press them up and hack them smal on a board. And take good almond milk and a little rice and do all these together and seeth and stir it well and do thereto sugar or honey and dress it in.'[27] White porrays were eaten on fast days with salted eels.

Pottages were more substantial and were usually made with pulses, dried peas, dried beans, lentils and even vetches in famine years, all stored after being 'frizzled' to prevent them from sprouting. Thick nourishing vegetable pottages were made of 'worts' or greens, such as colewort, cabbage and sprouts, particularly from Brussels. It may seem strange that England imported such lowly vegetables from the Low Countries, but trade between England and Holland was as regular as coastal traffic. Ships carried wool from England to trade for Dutch rape oil – rape being the acid-yellow crop so often mistaken for mustard – which the English used as a substitute for rich Mediterranean olive oil.

There was very little cultivation of rape in England until Tudor times, or indeed any vegetables at all. The market gardens of Flanders supplied the English, who were too busy conquering France to cultivate their own gardens. Apart from meat, sheep and wool, England was far from self-supporting and relied heavily on imports for food of all kinds, not only sugar, rice, spices and dried fruits. The first market gardens to supply the city of London were established in the sixteenth century, when Spanish galleons cut England's jugular vein and took control of the English Channel. Elizabethan England had to learn how to shift for herself.

With exceptional single-mindedness, Queen Elizabeth I dragged her subjects out of the dark ages and into the light. Trading companies were commanded to return with detailed reports of the resources of all the countries they visited. Timber and pig iron were of prime importance, to build her ships and arm them with cannon. Skills of all kinds were desperately needed: weaving and dyeing cloth, mining, smelting, casting, making brass and glass, breeding animals to produce better meat, improving sheep to increase England's only staple commodity of wool. When Gloriana died the pattern of life and trade had been laid down which was to govern England's success as a trading nation for years to come. The great trading companies had been founded – the Merchant Adventurers, the East India Company, the Levant Company, the Virginia Company, the Baltic Company – and sugar and spices, oil and wine, pig iron and timber were all coming into the country in exchange for wool.

Flemish, Dutch and German craftsmen were encouraged to come to England to teach their skills and English craftsmen began to make their first fumbling attempts at producing basic goods for their own people. Alone among metalworkers the bell-founders knew how to cast bronze

54 Cast bronze ewer with the familiar reeded legs and feet seen on many English cast cauldrons and skillets. This was probably made by a London bell-founder named William Elyot about 1400. The English inscription bears the name of his relative, Thomas Elyot. Height 10 inches. *Museum of London.*

55 Bell metal skillet with reeded handle and feet which are almost intact. Skillets were made in bronze, bell metal or cast brass over a period of two hundred years in England, from the sixteenth century to the eighteenth century. They were still being used even later, as old recipes show. Sealed pots were placed to cook in a skillet full of boiling water: glass jars were heated in skillets full of sand. Their earliest use was for heating milk and cream, because the metal heated slowly and did not burn; and for refining sugar, since even at high temperatures the poor conductivity of the metal meant that the handle remained cool enough to touch. This one has the number '3' on the neck of the handle, indicating that it was one of a set. *c.* 1680. Height 6⅛ inches; diameter 6¼ inches. *Colonial Williamsburg Foundation.*

and bell metal, and so to them fell the task of making cast metal skillets and cauldrons. The homilies cut crisply in the handles of these three-legged cooking pots such as 'Pittie the Pore' and 'In Christ was All Beganne' have the sanctimonious overtones of their origins, though the metal they used was not as pure as the thoughts they tried to impart. Today bronze, bell metal, gun metal and brass are immutable alloys with specific ratios of tin, copper and zinc. But the Elizabethan metal founders were far less particular. Shruff – scrap metal of all kinds – was thrown into the melting pot, and early English skillets are recognisable as much by their variation in colour as by the unevenness of their casting.

There was good reason for making skillets in expensive bronze and brass alloys, and not of iron, although the iron founders were technically far more advanced than the bell-founders. Brass is a poor conductor of heat, so that even when the contents of a skillet boiled fiercely the handle remained cool enough to touch. Iron on the other hand is an excellent heat conductor and the handle would have heated quickly to the same temperature as the rest of the pot. Milk and cream could be scalded in skillets without burning or boiling over. Costly sugar, with its high boiling point, could safely be clarified and refined without turning to caramel, and while it boiled, the impurities which rose to the surface could be skimmed off with a brass skimmer.

With central open-hearth cookery, cooking was a necessity rather than a pleasure for the average citizen of England. An inventory of kitchen equipment for a fourteenth century household shows how meagrely even manorial halls were equipped: 'A brandreth, or iron tripod for supporting the caldron over the fire; a caldron, a dressing board and dressing knife, a brass pot, a posnet or saucepan, a frying pan, a gridiron, a spit, a gobard, a mier for making breadcrumbs, a flesh hook, a scummer, a ladle, a pot-stick, a slice for turning meat in the frying pan, a pot-hook, a mortar and pestle, a pepper quern, a platter, a saucer for making sauce.'[28] A 'gobard' was probably a goblet of some kind and a 'mier' a sieve, most likely made of horsehair.

Brick-built chimneys changed the whole pattern of living in England. Farmhouses and manor houses separated their kitchens from the main living quarters. Where once it has been impossible to escape from the smoke, grease and dirt, there were Turkey carpets and fine linen. Brass, pewter and silver gleamed from proud polished dressers. In the kitchen there were iron 'ratchyngcrokes', whose notches held a rough ratchet so that the pot could be lowered or raised over the fire. Soon there were jibs and cranes, which swung towards and away from the fire so that the

56 Bell metal skillet with tapered handle, fleur-de-lys decoration and shaped rim. The casting is in one piece and, though pitted, it is crisp and clear. This flatter, wider shape is often found in bell metal and the form is distinctive for early skillets made up to the beginning of the seventeenth century. Height $5\frac{1}{2}$ inches; diameter $6\frac{1}{4}$ inches. *Michael Wakelin.*

57 Down-hearth cooking in the seventeenth century. Hearth death was second only to childbirth as the most common cause of death among women during this period. The scene is Dutch, but the conditions are identical to English down-hearth cooking at that date. *BBC Hulton Picture Library.*

pot could be hung over varying degrees of heat. Pot-cranes varied from plain iron struts with a simple swivelling arm set into sockets in the chimney brickwork to gloriously decorative wrought ironwork, often embellished with brass. Some of them were clumsily complicated, and combined the up-and-down mechanics of the ratchyngcroke with the hooks and chains which dangled sootily from them.

In time there were more refinements. Notched pot-hooks or trammels were forged, looking like a coarse-toothed saw, but more efficient than the old ratching crook. Some pot-cranes had small pulley-wheels running along the horizontal arm so that the cooking pot could be hung over any part of the fire. Decoratively speaking, the finest early pot-cranes were probably made in Scotland, where they were known as 'sways'. The Scots had been making decorative wrought ironwork toasters and roasters since the early sixteenth century, but as the coal and iron industries of Wales grew more technically advanced, Welsh smiths soon overtook the Scots, and in a country where firepits and hanging pots had been the traditional method of cooking for centuries, by the eighteenth century their ironwork was superb.

Iron pots were made with separate hangers which hooked on to lugs. It might be assumed that this was because of poor casting techniques, for those pots which have lugs are remarkably crude. But the Dutch, who were far more advanced, made their cooking pots in the same way, indicating a practical advantage. Perhaps it was because the pot-hangers became too hot, too dirty and too greasy to handle. Once it was possible to swing them away from the fire and lower them to the ground, the pot-hangers could simply be removed and scoured without having to empty the entire cooking pot to clean the handles. And a cold, clean pot-hanger could be exchanged for a hot dirty one with very little effort.

Iron pots were always round-bellied and made to hang over the fire. Cooking pots which stood in the embers of the hearth itself were cast brass, bronze or bell metal and often had three reeded legs usually

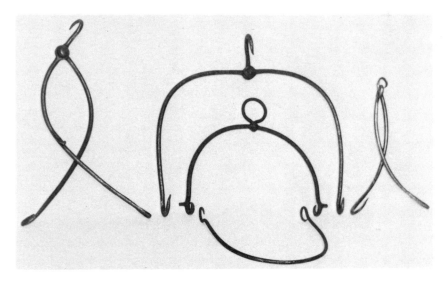

58 Detachable pot-hangers in wrought iron which were attached to hanging pots from the earliest times until cast iron hollow ware was manufactured with integral lugs and attached handles. Central pot-hook: width 30 inches. *Private collection.*

59 Pot-hooks, trammels, flesh-forks, ratchyngcrokes and salamanders. A collection of early wrought iron cooking equipment. *Private collection.*

ending in a hoof-shaped foot. A few survive today complete in their original shape and condition. Others have shortened legs where the feet have been completely worn away by centuries of use and heat, and there are some which never had a complete footed leg at all. These pots may have been made on the Continent as regular run of the mill pots for all sorts of uses other than cooking. Tanning, dyeing, brewing, candle-making – dozens of trades and crafts used metal pots to make a hundred and one different things, and there was no reason to make them with too much care since they were purely utilitarian. Their rough casting, however, makes them look very similar to the first of the best that England could make.

Domestic cooking pots on the Continent were often made with the lost-wax process, which gives them a smooth finish inside and out. But even when the English brass-founders were making considerable quantities of cooking pots and skillets, they continued to cast them in sand, as they cast bells. The mould was set upside-down, often in a pit in the earth, with a clay core, so that the inside was smooth but the outside was rough, often pitted and seldom decorated. Early 'gates' or 'sprues', as the pouring channels in the cast for pots and skillets were called, were oval or circular – later ones were rectangular or square. Larger cauldrons and skillets were sometimes cast in two halves and brazed together.

The reason why English founders did not use the lost-wax process remains a mystery. With foreign craftsmen working all over England from Cumberland to Sussex, it is hard to believe that they would not have used the Continental technique, which was so much less laborious, unless the materials themselves were not available. Perhaps the reason

60 A magnificent example of the blacksmith's art – a wrought iron pot-sway with a beautifully simple design in the centre, which shows how the bar iron was split and worked from a single piece. Early eighteenth century. Length 54 inches. *Victoria & Albert Museum.*

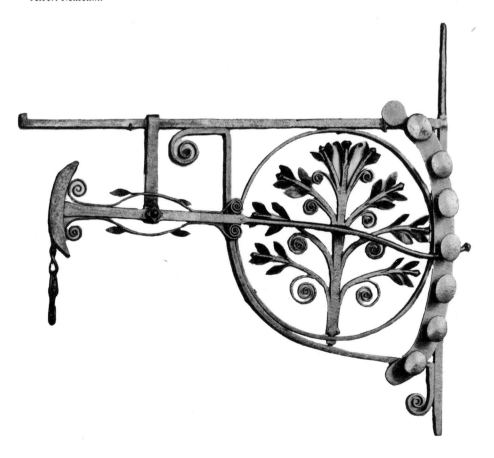

61 Kitchen at the Governor's Palace, Williamsburg, Virginia, an out-building away from the palace, a customary practice in most Colonial American houses. In front of the open hearth is a 'Dutch oven', sometimes known as a 'tin kitchener'. Note the absence of any pot-crane or spit-jack, even in such an important house. The Governor's Palace was completed in 1720.   *Colonial Williamsburg Foundation.*

62 Cast brass skillet, posnet or pipkin, shaped like a small cauldron, with three legs and stem handle. It is seamed and was cast in two halves and brazed together. This type of cooking vessel is typical of those made by English founders from the end of the sixteenth century to the end of the seventeenth century in the traditional shape. Height 6½ inches; diameter 4¼ inches.   *Michael Wakelin.*

dates back to the Dissolution of the Monasteries under Henry VIII, when the principal producers of beeswax and honey were disbanded and there was simply not enough wax available in England. The Catholic countries in Europe had no such problems. Cast brass and bronze cooking pots continued to be made and used in Spain and all over the Middle East and the Near East long after they had been superseded in Europe, and in many places they are still made today. The shape is a little different, but to a novice they are easy to mistake for ones made centuries earlier.

Jacobean England, with enclosed coal fires, separate kitchens, brick chimneys and a burgeoning industrial economy, was closer to the Continental way of life than it had ever been. Brick-built Continental cooking hearths were built into many country manor house kitchens,

63 Large cauldron in cast brass with traditional English sag-bottomed shape. Meat was often suspended from a hook into the cauldron so that it did not stick to the bottom. Bunches of vegetable were tied in cloths and hung round the edges. Sometimes earthenware pipkins containing 'spoonmeats' (morsels of meat or fish) stood inside the cauldron, which was filled with boiling water. This cauldron is seamed and has been cast in two halves and brazed together. *c.* 1620–1650. Height 19½ inches; diameter 15 inches. *Michael Wakelin.*

64 Cast brass cauldon with rudimentary raised design and date, 1658. Molten brass was an easier metal to cast than bronze which was slow to pour and quick to set. Cauldrons were sand-cast, upside down over a clay mould which produced a smoother interior finish. This example shows rare expertise in making the mould for the outer surface, which was usually rough and pitted from the sand. Height 15 inches; diameter 14½ inches. *Michael Wakelin.*

those same flat brick surfaces with charcoal fires burning in inset cavities in their brick tops, which the Romans had used. Here, where the heat was not so fierce, copper pots and pans could be used, and small side-dishes and sauces could be cooked over controlled heat. Copper posnets with turned wooden handles, copper frying pans and those flat oval dishes reminiscent of Roman *patina*, with cast brass or bronze handles, began to infiltrate English kitchens. On the Continent, where cooking had always been done over small braziers and brick-topped hearths, copper *batteries de cuisine* had been made and used for centuries, and England was at last beginning to catch up.

Hitherto copper had been made and used in England mainly for such things as jugs, measures, dippers, milk room pans and cream-setting pans where it was not subjected to much heat. Even over a fairly low heat the metal softens: brass handles were not just a decorative feature but a practical one, for copper handles, apart from heating up too quickly, would have bent if the pans were heavy and hot. The fact that copper was tinned to prevent tainting food presented another problem. Tin has a very low melting point, and will blister and bubble if heated too fiercely. The uncontrolled hearths of pre-Jacobean kitchens in England were totally unsuitable for anything but heavy iron, bell metal, bronze or cast brass.

Some attempt was made to meet the demand for frying pans lighter and easier to use than clumsy, long-handled iron pans by using sheet brass. In 1671 a Flemish family called Holland or Hallen set up a brass battery-works at Wandsworth in Surrey to mass-produce 'kettles' (or boiling pots) and frying pans, making up to nine at a time in a nest at one heating of the metal. It was obviously a successful venture, for they expanded all over the country, opening up manufactories at Keele in

65 Cast brass cauldron with traditional English sag-bottomed shape, though it has been cast using the lost-wax, or *cire-perdue*, process which would seem to indicate a Continental or Dutch origin. It may have been made, like so much fine English brass, by expatriot Dutch brass-founders working in London, Bristol, or one of the other English brass centres. *c.* 1740. Height 20 inches. *Rupert Gentle Antiques.*

Staffordshire, Newcastle-under-Lyme, Coalbrookdale, Stourbridge and, eventually, in Birmingham itself. But brass was expensive and the supply of raw brass was erratic. Smaller domestic items such as strainers and skimmers could be made economically from sheet brass; cast brass ladles and spoons of that period were probably imported expensively through Flanders. But in the main kitchen pots and pans were made of iron, and ladles and spoons of wood, or copper with iron handles riveted onto the bowl.

As the pattern of life changed in England, so too did the food which was prepared and cooking in the separate kitchen quarters. Consistency had played a vital part in determining what could be served up on squared-off trenchers of stale bread, but by the beginning of the seventeenth century pewter and silver became the rule for plates and dishes in all but the poorest households, and even they had wooden

66 A woman in her kitchen. An illustration of a seventeenth century kitchen with a raised brick cooking hearth built on exactly the same principal as Roman hearths. The introduction of raised hearths made kitchens slightly safer for women, whose trailing skirts and sleeves endangered their lives if they cooked over a low spreading fire. *c.* 1618. *BBC Hulton Picture Library.*

platters and wood or horn spoons. The Reverend William Harrison, the Elizabethan chronicler, bears out the fact, recording the change from treen (wooden) platters to pewter and of wooden spoons to silver or tin. 'The age of forks was not yet come; where knife and spoon would not avail even the Queen picked up the chicken bone.' Until the reign of Queen Elizabeth I 'a man should hardly find four pieces of pewter in a farmer's house. Of china there was no question.'[29]

Consequently meat pottages became more sophisticated: meat was cut up into small pieces, seasoned with saffron and herbs and served

67 Copper and cast iron water cisterns. With the advent of enclosed bar grate fires and hob grates the shape of water boilers changed from wide-mouthed vessels to enclosed cisterns with brass taps so that hot water could be drawn off without removing the hot vessel from the fire. Copper cistern: height 10 inches; diameter 10 inches. Cast iron cistern: height 10 inches; diameter 12 inches. *Private collection.*

68 A punched sheet brass colander with cast brass handles. Although brass corroded and sometimes tainted food, it was a far more satisfactory metal than copper from the point of view of withstanding heat. *c.* 1750. Diameter 14 inches.   *Rupert Gentle Antiques.*

with rich gravy thickened with flour. In Northern Britain there were echoes of more barbaric days. In Scotland meat pottages were served with a singed sheep's head stewed in it which gazed blindly at the diners when it was proudly brought to the table. But apart from such regional lapses, cookery in Jacobean England was refined and imaginative. Wheat and corn grew and flourished in the empty spaces once covered with forest. Corn laws and bread controls were relaxed and flour, once reserved for the privileged, was freely available. Most cottages had small brick ovens built into their chimneys, and even the most lowly hearths had pans of bread dough set to rise in the warmth.

Basic grain-based pottages or porridges, known in Scotland as 'crowdie', in Wales as *'llymru'* or 'flummery', were still the staple diet of the poor in the seventeenth century. Whole grains were boiled to a soft jelly and eaten with butter or honey and in towns street vendors sold buttered wheat and buttered oats by the dishful. Flour-based sauces swept the country with the dubious results that a universal white sauce smothered every dish from meat to vegetables to puddings. 'Puddynges' made of dough, sweet or savoury, were served as a first course to take the edge off over-enthusiastic appetites in much the same way as 'rowly-powly pudding' was dished up in the nineteenth century. By the seventeenth century, dumplings bobbed in broth to stretch the meat.

There were no potatoes in those days to bulk out the meagre contents of the cooking pot. Although, as everyone knows, Ireland virtually subsisted on them from the seventeenth century onwards, these versatile tubers from high in the South American Andes took a rather more circuitous route into England. Spanish ships brought them to Europe, where they took root in the Spanish Netherlands rather than in Spain itself. When the Dutch fought wars, they grew potatoes as a war crop to feed their soldiers and in 1689, with the Dutch King William, potatoes came to England. By the eighteenth century they fed the English peasant almost as exclusively as they did the Irish.

Until then it was dumplings. At first they were made separately and not dropped into the stewpot, as this recipe dated 1653 shows: 'To make dumplings, season your flour with pepper, salt and yeast, let your water be more than warm then make them up like manchets but let them be somewhat little, then put them into your water when it boileth and let them boil an hour then butter them.'[30] The medieval 'manchet' was a small loaf or bread bun. Across the centuries many things had changed but not all.

Shortly after the death of Queen Elizabeth, the Scot Fynes Morison reported that:

'The English have abundance of white meats of all kinds, of flesh, fowl and fish and of all things good for food . . . In the seasons of the year the English eat fallow deer plentifully, as bucks in summer and does in winter which they bake in pasties, and this venison pasty is a dainty rarely found in any other kingdom, yea perhaps one country thereof, hath more fallow deer than all Europe that I have seen. No kingdom in the world hath so many dove-houses. Likewise brawn is a proper meat to the English, not known to others.'[31]

Venison was still kept for the tables of land-owners, and sold in towns, but thrifty cottagers made brawn from the head and tougher parts of their home-reared pigs. The Reverend William Harrison again:

'When the boar's foreparts are thus cut out, each piece is wrapped up, whether with bullrushes, osiers, peels or suchlike and then sodden in a leaden cauldron together till they be so tender that a man may thrust a bruised rush or straw clean through the fat; which being done they take it up and lay it abroad to cool. Afterwards, putting it into close vessels, they pour either good small ale or beer mingled with verjuice and salt thereto till it be covered and so let it lie now and then altering the sousing drink lest it should wax sour till occasion serve to spend it out of the way.'[32]

For the countryman there was jugged hare, now that hares bred freely in the wild again. It was stewed in cider, laid in an earthenware pot or jug within a larger kettle of boiling water and left to simmer for three hours. The habit of wrapping meat in leaves, bark or rushes was common. What more natural than that bread dough should be substituted? Apple dumplings and meat puddings were wrapped in a pudding cloth and bubbled in a broth of vegetables, all cooking at the same time. Earthenware or clay pots had also been used for the same purpose, as the recipe for jugged hare shows. There were special containers for the purpose, often mistakenly thought to be cider owls or mead jugs. They were wide-necked, jug-shaped vessels with a small spout to one side and a tightly fitting lid. The lid was sealed with dough and the small spout allowed the steam to escape so that the earthenware pot did not burst as the pressure built up inside. The vessel was lowered into a cauldron of boiling water to cook.

This method cooking was brought to an extreme refinement in the mid-seventeenth century by de la Varenne's *poulet en ragout dans une bouteille* which he described in his book *The French Cook* in 1673.[33] A whole boned chicken was stuffed with a forcemeat of mushrooms, truffles, sweetbreads, pigeons, egg yolks and seasoning and inserted like a ship in a bottle. The mouth of the bottle was sealed with pastry and it was then immersed in boiling water and left to cook. The final touch of sheer extravagance was that a diamond was needed to cut the bottle open so that the entire *poulet* could be served whole.

The French indeed were making huge technical strides in their culinary progress. John Evelyn recorded a visit to the Royal Society in 1682 to sample food cooked over less than eight ounces of coal in Denis Papin's 'digester'. Papin, a French physicist, was the originator of the pressure-cooker: his 'digester' was a closed vessel with a tightly fitting lid and a safety valve to release excess pressure which built up as the contents boiled, but though he invented the 'digester' in 1679 no one thought of it as more than a scientific novelty and it sank into oblivion.

While the French made such culinary leaps and bounds, Cromwell's Puritannical rules brought English cooking up on its heels. Pies and puddings were forbidden as inventions of the devil, sauces and spices condemned as Papish corruptions. It could be that these harsh laws were rooted in politics rather than religion, and governed by expediency rather than the desire to deprive. All trade with Catholic countries, the source of most dried fruits and spices, ceased and England was ravaged by civil war. Crops went untended, corn unharvested, and there might have been a rebellion if the demand for flour had continued to rise and the citizens insisted on raisins and currants to put in their puddings. Whatever his reasons, Cromwell inflicted great damage to progress in the kitchens of England from which it never fully recovered. With the Restoration of Charles II and his arrival in London with a foreign queen and a foreign court, the rest of England took its fashionable cue from their king and French influence reigned supreme.

Once again, raw metal for industry was running short in England as a result of Cromwellian trade policies. Sweden was asking far too high a price for pig iron and Parliament was petitioned to encourage mining in the new colonies. It must have gone hard with Colonial Americans, who were forbidden to manufacture their own goods, to see their iron carried away to England as ballast. There it was made into pots, pans and kettles, implements and tools, and sold back to America at a high price. Denied the opportunity of self-improvement, the settlers used what equipment they were given and improvised as best they could.

With very little iron available, Colonial kitchens were equipped with nothing more than a stout lug-pole made from green beech or maple, from which hung pot-hooks and trammels. Without pot-cranes or sways, iron pots were lifted off the fire with long iron levers. Americans made special trivets for their long-handled frying pans and in them cooked pan-bread and 'johnny cakes', or journey cakes, made from maize meal mixed with rye. Mostly they subsisted on a diet of samp or hominy and barley broth or bean porridge. They ate from wooden bowls with wooden spoons, and when they were lucky their broth was made from woodchuck and wild turkey, salt beef and moose meat. Their diet also included two basic ingredients still vitually unknown in the Old World: Virginian potatoes and sweet potatoes from the West Indies, which they baked in the hot ashes or boiled in their broths. Without scales and weights, they used volume to measure quantities: a cupful, a wineglass, a piece the size of a walnut.

After the Revolution of 1776 small mining and smelting concerns sprang up and America began to make desperately needed goods of all kinds. The accounts and day-books of the Pine Grove Furnace, Pennsylvania, show that besides making kettles, skillets, Dutch ovens, cooking pots and frying pans, it was turning out everything from hatters'

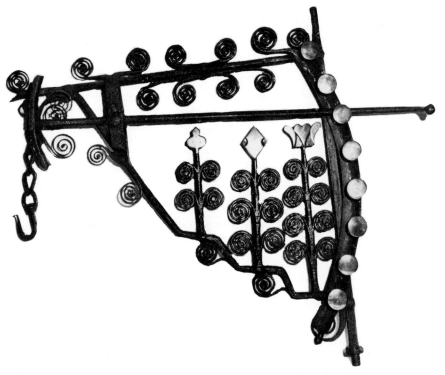

69 Wrought iron pot-sway or pot-crane. A fine example of a complicated mechanism incorporated into a beautifully swirling design of wrought iron with brass decoration. The lever could be adjusted up and down the brass studs to raise or lower the pot, which hung from the end of the chain. The whole pot-crane swivelled on a heel set into the chimney brickwork so that the pot could be swung away from the fire. Although ornate, it is a little more restrained than Scottish iron work of the period, and may be Welsh. *c.* 1700–1750. Height 36 inches; length 45 inches.   *Vermoutier & Bankes.*

irons to waggon boxes, windmill wheels, swedge anvils, small firedogs, clock weights, chamber pots, mortars and pestles and even steleyard weights and paper-mill spindles. They also slaughtered beeves for meat, hide and tallow. All the metal goods were manufactured with one casting a week. It was a small concern, employing men to break stones at the mine bank, labourers to cart the ore, wood and coal, team drivers, furnace men and smiths. On Sunday the furnace was fired, achieving a high enough temperature by Wednesday to smelt the ore, and on Fridays, often late in the afternoon, they cast.[34]

Mid-eighteenth century England was a country of very uneven development. Inland, and in more remote parts of the countryside, life had changed very little since the days of Elizabeth, but where there was water transport, by river, canal or sea, merchant travellers sold their goods in bulk to warehouses in towns and cities. Innovations from all over the world were available to the rich merchant class as well as the aristocracy, and English craftsmen were quick to adapt and improve on almost every kind of merchandise.

Scotland, though united with England since the beginning of the century, was still very much under French influence in its way of life and

70 Heavy cast iron cooking pot, with typical squared lugs incorporated in the casting and a detachable hanger with spoon spur. The feet have been considerably worn down and, unlike the previous example, it may originally have been intended to stand in the hearth. Height 9 inches; diameter 10 inches. *Private collection.*

in its kitchens. A Scottish housewife, Elizabeth Raper, published *The Receipt Book* for women, with such success that a number of editions were printed, spanning fourteen years in all, from 1756 to 1770. The inventory included shows how many more implements of all kinds were being used, and the recipes in the book include marinating vegetables and making 'daubes, fricassees, pillaus and chicken *à l'Aspicq'* – all very French. She lists the following equipment for a well-furnished kitchen:

'8 copper stewpans, two of 1½ gal. one of 1 gal. etc. down to small size. 1 oval fish kettle, 1 middle sized braising pan, 1 preserving pan, 1 round bowl for beating whites of eggs, 2 sauté pans, 1 omlette pan, 1 frying pan, 1 bain marie, 6 saucepans, 1 middle sized tin pie mould, 2 tin jelly moulds, 1 tin flanc mould for fruit, 1 freezing pot and requisites, 2 baking sheets, 1 gridiron, 1 small salamander, 1 colander, 1 spoon, 1 bottle jack, 2 spits, 1 dripping pan, 1 screen, 1 sugar pan, 2 soup ladles, 8 copper spoons (two pierced for straining), 2 wire baskets, 1 wire sieve, 2 hair sieves, 24 tartlet pans, 2 tammie cloths, 1 jelly bag, 12 wooden spoons, 2 pastebrushes, 1 pr. scissors, 2 kitchen knives, 6 larding needles, 1 packing needle, 1 box vegetable cutters, 1 box paste cutters, 1 meat saw, 1 cutlet chopper, 1 meat chopper, 6 tinned meat hooks, 1 rolling pin, 8 kitchen basins, 6 china pie dishes, 6 earthen bowls for soups and gravies, 4 kitchen tablecloths, 18 rubbers, 12 fish napkins, 6 pudding cloths and 4 round towels.'[35]

Copper and iron began to compete for favour in the second half of the eighteenth century. New smelting techniques made it possible to run iron much thinner, resulting in lighter hollow ware, tinned on the inside and blacked and stoved on the outside. Until the mid-eighteenth century copper was still relatively scarce and expensive and to a great extent had been commandeered to make brass for ordnance and other essentials. But in 1763 a positive El Dorado of copper was discovered in Wales – the famour Parys Copper Mine in Anglesea, known locally as Parry's Mountain. The price of copper plummetted, bringing it into direct competition with iron. Quite naturally, cooks preferred light, pretty copper saucepans, posnets and frying pans to heavy iron utensils

71 A finely wrought steel pot-hook inlaid with brass and copper in the tradition of gunsmiths and swordsmiths. Here the mechanism has been refined so that the clumsy ratchets of wrought iron trammels form part of the overall design. *c.* 1770. Height 28 inches. *Rupert Gentle Antiques.*

and most 'black' ironware of that date went abroad to the colonies who had little choice in the matter.

Industrial Wales had begun to stir its giant frame at the beginning of the century. In 1720 John Hanbury started to make tinplate at Pontypool, and by 1728 tinplate rolling machines replaced the ancient methods of beating metal into sheets with hammers, either power-driven or wielded by labourers. Methods of tinning iron hollow ware improved, and in 1776 John Izon, who had been making tinned hollow ware with modest success, purchased a patent from John Taylor for 'casting oval-bellied cast-iron pots' and 'nealing, tinning and finishing such kinds of round cast iron pots and saucepans as are made with a head or rim round the top'.[36]

John Izon moved his hollow ware manufactory to West Bromwich, and was soon making quantities of 'sweet' tinned cooking pots and saucepans and all manner of fine cast iron hollow ware, which began to come into more popular demand as the English palate mellowed and lost its appetite for strongly spiced food, preferring the sharp fresh taste of citrus fruits. Georgian dishes were far more bland than the heavily-flavoured dishes of earlier generations. *Andouilles,* known in England by the far less appetising name of chitterlings, were boiled in sage to take off the 'hoo-goo' (*haut gout*) and gooseberries, lemon juice, lemon peel, red currants and other acid fruits were used to flavour and help to tenderise the meat. 'Boeuf Alamode' was an extremely popular and fashionable dish of the day:

'Take some of a round of beef (the veiny and small round) and cut it 5 to 6 inches thick, cut some pieces of fat bacon into long bits, take an equal quantity of beaten mace, pepper and nutmeg. Double the quantity of salt if wanted. Dip your bacon in vinegar (garlic vinegar if agreeable) put in the spice, lard it with a larding pin very thick and even, put the meat into a pot just big enough to hold it with a gill of vinegar, 2 onions (large), a bunch of herbs, $\frac{1}{2}$ pint of red wine and some lemon peel, cover it down close, put a wet cloth round the edge to prevent the steam from evaporating when $\frac{1}{2}$ done turn it, cover it again, do it over a slow fire it will take 5 hours and $\frac{1}{2}$, add truffles if aggreable.'[37]

With dishes like this on every handsome dinner table, the problem of copper poisoning again reared its head.

'Acid contained in stews and other made dishes as lemon juice, though it does not dissolve copper by merely being boiled in it . . . if allowed to cool and stand in it for some time will acquire poisonous matter, as verdigris in the form of a green band or crust inside the vessel . . . Weak solutions of salt act powerfully on copper, strong solutions of brine do not.'[38]

So said Sarah Josepha Hale in her cookery book published nearly a hundred years later. The argument continues, with experts contending that copper carbonate, the chemical released if copper is brought to boiling point, is eliminated by the body normally and causes no harm, whereas copper acetate, released when acid foods are allowed to stand in copper pans or when fruit juices and other acidic ingredients are cooked in copper, is poisonous. To reduce the risk of poisoning, copper pots and pans were tinned, but this also presented problems, as Sarah Josepha Hale warned. She advised her ladies not to fry in a stewpan 'or else with great care and sufficient butter to save the tinning from melting.'

The only other innovation in English cookery which deserves a mention before the great revolution of enclosed fires, hob grates and kitchen ranges was the invention of the bouillon cube. It was known unattractively as 'veal glue' and was used not for making jelly, but for flavouring soups and stews. Strong veal stock made from calves' feet was simmered, strained, simmered again, left to set, scraped free of sediment and cooked again. 'When the jelly grow of a gluish substance . . . put it into little sweetmeat pots till it is quite cold, then you may take it out and wrap in flannel and afterwards in paper and it will keep many years. A piece the bigness of a nutmeg will make half a pint of broth . . .'[39]

The French Revolution, which began in 1789, caused an influx of French chefs into England, among them Carême, Escoffier, Ude, Franatelli and Soyer, the man who caused his own personal revolution in the kitchen with his designs for the Reform Club kitchens and those of the Prince Regent's exotic Pavilion at Brighton. Alexis Soyer's kitchens at the Reform Club attracted such attention that tours of them became fashionable for both ladies and gentlemen. Not for M. Soyer the heavy cast iron utensils of the average contemporary kitchen. Only copper, gleaming rank upon rank on shelf and wall: nests of oval entrée dishes, omelette pans and frying pans, saucepans in graduated sizes, deep boilers, *bain-maries*, braising pans, fish kettles and stewpots. If tours of Soyer's kitchens were fashionable, so too was his *batterie de*

72 Cast iron hot water kettle with spout. The familiar shape evolved in the second half of the nineteenth century when cast-iron hollow ware manufacturers began to mass-produce them for the colonies as well as for the home market. They were extremely heavy to lift, and were hung on kettles tilters or 'Lazy backs' so that they could be tipped and poured without taking them off the fire. Height 10 inches; diameter 8 inches. *Private collection.*

73 Hanging frying pans and baking irons. Every region had its own variation on basic cooking methods; a great deal depend on the food and fuel available. The circular iron baking iron with folding handle and accompanying brandreth is from Wales, where cooking fires were coal or peat. Both fuels produced a thick, acrid smoke and were not very suitable for cooking over at any height. Hanging frying pans were more suitable for the glowing charcoal of a wood fire. Griddle with brandreth: diameter 15 inches. The rest to scale. *Private collection.*

cuisine. One of the best-known suppliers of copper ware was the firm of Jones Brothers, who originated in Wales and who made pots and pans for the embryo catering trade. Their catalogues show that those original designs continued to be manufactured, almost unchanged, until the firm became defunct in the 1920s. Jones Brothers also manufactured spit-engines and smoke-jacks of great engineering complexity.

Although the makers of cast iron hollow ware struggled to make their products lighter and more attractive, copper had advantages with which they could not compete. Cast iron is a dirty metal, and it cracks and breaks extremely easily. Although it retains heat, cast iron takes some time to reach a satisfactory cooking temperature and is therefore not very economical to use. Copper, on the other hand, heats up very quickly, and though it has to be retinned regularly, it is virtually indestructible. Battered, dented pans could be beaten out to look like new, making copper an extremely economical proposition. Retinning was a simple, inexpensive process: a small quantity of tin was melted in the vessel itself and simply swirled around until it covered the entire inner surface. The surplus was poured off and the coating left to dry, and that was all. Methods have not changed and the same retinning process is still used today.

The only problem which remained unresolved to tinners of copper and cast iron was the difficulty of refining tin itself, which occurs naturally with lead, which is poisonous. Although cast iron hollow ware improved beyond recognition in the first half of the nineteenth century, alternative ways of coating the inner surface were being sought by manufacturers all over Europe. Archibald Kenrick, one of the most famous English names in latter-day kitchen equipment, first made his mark by producing rimmed saucepans for easier pouring and began experiments with enamel as an alternative to tin for coating the inner surface of cast iron cooking pots. These efforts were stimulated by competition from the Germans who had been experimenting with enamelling for some years.[40]

On the face of it, the ancient process of enamelling was not entirely suitable for cooking pots. The process consisted of grinding silicates of lead and soda of potash finely together and mixing oxide of antimony and arsenic into the resulting powder to produce a white finish. This combination of chemicals had a lethal potential, far more dangerous than the presence of lead in tin, since fruit and vegetable acids and fatty acids released poisons to a dangerous extent. German manufacturers encountered an additional problem: they were unable to prevent the enamel coating from flaking off when the pots were heated.

The first British patent for enamelling was taken out in 1799, substituting borax for some of the more poisonous elements, and using china clay as an undercoat. But the true innovators, on a commercial scale, were Thomas and Charles Clark, proprietors of an old-established firm of hollow ware manufacturers in Wolverhampton. T. & C. Clark succeeded in producing a lead-free enamel coating in the 1840s. The impetus for new developments came from the increasing amount of competition for overseas markets and the need to supply ships' galleys with sturdy pots and pans which would not rust and which could withstand the vagaries of ships' cooks whose talents were hardly those of *haute cuisine*. Old-fashioned 'black' hollow ware, now being mass-produced in South Staffordshire, was no longer suitable for the home market, but was still much-needed in the colonies where life was rough and there were few forges or smiths.

In the modest homes of nineteenth century England, things changed more slowly. Heavy black pots still hung from simplified pot-cranes over fires which were by this time enclosed, but now they only heated water

74 A kitchen in 1830. In spite of the many advances made as the Industrial Revolution gathered speed, raised brick hearths were still being used in the nineteenth century identical to those installed by the Romans. *BBC Hulton Picture Library.*

75 Copper half-kettle which sat on a narrow bar grate trivet with its flat side pressed against the fire, thus keeping the contents hot most efficiently. Height 6 inches. *Private collection.*

and the stockpot had a new place on the hob. The basic 'kittle' of medieval days had undergone many changes. Small brass taps had been added to the base of the pots, which were no longer cauldron-shaped but had narrow mouths with lids. Hot water was available without having to reach a dipper into the steam and risk a scalded hand or arm. Some 'kittles' were made of copper, similar in design, quicker to heat but more expensive. The true kettle of today with a pouring spout had begun to emerge, though it was still likely to be made of cast iron and was too heavy to lift from the fire. Kettle tilters, known as 'idle backs', 'lazy backs', 'Lazy Susans' or 'Lazy Bettys' solved the problem. They allowed the kettle to be tilted without taking it off the hook.

The Great Exhibition of 1851 probably marks the watershed between the last of the old hand-made equipment and the beginning of mass-produced, highly competitive domestic articles of all kinds. Steam power hastened progress: between 1805 and 1812 Kenricks installed their first steam-powered lathes for turning and finishing rough-cast iron pots, and the horses which for centuries had provided power for industrial machines were at last put out to grass. Competition for overseas markets was fierce – the Empire had expanded, new colonies were born, and from Buenos Aires to Adelaide, across Europe to Russia, the whole world was a market place for domestic articles of every shape and size.

Kenricks recognised the importance of publicity in this world of cut-throat competition and by 1840, years ahead of their rivals, the company began to produce illustrated catalogues for their salesmen. Kenricks also recognised the importance of having their name and their products constantly in the public eye. In 1868 they began to stamp pot lids and saucepan lids from pressed sheet steel, and soon the name 'Kenrick' was stamped on every article which left the factory and incorporated into the base of every pot as well as every lid. Other manufacturers such as Baldwins, Pugh, T. & C. Clark and many others quickly followed suit.

By the 1870s innovations were coming thick and fast. The Bessemer and Siemens-Martin processes meant that cast iron was superseded by pressed mild steel. The London Aluminium Company was in operation by 1879, in an attempt to bid for the American market which preferred lighter, easier to clean pots and pans made from this new alloy. Cooking with coal-gas had been pioneered by the Aetna Iron Works as far back as 1824 when they produced a gas griller. James Sharp of Southampton had also produced a cylindrical gas cooker to be shown at the Great Exhibition, but it was turned down by the Crystal Palace authorities as being far too dangerous. Undaunted, Sharp took it to America where it had a modest success. By the 1880s Bunsen's work on gas burners made town gas a safe and controllable fuel for big Victorian kitchens.

Gas cooking brought new problems to the hollow ware manufacturers. Enamelled iron saucepans became unpredictable and extremely unsatisfactory. Milk burned and pots boiled over as the uneven conducting properties of iron and enamel fought each other, and thinner coatings had to be devised to allow for the poor heat-conducting properties of enamel. Eventually British manufacturers abandoned enamelled iron saucepans in favour of steel and aluminium, though in America imaginative manufacturers began to produce saucepans enamelled in bright colours on the outside, which greatly appealed to American women. Everywhere the market for cast iron declined dramatically, except for the colonies where living conditions excluded anything more sophisticated.

The first Ideal Home Exhibition was held in London in 1909, with manufacturers vying with each other for a buoyant home and kitchen market, and was such a success that a second one was held in 1912. Then came World War I, and many hollow ware manufacturers went into government contracts for supplies for the armed services. When the war ended the entire industry was technically greatly advanced, a sad spin-off from years of making shell cases and weapons of war. By the 'twenties modern kitchens were equipped with 'Diamond Brand', 'Swan', 'Goat' and 'Tower' cast aluminium pots and pans. But yet again, although thousands of households 'modernised' their kitchens and, to the eternal sorrow of today's collectors, threw grates and ranges, pot-hooks, trammels and chimney-cranes onto the scrap heap, thousands more still kept to their old-fashioned Victorian ways, particularly in the country, where cast iron and brass kitchen ranges were blacked and polished until they shone.

Solid-fuel cookers, pioneered by Aga, revived the demand for heavy cast iron pots, pans and casseroles, and one firm in particular began to specialise in making brightly coloured ovenware, saucepans and cooking pots for this relatively small market. Ernest Stevens Ltd, founded in 1909, made 'Judge' and 'Jury' ware in the teeth of all logical argument and has continued to do so profitably until the present day. The wheel has turned full circle. Contemporary kitchens glow with copper pans almost identical to the ones used two hundred years ago. Almost, but not quite. These days they are often made of stainless steel which has been copper-plated, and many modern copper dishes, jelly moulds, casseroles and saucepans are no longer tinned inside but nickel-plated. Still, they look almost the same.

5 Baking

76 Kitchen boy pounding grain for flour – from an illumination in the Louterell Psalter, 1340. *Mansell Collection.*

THE HUMBLE LOAF looks far too innocent to be the cause of rebellion and revolution, martyrdom and persecution. Yet down the ages bread has been a political and religious issue. Kings, governments, popes and Churches were dependent on the feasts and famines of their people for their power. There have been corn laws, bread laws, assizes, controls and legislation, some just, some unjust, to keep the people pacified and submissive, while power remained in the hands of those who owned the land and cut the corn and milled the flour and made the bread – symbol of nourishment, well-being, freedom from starvation and the basic rights of man.

In England's Anglo-Saxon open-field system, harvests were thin and poor and frequently failed altogether because of blight and disease. To ward off famine, which stalked the land one year in ten, peasants grew a mixed crop of cereals, beans, vetches and weeds, so that if the corn failed there was still something to feed them and their beasts through the winter. They ground up dried beans and peas with whatever grain there was and mixed it with beer barm to make coarse black bread, and fed the rest of the crop to the animals.

In good years, when the grain fattened on strong upstanding stalks, the crop was reaped several times. First the ears were harvested in short sheaves, then the good straw was cut to make ropes and baskets, thatch for houses and skeps for bees. The stubble was left uncut and was reaped later in the year with the second flush of grass for cattle fodder. Finally, sheep, goats and pigs were turned out to forage on whatever was left. Not a blade of grass was wasted. Corn was stored in the driest place in the house to prevent it sprouting in the damp which seeped inexorably into house and hovel. The husks gave some protection, so the grain was stored in the ear and threshed as it was needed. If it was not dry enough to thresh and winnow, it was parched.

'A woman sitting down takes a handful of corn, holding it by the stalks in her hand, and then sets fire to the ears, which are presently in a flame. She has a stick in her right hand, which she manages very dexterously, beating off the grain at the very instant when the husk is quite burnt; for if she miss of that she must use the kiln, but experience has taught them this art to perfection. The corn may be so dressed, winnowed, ground and baked within an hour after reaping from the ground.'

That is a description of 'The Graddan' in the Western isles of Scotland, where they were still parching corn almost within living memory.[41]

The grain was then ground up, sometimes in a mortar, sometimes in a grooved stone trough with a round stone, and sometimes in a hand-quern – a stone disc with a couple of pegs driven into it, one as a central pivot and the other as a handle. The quern was set on a flat stone surface and rubbed backwards and forwards to crush the grains beneath. Up at the manor, corn was ground in a mill turned by oxen, donkeys, men or water-power, and then sieved into grades by being bolted several times through a series of coarse woollen and linen cloths. The finest grade made white bread, the next, bran bread, and the remains were baked as coarse trencher bread. The peasant's loaf of mixed pulse and cereal, was aptly called 'horse bread' because it needed a very strong digestion to stomach it.

Controlling the bread supply was the quickest way of bringing a conquered country to heel. After the Norman occupation, fierce legislation and appalling penalties were imposed to outlaw the use of hand-querns and force the serfs to obey the law and bring their corn to the manorial mill to be ground, paying taxes for the privilege. If the land they tilled belonged to the Church they had to take their corn to the

monastery, where tithes were exacted for milling. The great millstones
of the Norman barons were brought specially from Caen in their own
homeland in 'stone boats' which frequently foundered during the
crossing.

It was a legacy of another, older invasion of Britain which made
complete control of hand-milling impossible for the Normans. When
the Romans sent out their cohorts to subdue the ancient Britons, they
carried a hand-quern to every ten soldiers so that they could grind their
grain, mix it with water and make and bake flat bread on the march.
Legend has it that they used their breastplates to cook it in. Thus,
unwittingly, they spread the knowledge of milling from Gravesend to

77 Pie peel, oatcake spittle, dough scraper and salamander. In large households pie
peels and bread peels were often made of iron with a long wooden handle, but in farms
and smaller houses wood was the most common material. This pie peel is elm and
strongly resembles boards on which cheeses were laid to drain, but cheese boards
usually had a groove in the handle for the whey to run out. Oatcake spittles were used for
draining wet oakcake mixtures before they were flicked on to a bakestone or baking iron.
Dough scrapers were often no more than a flattened shell or flat stone. Salamanders
were used almost exclusively in large households, where they were heated in the fire and
used to brown the tops of pastries, pies and macaroni cheese (a favourite of Richard II).
Pie peel: diameter 21 inches. Spittle: length to end of handle 21 inches. Dough scraper:
5½ inches. Salamander: 28½ inches.   *Private collection.*

78 Sycamore butter bowl and carved elm spoon. Most bowls in the kitchen were used for a variety of purposes, with the exception of dairy equipment. All utensils for butter and cheese-making were kept scrupulously clean, scalded in salt water after each use and kept entirely for the dairy. Bowl: diameter 19 inches. Spoon: length 8 inches. *Private collection.*

Hadrian's Wall and beyond, and no future conqueror could stamp it out. During the fourteenth and fifteenth centuries the Scots used the same method to feed their raiding parties. The moss troopers hung flat iron bake-pans and leather bags of oats on their saddles and messed up oatmeal and water to make oatcakes which they baked over small fires. Thus they fed themselves without depending on supplies from headquarters or having to waste time and give away their positions by foraging in the countryside.

The 'mystery' of bread-making was jealously protected under the Normans by guilds of white bakers and brown bakers, each one scrupulously supervised by the Assize of Bread which laid down the weight and size of every loaf baked for sale in England. If a baker gave short measure, he was punished; if he offended a second or third time the penalties were extremely severe:

Item, if default shall be found in bread, the first time, let the baker be drawn through the streets on a hurdle, and the loaf about his neck; the second time, let him be drawn and set upon the pillory; and the third time, let him be drawn, and his oven pulled down, and let him foreswear the trade within the city'.[42]

Such fearsome laws probably gave rise to the baker's dozen – thirteen for twelve was a reasonable protection against the possibility of losing his livelihood.

A brown farthing loaf weighed twice as much as the finest white wastel farthing loaf. Wastel bread or pandemain (*panis domini* – sacramental bread) was stamped with the figure of Christ and baked in monastery ovens. A manchet loaf, also white, had to weigh eight ounces going into the oven and six when baked. A farthing wholewheat loaf must weigh one and a half times as much as a cocket loaf – the finest white bread of all, made from flour which had been sieved three times through woollen and linen bolting cloths.

Baking ovens in monasteries and manors were vast and cavernous, for they had to bake bread for the entire community. Few of them have survived in their medieval state, for most of them were bricked up and considerably reduced in size as the peasants gained the freedom to bake their own bread. But at Stanton Harcourt the original stoking sheds built outside, against the walls of the high kitchen, still stand. Great bundles of faggots and brushwood were heaved into the ovens and fired from these outside stoking sheds. When the ovens were hot enough, the hot ashes were raked out from the stoking sheds on to the ground outside. The master baker could then stack his loaves from the relative cleanliness of the kitchen through the arched openings to the ovens inside. Huge paddle-shaped peels were used to shovel the uncooked loaves into the furthest recesses of the vaulted furnaces. Doors of wood, clay or iron were clamped shut on either side and made airtight with clay. In due course the fresh baked bread was shovelled out into the kitchen and laid on racks to cool.

79 Steel bread-scales consisting of a pan suspended from three chains which held the correct weight, and a pair of hooks which grappled the loaf. They were almost certainly used in a bakery, for they date from the latter half of the eighteenth century – far too late to have been used in communal manor ovens. They weigh loaves of up to 4 lbs. Length of balance arm: 12 inches *Private collection.*

Prodigious amounts of wood were needed to keep monastery bake ovens hot. In Glastonbury the Abbot's kitchen used no less than 27,000 bundles of firewood for the last three months of 1538. During this festive winter season they baked fourteen hundredweight of bread which, at an average loaf-weight of one pound, works out at over five hundred loaves a week. Early baking equipment for these huge ovens was Brobdingnagian: the dough was set to rise in enormous elm chests, kneaded on trestle tables and stirred with wooden spoons the size of oars. Mountains of flour were mixed with buckets of water hauled from the nearest spring and seasoned from salt bins the size of milk churns. Wooden moulds pressed the sign of the cross on every loaf to drive out any evil spirits which might prevent the bread from rising – a custom

80 Elm dough bin. These sturdy chests sometimes have lids which hinge in two parts so that two batches of dough could be set to work at different times. They continued to be made with little change from the end of the sixteenth century to the end of the nineteenth century. Overall height 33 inches.   *Private collection.*

81 Wooden trough in an early nineteenth century Welsh farmhouse. The position of the trough, near the cooking fire, indicates that it was used for dough and not for salting meat. Similar troughs, sometimes lead-lined, are found in sculleries for that purpose. The picture shows how little conditions in the country changed over the centuries. *BBC Hulton Picture Library.*

which was only forbidden in the seventeenth century by Cromwell, who judged it to be Papish.

Not only was it unlawful for a peasant to grind his own corn, it was also unlawful for him to bake his own raised bread. But away from the watchful eyes of their lords and masters, country wives made flat cakes of yeast dough, laid them on hot stones and covered them with an iron pot, or 'kytel', over which they heaped hot ashes or peat, as they had done for centuries, and even succeeded in making unleavened bread rise a little. Under the iron pot the warmth from the baking stones circulated round the dough, so that some moisture was retained and the bread rose like small buns, lighter and more digestible than flat hearth-cakes. In the West of England, in Devonshire and Cornwall, where the people lived in poverty and isolation 'clome ovens' were still being used in the nineteenth century.

The frenchified barons of the Middle Ages lived in relative comfort and great style in halls and castles hung with tapestry to keep out the draught and damp. They dominated the landscape and the people, feasting frequently, fasting sometimes. They brought all manner of breads and doughs with them from France, the Low Countries and Italy and their Norman bakers made them all in England. There was 'pain perdu', white bread dipped in egg yolk, fried on a griddle and sprinkled with sugar. There were 'rastons', dough baked with a fist of butter in the centre; and 'pain farci', when the crumb was removed and the loaf stuffed with lobstermeat and oysters, herbs, butter and spices. There were 'tostes' too – white bread browned on a gridiron, soaked in wine, crisped and served with almond milk. And 'toste rialle', a thick paste of sugar, spice, sweet wine, quinces, raisins and nuts, bound with rice-flour and spread on hot toasted trenchers of white bread, decorated with sugar plate dipped in gold.

Later, there was French bread of puff – milk bread mixed with butter and raised with eggs – and spiced buns. There were 'gauffres', or wafers, too, made from a rich batter mixed with wine and run between two greased wafer-irons, which were thrust into the fire. Those same wafer-irons, cast with holy symbols to mark sacramental bread in monasteries, were soon decorated with secular designs and put to better, more appetising use. They travelled across the Atlantic centuries later to make American waffles, a corruption of the word 'gauffres'.

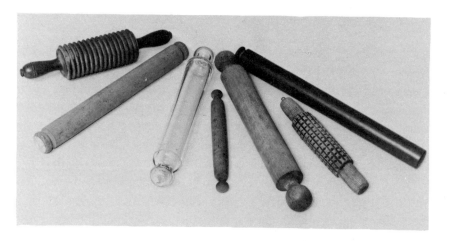

82 Rolling pins and oat crushers. Ridged rolling pins were often used with grooved 'riddle boards' for crushing oats for oatcakes. They were made of hardwoods and fruitwoods. In the nineteenth century oat crushers were sometimes of pine with a ridged tin or sheet brass jacket. Glass rolling pins were filled with cold water and used to roll out puff pastry. The pin on the right is not in fact a single-ended rolling pin but a late nineteenth century truncheon or nightstick. Oat crusher: length 13 inches. Glass rolling pin: length 18 inches. *Private collection.*

Twice-cooked bread was made in great quantities for armies and fleets, known by its Latin name *panis biscoctus* which gave us the name 'biscotte' or biscuit. There were simnels and cracknels too, glorified versions of plain flour-and-water ship's biscuits: 'Take best wheat flour and cook it in hot water so it forms a very hard paste, then spread it on a plate. When it is cold cut it up for sweets and fry it in best oil. Lift out, pour honey over, sprinkle with pepper and so serve it forth.'[43] With the exception of 'horse bread' and brown breads, most white bread was enriched one way or another, with butter, sugar, raisins and honey. This enriched bread still lives on in almost every region of the British Isles, as heavy cake, lardy cake, currant bread or fruit loaf – not quite cake but more than bread.

In the end it was charity which undid the barons and all-powerful manors and monasteries and gave the poor a taste for white bread. Alms bread was made from the finest white flour, boon workers were paid in white bread at harvest time – even the crumbs from the rich man's table dispensed at the castle gate were white. By the middle of the fourteenth century the peasants began to demand white bread as their right. At the end of Queen Elizabeth's reign there was scarcely a peasant in the land who would stand for his miserable diet of 'horse bread' and they had risen in revolt several times over the years to make their point. Wheat and corn, improved beyond measure from the miserable thin grains of the Middle Ages, now grew in wide fields where the forests had been felled, and the peasants would no longer put up with barley bread or black rye bread. Nor would they accept flour that was less than two-thirds wheat. Driven off the land by enclosures, their goat-like digestions had been weakened by inactive life in towns and cities. People who lived and worked in cramped conditions could not digest the heavy, lumpy loaves any more than the idle rich.

In the country, cottagers refused to buy flour that was less than four-fifths wheat. They had their own brick-built ovens now and would no longer be dictated to by the millers. The bakers had no sale for coarse-mixed brown bread, and would buy nothing but the best white flour. The Guild of Brown Bakers declined drastically and by the seventeenth century had faded into oblivion. In order to keep the people happy and unrebellious, England imported grain from abroad, at a price, and the millers acquired a new unpleasant image. No longer the jolly miller, but a mean, cheating, miserable arbiter of the nation's bread, he began to adulterate his flour to make a bigger profit. He burned alum in a shovel and beat it to a fine powder to mix with the flour to make it look whiter. Chalk, lime, bones from the charnel house, and even white lead were all grist to his mill. Though the miller might not be as pure as the driven snow, his bread must be white at all costs.

A few cookshops were established in London by 1183, mostly selling cooked meats and birds. By the fourteenth century any customer could have his own capon baked in a pastry for sixpence for 'the paste, the fire and the trouble'. It would seem that this way of cooking meat owed more to the ancient methods of wrapping it in clay and baking it in the ashes than to pastry as we know it today. Paste was an indigestible mixture of oil and flour, which was wrapped round fowls and white meat to keep in its natural juices and prevent it from drying out in the oven. Paste 'coffins' and pie-shells were made with the same mixture, and served as containers to hold the rich mixtures of curds and dried fruits. The paste was mixed in earthenware, stoneware or wooden bowls. For many their stone mortars were the only mixing bowls they owned. As often as not, they made paste straight on to the trestle table, pouring oil into a small well in a heap of flour and kneading it in with their hands. There were special pins for rolling out the paste, but a straight-sided stoneware flagon or a horn beaker served almost as well.

A cross-breed between this crude paste and the French puff mixture produced a richer, shorter paste which was used by the ubiquitous pie-shops of Elizabethan towns. Scarce fuel heated communal ovens to cook meats and sweetmeats, either brought in by the 'goodwife' – the mistress of the kitchen – or made and sold by the pieman. The custom of decorating paste pies with individual markings, flowers and leaves originated in the cookshops as a means of identifying the goodwife's own pies from her neighbour's or the ones made by the pieman himself.

In the huge bake ovens of manor houses, great pies were made and filled with capons, hens, mallard, woodcock, teal and squab (young pigeon). The birds were parboiled and then laid inside the pastry coffin in alternating layers with minced beef, suet, marrow, egg yolks, dried fruit, spices and wine. Chickens were yellowed with saffron and then 'couched in their coffins' with spices, verjuice and diced pork fat or lard. There were problems with preventing the lids from sinking, particularly with the heavy paste crust that was used. Oddly, no one thought of supporting them from the inside, though by now there were plenty of pots and funnels which could have served the purpose. Remedies were far more unreliable, as can be seen from this one for a lamprey pie:

Then cover him fair with a lid, save a little hole in the middle, and at that hole blow in the coffin with thine mouth a good blast of wind. And suddenly stop the hole, that the wind abide within, to raise up the coffin that he fall not down and when that he is a little hardened in the oven, prick the coffin with a pin stuck on a rod's end for fear of breaking of the coffin and then let it bake, and serve forth cold.'[44]

Distinctions were made between the various pastes required for different dishes: crusts for raised, freestanding pies were best made from rye flour, which made a good strong coffin for pies to be served up more than once. White fowls needed a thick wheat flour paste and pies to be eaten hot needed a thin short crust of fine wheat flour, which had first been dried in the oven. There were open tarts, flathons and crustards as well as meat pies and patties, but their 'coffins' were still not much more than paste containers for the rich custardy mixtures they held. 'Take and make fair coffins and let them harden in the oven. Then take the hardened coffins, and fill with egg yolks, fruits and spices.' There were spiced cheese tarts too, known as curd tarts or cheese cakes, and curd fritters made by dipping curds in batter and frying them, and heavy, curd-enriched loaves eaten hot with sugar and butter.

By the end of the sixteenth century the fillings were so numerous and delicious that a little more was demanded of the coffins than a strong paste container. Pastry proper, in its most buttery form, was made to be eaten by itself, like crumbly shortbread. Butter and lard replaced the oil in pastes for meat pies and, in the right consistency, was made into deep, commodious standing pies, for pie-meat was chopped and mixed with herbs and gravy now that there were wooden platters and pewter plates to eat from. These great pies were the forerunners of England's famous raised game pies which had such a glorious renaissance in the eighteenth and nineteenth centuries.

The art of making puff pastry came to England when Charles II returned in triumph with a train of foreign chefs. Up and down a country whose people had been starved of all but the heaviest suet crusts since the beginning of the Commonwealth, delicate, crumbling, melt-in-the-mouth pies and pastries rose in thin golden leaves. Fine flour was mixed with butter, eggs, rosewater and spices. The paste was divided into two or three pieces and then, as a contemporary recipe book instructed: 'Drive out the piece with a rolling pin and so with butter one piece by another, and then fold up your paste upon the butter and drive it out again, and do so five or six times together.'[45]

The eighteenth century was the age of the pie and the pastry, of the

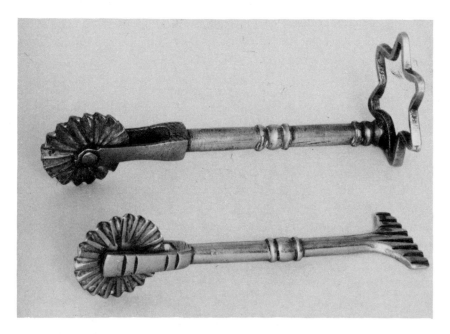

83 Two fine cast brass pastry jiggers and cutters dating from the end of the eighteeth century. Pastry jiggers of all kinds were made from earliest times, in varying sizes, depending on the thickness of the pastry to be cut. Before the Elizabethan age and the introduction of shortcrust pastry, jiggers had to cut through the thick 'paste' from which paste coffins were made. Pastry jiggers are found in boxwood, bone, horn and tinplate, as well as brass. Length 4 inches and 4½ inches. *Rupert Gentle Antiques.*

light cool hand and the delicate touch. In the elegant country mansions of the landed gentry, in farmhouses and in cottages, every region had its own specialities. Pies were appetising, pies could be hot or cold, raised or flat, and, lower down the social scale, they were marvellous for stretching meagre supplies of meat and wondrous containers of a good square portable meal for the working man. In Cornwall tin-miners' wives made pasties with meat at one end and fruit at the other. In Wales and Gloucestershire they made lamprey pies and sent them down to London. There were fish pies with herrings bursting through the crusts to stare at the sky, called 'Star Gazey' pies. There were pork pies in the North, veal and ham pies in the Midlands, steak and kidney pies, rabbit pies and chicken pies, eel pies from the Lake District, venison pies for the gentry and pigeon pies for the poor. Pie-moulds like flat-sided mallets, usually made of sycamore, were made in all sizes. The pastry was wrapped round and under them, decorated and scalloped, and then the mould was lifted out and the centre filled before the pie was lidded, pricked and baked.

Baking equipment had improved a little by the beginning of the eighteenth century. Open tarts and pies were baked in 'hoops' or 'traps', wooden or metal bands which held the pastry while it hardened and baked. Flat pies were made in earthenware slipglazed shallow dishes. But as the tinplate mills began to roll in Pontypool, Kidwelly and up the Vale of Neath, all manner of new equipment flooded into the kitchen. There were nests of baking hoops, patty pans and paste-cutters, 'spatlas' and rowel-wheeled pastry jiggers of every shape and size. There had been some pastry jiggers made in cast brass or boxwood with bone cutting-wheels, but by the mid-eighteenth century they were made with pincers or shapes at one end and metal cutting wheels at the other, large

84 Wrought iron hanging griddle. Griddles were made locally in a multitude of shapes and designs, and were used for suspending baking irons, flat earthenware dishes and griddle pans over a log fire where there was not too much smoke. They were also known as 'hanging trivets' or 'branders'. Width 19 inches. *Private collection.*

and small depending on the thickness of the pastry to be cut. Old pastry moulds for decorating the outsides of raised pies had been clumsy wooden affairs, bound together with iron, but now they were made of tin, stamped with bas-relief designs into which the pastry was pressed before being baked with the patterns raised on their golden sides.

Small pie-peels in wood or iron, miniatures of the huge shovel-shaped iron peels which cooks in grand medieval kitchens used to load their enormous ovens, were now made in great quantities for domestic use. Tin baking sheets replaced the insubstantial buttered paper for biscuits and little tarts and pies. Elm dough-bins stood in the warmth of the kitchen. In cottages glazed earthenware bowls held the miraculously rising dough, covered with a damp cloth. Whole days were set aside for baking and the air was rich with the heady, yeasty smell of fresh-baked bread and buttery pastry.

It is said that the first pottery pie dishes came from the Black Country, in Staffordshire, where the pottery-makers' wives could not afford the flour and butter to make standing 'coffins', and used glazed pottery instead. Josiah Wedgwood was among the first to understand the cook's

85 Tinplate and iron wire 'easel' bar grate toaster, used for drying oatcakes cooked on a bakestone or baking iron, on the same principal as 'twice-cooked' bread or 'biscoctus'. Height 10 inches; width 12 inches. *Private collection.*

86 Two elaborately-wrought iron gridirons. The one on the left is almost certainly from Scotland; the one on the right is less ornate and may have been made by an English blacksmith. Gridirons were placed over hot ashes and used for cooking bannocks and flat hearth-breads, sometimes covered with an iron or earthenware pot to encourage the dough to rise. *Left:* 20 inches × 15 inches. *Right:* 27 inches × 18 inches. *Victoria & Albert Museum.*

special needs and he began to make a whole range of pie dishes and ovenware, faithfully following the crimped pastry designs, making pottery in the shape of animals and birds baked in a crust. His potteries had already made a series of meat-roasting screens, but they were impracticable and very few of them have survived. Tinplate stamping machines turned out millions of cutters, patty pans and moulds, some in nests inside a tin case, some with handles, some without. At the back of some kitchen cupboard there may still lie some original eighteenth century cutters, but it is doubtful. They were probably replaced, time and again, with identical sets by succeeding generations of cooks and housekeepers, and the earliest that one can hope to find are probably late nineteenth century.

Recipes are more lasting than artefacts and Yorkshire Christmas pie, itself a descendant of the great banqueting hall pies of the Middle Ages, lingered on as a grand feast-day dish:

'First make a good standing crust, let the wall and bottom be very thick; bone a turkey, a goose, a fowl, a partridge and a pigeon. Season them all very well . . . Open the fowls all down the back and bone them; first the pigeon, then the partridge, cover them; then the fowl, then the goose and then the turkey which must be large; season them all well first, and lay them in the crust one inside the other, so as it will look only like a whole turkey; then have a hare ready cased and wiped with a clean cloth. Cut it to pieces . . . and lay it as close as you can on one side; on the other side woodcocks, moor game, and what sort of wildfowl you can get. Season them well and lay them close; put at least four pounds of butter into the pie, then lay on your lid, which must be a very thick one; and let it be well baked . . . These pies are often sent to London in a box as presents; therefore the walls must be well built . . .'[46]

This architectural triumph was revived by Edward, Prince of Wales, and was said to be his favourite dish.

On the other side of the Atlantic things were very different. Thick raised pies were considered to be extremely wasteful and were seldom

87 Wrought iron Irish harnen, also known as a 'cake stool'. Peat fires were being used in many regions of the British Isles until well into this century, and it is hard to date items such as this beyond the dividing line of the wrought iron/mild steel date of 1850–65. Even then this is not entirely reliable. Height 15½ inches. *Private collection.*

88 Two baking irons and a long-handled frying pan. Baking irons were known as 'plancs' in Wales, which gives 'plank bread' its name and has nothing to do with wood or timber. Also known as griddles, they were used for making pancakes and for grilling or broiling collops of bacon and steaks of meat or fish. Long-handled frying pans were widely used in Britain, but in Colonial America they were almost the only utensil available for cooking all manner of things. Large baking iron: 22 inches diameter. Smaller baking iron: 11½ inches. Long-handled frying pan: length 42 inches; diameter 10 inches. *Private collection.*

made in thrifty Colonial America. Without benefit of a household of well-trained servants, young ladies setting up house learned the art of pastry-making in special schools. Their imported black servants could scarcely cook at all and had to be taught by the lady of the house. Supplies of wheat flour were meagre in the new colonies, and maize flour was the main ingredient of small bread buns and cakes. Ale yeast was not easy to come by, as it was in England, and in order to keep yeast 'alive' it was mixed with brown sugar, which made most bread sweet and almost indistinguishable from cake. Everyday loaves were often 'sour-

89 Sheet iron American 'spider pan'. Special trivets were made to hold long-handled frying pans in Colonial America, and the evolution of 'spider pans' was a logical progression. The legs were welded to the pan itself. Unlike in England, down-hearth cooking in America continued until after the War of Independence, when enclosed cooking stoves were introduced. Length 29 inches; diameter 13 inches. *Colonial Williamsburg Foundation.*

dough' bread, made by keeping back a little dough from the previous day's baking and adding it to the next batch.

There was a dearth of metal equipment almost everywhere in America, especially after the War of Independence, when for a time regular shipments of domestic articles from the old country virtually ceased. Undaunted, American housewives baked cakes and 'biscuits' in paper coffins and found them quite satisfactory. Their pastry traps were of wood, until tin-mining brought the first flush of home-produced domestic articles on to the markets of the newly-independent states. Then, almost everything that could be made of tin was made of tin. There were toleware pastry moulds, traps, baking sheets, pie plates, pastry jiggers, spoons and forks, ladles, tin trays – there were even tin chandeliers.

The difficulties inherent in breaking and planting virgin soil to grow enough wheat persisted from the earliest colonial days until the middle of the nineteenth century, and even then America was still dogged by crop failure and poor wheat harvests. The great fertile plains of the Mid-West only began to produce enough grain for the nation when the steel plough and the railroads cut through the land. Then at last there was enough wheat and cheap transport to carry it to New England so that there was plenty of good fine flour for every household. The legendary apple pies on which all American children are raised were born after the Civil War of 1861.

There were islands of privilege, of course, as there are in any community. Traders in fish, lumber and iron imported spices and raisins, currants and 'sweet' olive oil as return cargo from the earliest days of colonial life. Their ships carried many private orders for goods of all kinds which were otherwise unobtainable – fine furniture and porcelains, beautiful clocks and instruments, copper and brass pots and

90 Cast iron hanging baking iron. In Colonial America, where often there was only a green wood lugpole from which to suspend cooking pots and pans, and a fierce open fire to cook on, hanging griddles were in far more widespread use than in England. They were used for broiling steaks and fish as well as for making waffles and batter-based cookies and biscuits. Height 17½ inches; diameter 12¾ inches. *Colonial Williamsburg Foundation.*

pans, pewter dishes and silverware. There was a small copper-mining venture in New York State, originally intended to be exploited for export, but the ore was sparse and it was soon abandoned. But a few copper pots and pans may have been made there for the exclusive First Families.

Mostly, however, houses were equipped with tin and toleware, for tin was relatively easy to mine and smelt. A tinsmith named Edward Pattinson is on record as being in business in Hartford County as early as 1750; and after the War of Independence tinsmiths set up businesses wherever tin was to be found. Their travellers sold all manner of goods from house to house – journeymen with journey cakes to sustain them, no doubt, made from cornmeal mixed with rye flour. Basic ingredients were still scarce for many years to come, however, and even when supplies were good there was no way of distributing them among the scattered homesteaders. For most of the settlers it was corn pone and hominy grits, potato flour and black 'ryeaninjun' bread most days of the year.

Eighteenth century England suffered no such deprivations – at least

91 Early tinplate biscuit cutters, with rolled edges and iron wire frames. As the technique of stamping tinplate improved, edges were machine-pressed to join the metal. The centre biscuit cutter with handle has been roughly soldered together. Diameters 2½ inches, 2¼ inches and 2 inches. *Jeremy Le Grice.*

92 Kitchen at St James's Palace in the time of George III. The arches of the huge old baking oven have been bricked up to accommodate a smaller oven with cast iron doors and a firebox beneath. There are at least three methods of cooking going on simultaneously: spit-roasting, oven baking and *(on the right)* a flat-topped raised brick hearth for stewing and sauce-making. Shortly after this date the great kitchen revolution took place and the huge, impractical kitchens were modernised. *BBC Hulton Picture Library.*

not in the dreamlike rose-brick country houses which stood in land-scaped parks and breathed culture into the gentle countryside. Servants recruited from nearby farms and villages scurried about their business, which was to make life even more gracious for their masters. Biscots, biscakes, puffs, macrooms, whiggs, plumb cakes, seed cakes, queen's cakes and pies were baked in the spicy warmth of brick-built ovens, produce of hours of sifting, beating, sieving and whisking. Biscuits in those days were leavened and more like American cookies or sponge fingers than the hard, sweet, unleavened English biscuits of today.

Simpler versions made of a more doughy mixture were baked in clean, well-buttered mussel shells and known as 'shell bread', but the average recipe for biscakes of that date is a testament to a cook's patience and strong right arm:

'Take half a pound of the finest flower scarfed [sieved] and three quarters of a pound of double refined Sugar scarfed. Take 8 new laid Egg Yolks and Whites beat the Eggs by themselves as the froth rifeth take it off with a Spoon soo that you take nothing but the froth put it to the flower and Sugar. Stirr it round to Mingle them soo doo till you have froth enough to make it as thin as bifcott batter then put it into your plates being buttered doo not fill them too full lett the oven be quick but not too hott when they are enough they will rife to the Top . . .'[47]

A good brick-built oven retained the heat for up to twenty-four hours. Bread was baked first, when the oven was hottest, then small bread, buns, cakes and biscuits. In the last of the heat when all the baking was finished, feathers and down for pillows were dried and fluffed, and rose leaves and herbs dried for pot-pourri and the store cupboard. Without thermometers there were only rough guides to knowing the heat of the oven. Cooks must have relied entirely on habit and instinct: old recipes occasionally mention 'nott soo hott as for Manchetts' and 'lett your oven be so Cool that a Wafer bread may ly in a minute and be but just Coloured.' Oven-stones set into the baking chamber could be adjusted to allow a little heat to escape or to seal it completely, but there was no substitute for experience and intuition. In any case, most cakes were leavened twice, with beaten eggs and ale yeast, and set to rise like bread, before being transferred to a buttered hoop with a paper base and put in the oven.

Here is an eighteenth century recipe for a 'Plumb Cake' in all its full glory:

'Take 9 or 10 pound of flower and set it in the Oven to dry. 12 pound of Currants wafht and dryed a pound of almonds beaten very fine in a stone Mortar with a little water to keep them from Oyling rub them well into the flower then put in your Currants, Nutmeggs, a litle Mace a quart of Ale Yeast half a pound of sugar 40 eggs leaving out halfe the Whites beat them very well with a pint of Sack 3 quarts of Cream 3 pound of Butter. Put the butter into the Creame sett it over the fire till its all melted then take it from the fire and lett it stand till its blood Warm put it to the other things and mix them well together. Lay a Cloath over it and sett it before the fire while the Oven is sweeping then mix it well together then butter paper and Hoop and put it in. Prick it to the bottom with a knife in severall places set it in the Oven 3 hours then Draw it and to Ice it take the Whites of 6 eggs and beat to a froth then put to it a pound and a halfe of Double refined Sugar beaten and scarfed 2 or 3 spoonfulls of Orange flower Water beat all these together almost an hour and when the Cake comes out lay it smooth all over and sett it in the Oven a little while to harden.'[48]

Again and again in recipes for light biscuits made without yeast – such as macrooms (macaroons), Savoy biscuits and Portugall biscuits – the eggs are beaten with rosewater or orangeflower water. Since these fragrant essences were made by steeping rose petals or orange peel for three days and nights in brandy, perhaps those eighteenth century cooks stumbled on the secret of a raising agent without knowing it. It may well not have been the beaten eggs as they most certainly thought, but the tartaric acid in the brandy. Cream of tartar is made from acid salts deposited by grapes during wine-making and may have been present in these essences.

Whether this property was known or not, Sarah Josepha Hale gives an almost identical recipe for a rich plum or wedding cake for her nineteenth century American sisters. The ale yeast is missing, she used very few eggs and more than double the amount of rose or orangeflower – nearly a teacup full. Her predecessor, Miss Eliza Leslie, some twenty years earlier, was trying out something entirely new as a raising agent; bicarbonate of soda, otherwise known as pearlash or *sal aeratus* (aerated salt). Between them, Sarah Josepha Hale and Miss Eliza Leslie had the answer, but it was not until the 1860s that cream of tartar and bicarbonate of soda were scientifically mixed in the correct proportions and put on the market as baking powder, and many more decades before it was incorporated into flour and marketed as self-raising flour.

Towards the end of the eighteenth century in England, cottagers and artisans were making slow-cooking dishes such as rice pudding and Devonshire whitepot which cooked in a cooling oven after baking was finished. But in Carolina, where they grew the rice which was now exported to England, rice puddings were made quite differently. Rice was gently boiled with milk in a pan till it was thick. Cinnamon, nutmeg, a little lemon peel, some chopped apple and egg yolks were added. The pudding was turned into a bowl, tied up with a cloth and boiled. There

93 M. Alexis Soyer's practical and revolutionary design for a ship's kitchen 8 ft × 17 ft
for the SS *Guadalquiver* in 1840. M. Soyer opened his first restaurant in the Boulevard
des Italiens in Paris, and then came to England and carried out contracts for redesigning
the kitchens of the Reform Club. Their design is contemporary with the previous
illustration and shows the revolutionary ideas M. Soyer introduced into England. The
caption to this illustration of 'Soyer's Miniature Kitchen' reads: 'This commodious and
compact kitchen has been fitted up on board the *Guadalquiver* steam-vessel (which lately
left Liverpool for the Spanish Main), by Messrs Bramah Prestage, 124 Piccadilly, under
the superintendence of M. Soyer, of the Reform Club. Like all similar contrivances by
M. Soyer, the present one combines great economy of space with the most methodical
arrangement; since it affords every possible convenience for cooking large dinners if
required, and without confusion, in the small space of eight feet by seventeen long. The
accompanying illustration shows the interior; the figures aiding the understanding of the
plan.'

1 The roasting fireplace.	8 The pounding pestle and mortar.
2 A Bainmarie-pan.	9 The kitchen table.
3 Two charcoal stoves.	10 Small cupboard under the mortar.
4 Charcoal stove.	11 Black-tin spoon drainer.
5 Charcoal stove, drawers and	12 Shelves for saucepans.
ventilators.	13 Boxes for vegetables.
6 The hot plate and gridiron.	14 Door leading to the deck.
7 The oven and hot closet above.	*Mansell Collection.*

were still no ovens in most houses and cooking equipment was restricted to saucepans, spiders, griddle pans and Dutch ovens, plus a cauldron or kittle.

Fifty years later it was quite a different story. A wave of German immigrants had settled in Pennsylvania and opened ironfoundries, where they manufactured traditional freestanding wood-burning stoves, known as six-plate stoves. These were square boxes with enclosed fires and a flat cooking top. They made ten-plate stoves too with integral ovens, also freestanding, with iron flue chimneys to take the smoke away. These stoves produced a far more controllable heat than the hob grates and first unevenly heated enclosed ovens of the old country. Unlike England, America went straight from down-hearth cookery to 'kitcheners' or cooking stoves without the transitional stage of bar grate kitchen ranges.

By the middle of the nineteenth century there were dozens of cookstove manufacturers in America, producing illustrated catalogues to advertise their wares, which were in great demand. Among them were Mr F. D. Tucker of Williamsburgh, Brooklyn, New York, and Mr Currier of Haverhill, Massachusetts, who made 'The Model Cookstove' and the grand 'Kitchen Queen'.[44] American kitchens of the 1840s and 1850s were equipped with far more efficient cookers than most of the smoky, sooty English kitchen ranges with open chimneys and no controlling flues.

The tide had turned. Britain began to import American designs and manufacture them herself. The famous Canon ironfoundry produced a freestanding 'American' kitchen stove in the 1840s and was still manufacturing it and advertising it in their catalogue as late as the 1930s. Yet evidently the British still preferred to see the fire they cooked on, however inconvenient and inefficient it might be. In 1860 one of England's foremost foundries was making and selling superior versions of the old-style hob grate with sliding cheek and pot-crane which had first been introduced by Thomas Robinson nearly a century earlier. For all its grand crests and inscriptions, the 'Albert Kitchener' made by William Tomlinson Walker, Founder to the Queen, at the Victoria Foundry, Walgate, York, was little better than the coal-devouring Bodley Range of 1802.

There must have been many a frustrated cook and housewife during that time, for the first enclosed ovens were very unevenly heated and it must have been almost impossible to bake a pie or raise a cake without burning it on one side and undercooking it on the other. Some kitchens had separate ovens with fireboxes beneath them. Others daringly installed gas ovens as auxilliaries to their grimy ranges, and many more still used their old wall-ovens, though in towns this was hardly practicable. Relief was at hand.

94 The 'Albert Kitchener' designed and built by William Thomlinson Walker of the Victoria Ironworks, York, built in the 1860s with a sliding cheek to press the fire close to the side of the roasting oven. The old chimney crane is still in evidence, though small and simplified. From it hung new cast iron versions of old utensils such as hanging frying pans and griddles. The range has an L-shaped water boiler built into the chimney behind the fire, and hot water was drawn off from the brass tap on the right-hand side of the fire. Width 53½ inches. *Castle Museum, York.*

95 Combination coal-and-gas kitchen range by John Beverley of Mark Lane, Leeds. John Beverley began making combination kitchen ranges as early as 1827, when gas was still not wholly suitable for domestic use. The risk of accidents and explosions from those early combination cookers much have been high. Gas was used on the hob for economy and fast heat, since the coal fire was still without a built-in flue and consumed great quantities of coal. Width 56 inches. *Castle Museum, York.*

Paraffin is so commonplace today that few people realise what a tremendous difference it made to the lives of people living in the nineteenth century. If anyone gives it a thought at all, paraffin is probably attributed to America and some bright New World inventor. In fact, though German scientists and physicists discovered this by-product of petroleum in 1830, it was a young Scotsman, James Young, who discovered a refining process in 1847 and patented it in 1850. It was he who founded Young's Paraffin Oil Company, ten years ahead of American oil drilling and refining. It was a smokier, less clean fuel than paraffin refined from natural petroleum, since it was distilled from coal-bearing shale, but nevertheless the new fuel made an immense contribution towards improving living standards. The Aladdin Company was the first British manufacturing venture to produce oil-burning paraffin lamps and those invaluable auxilliary cooking stoves with tin biscuit-box ovens.

America first struck oil in the spring of 1858 and was soon refining kerosene or paraffin for its adventurous homesteaders, who pushed steadily further and further West. By 1870 oil-stoves were to be found all over America. Paraffin lamps lit almost every house in the land where there was no gas or coal to be had, and paraffin wax made candles. It was cheap and easy to supply now that the railroads had opened up the entire continent of America. Though it was liable to layer the entire kitchen with blackened cobwebs of greasy soot, paraffin was reliable and easy to use, providing the wicks were kept properly trimmed and clean.

Meanwhile, ironfounders tried all manner of means to get the heat from the fire to circulate round the enclosed ovens. They designed flues which drew the heat off the fire almost at right-angles, so that it passed behind the back of the oven. They advised draught-pits underneath the range which sucked the heat down and round the oven before it rushed up the chimney. They grappled with the laws of convection and air currents, but until Count Rumford's scientific application of thermo-dynamics was properly understood, manufacturers had little success. The greatest practical advance in those years was the addition of a water-boiler on the opposite side of the hob to the oven, with a brass tap to draw off hot water at ground level, which was far less hazardous than tipping it from hanging kettles. Soon after, back-boilers were built into bigger ranges as the civilised world began to investigate and understand the mysteries of plumbing and hot water circulation. Back-boilers heated a tank in the kitchen quarters, and hot water was drawn off and carried in brass jugs up to the bathrooms and bedrooms of the master and mistress of the house.

Town gas had been used for street lighting since the beginning of the nineteenth century. Pall Mall was entirely lit by gas in 1807, and theatres and opera houses shone with harsh, hissing naked flames in glass shades, but gas was not seriously considered as a domestic fuel until the 1850s. America, ahead of Britain in daring innovation, was making gas ovens for domestic use at least ten years before Britain. In 1856 the firm of Cox, Hagar & Cox advertised regularly as wholesalers in stoves and gas ovens. In England, John Beverly of 9 Mark Lane, Leeds, was making a recognisable gas cooker by the 1860s, but it was of cast iron and difficult to keep clean. W.H. Micklethwaite & Co. Ltd of Rotherham produced a combination gas and coal range in the 1890s with an oven,

96 Freestanding 'American kitchener' with cast iron flue pipe, side oven and two boiling rings, dating from the 1840s when they were first introduced into the British Isles. The famous iron-founding firm of Canon was still illustrating an almost identical model in their catalogues of the 1930s. Width 35½ inches. *Castle Museum, York.*

The Easiest
The Cheapest } **Mode of Cooking.**
The Cleanest

"Upwards of **ONE MILLION** of our Stoves in ACTUAL and SUCCESSFUL use at the present time in all parts of the World!"

THE "ALBIONETTE" Is THE COOKER OF THE FUTURE

THE "ALBIONETTE"

THE only perfect Oil Cooking Stove, performs every Cooking operation *at one and the same time* at one-third the cost of COAL or GAS. Heat regulated to a nicety.

Lit and Extinguished in a moment.   **" Our Latest and Best,"**

The result of **25** *years' experience.*

All other Oil Stoves are now old-fashioned.

Sold by all Stores and Ironmongers. Prices from 27s. to 90s. Illustrated Catalogue free, from

Rippingille's Albion Lamp Co., BIRMINGHAM.

ORIGINAL Inventors of Oil Cookers. Contractors to H.M. Government.

London Depôt and Show-rooms: 65, HOLBORN VIADUCT, E.C.

97 Advertisement for the 'Albionette' oil cooking stove 1897. Although the process of refining petroleum to paraffin was patented in England in 1850, it was largely ignored as a fuel on this side of the Atlantic. But when the first oil well in America came on stream in 1858, refining paraffin or kerosene was instantly taken up as an ideal fuel for the new frontiers of the West and by 1870 oil stoves and oil lamps were to be found all over America. *Mansell Collection.*

gas grill and boiling burners incorporated into the traditional coal-burning kitchen range which, considering the relative novelty of gas as a domestic fuel, would seem to have been highly risky.

By the end of the century, Bunsen's work with gas had made it a safe domestic fuel and W. Parkinson & Co., one of the oldest manufacturers of cooking stoves and ranges, began work on producing a gas cooker with an easy-to-clean enamel finish. Kenricks, hedging their bets on the evanescent popularity of gas, bought the necessary factory tools for making 'American' cookstoves from the Perfection Stove Company of America in 1908, but by the following year their rivals, Cannon, plunged into the wholesale manufacture of gas stoves and ranges. The Gas Light and Coke Co., founded in 1812, also began work on domestic appliances.

There was, however, a new competitor in the kitchen cooker market to be reckoned with. While the ironfounding industry was still struggling with the problems of heating enclosed ovens properly and millions of people lived under a pall of soot and smoke, the pioneer firm of Crompton began making the first experimental electric hotplates at the end of the nineteenth century, in keen competition with the General Electric Company, who produced the 'Archer' electric cooker in the 1890s. The 'Archer' was an amazing affair with huge wooden plugs and a distinctly Martian air about it. The first all-electric kitchen was on show at the Chicago World Fair in 1893, goading manufacturers on both sides of the Atlantic into fresh activity. The search for novelty and technical advance produced one invention which was a long way ahead of its time – the Carron Iron Company's double-doored cooker with an inner door made of glass.

The race was on – gas versus electricity fought their battle grimly at trade fair after trade fair all over the world. The first post-war Ideal Home Exhibition saw for the first time names which are so familiar in Britain today: Creda and Crompton, GEC and Belling, Parkinson New World, Kingsway and Radiation. In 1923 Radiation cracked the last problem of all – that of controlling oven heat in gas stoves – with the 'Regulo' thermostat, which is still used today. In spite of all these advances, however, a house to house census in 1924 produced the amazing fact that there were still 1,515,000 cast iron stoves, grates and ranges in everyday use. Perhaps the fondness of the British for solid fuel prompted the makers of the Aga solid-fuel cooker, invention of Swedish physicist Gustav Dalen, to launch a brand new version of the old favourite on to the English market that same year. Electricity had long since replaced the old gas street lights and the gas companies redoubled their efforts to improve their products, sensing that progress was overtaking them.

For another ten years they still had the edge on electricity, with thermostatic control for gas ovens. But in 1933 the Simplex Electric Co. of Birmingham, makers of Creda cookers, at last triumphed and put their newest cooker on the market complete with 'Credastat'. Electric cookers began to gain ground. In 1934 there were only 200,000 electric stoves in use in Britain, and over a million gas cookers. By 1939 the number of electric stoves had crept up to one and a half million. But in the cities, town gas was still the cheapest and most popular fuel, and nine million gas cookers boiled and baked hot dinners for the acres of Victorian back-to-back houses built for artisans in all the major industrial cities of England.

Out in the countryside, where neither gas nor electricity was available, smaller, cheaper versions of the Aga solid-fuel cooker, incorporating back-boilers to heat the water, began to replace the shining brass-knobbed, black-leaded kitchen ranges and old hob grates which had

98 An all-electric kitchen designed and built in France by Auguste Perret. It is equipped with electric cooker, dishwasher and water-heater, but with all this ultra-modern gadgetry the French cook would not be parted from her mortar for grinding herbs. *Mansell Collection.*

been loved and cherished, inconvenient as they were, for generations of British country wives. The pity is that when they were torn out to make way for the sleek new enamel cookers, they were simply regarded as old-fashioned and out-of-date and thrown on the scrap heap. With them went a whole chunk of history and industrial development which can never be replaced.

—6 Puddings and — Drinks

99 Carved hardwood gingerbread mould. Gingerbread moulds, like butter-prints show a high degree of skill in carving and design. Early gingerbread moulds were long, rectangular carved boards. Length 4 inches. *Castle Museum, York.*

IT IS CURIOUS TO IMAGINE THE CELTS chewing gum as they trudged behind their herds of cattle, driving them up to the high pastures in early summer, but they almost certainly did. They were great bee-keepers, and took their skeps with them on their summer migrations into the heather hills, thus discovering that the amiable bee could be persuaded to produce different flavoured honeys. At honey-gathering time the combs were drained in deep linen sacks and the thick, amber syrup dripped into earthenware pots and bowls. When the last drop had fallen, the sack was hung in front of the fire and beaten to drive out any honey which might still be lurking in the battered combs. Finally, the sack was pressed between two stones, then the combs were washed and the liquor fermented to make mead. The unwashed wax from the honeycombs was chewed on expeditions and marches, and could fairly be called the first chewing gum in history.[50]

Sugar, as already mentioned, had first come to England in spice ships which traded with Mediterranean countries, and by the Middle Ages it could be bought from spice merchants by those who could afford it. Sugar loaves varied from 3lbs to 18lbs, but the sugar was poorly refined. Long before England had sugar colonies of her own, there were sugar refineries in several seaports which refined imported sugar, separating the white from the brown, and the brown from the sticky molasses in the very centre of the sugar loaf. The greatest attraction of sugar compared with honey was that it could be used as a powdery, glittering decoration or made into 'sugar plates', which were like transparent toffee. The medieval barons loved displays and showy centrepieces, and anything which glittered or shone was irresistible.

The jelly which served as the foundation of their grand 'sotelties' could hardly be called dessert, made as it was from boiled swines' feet, snouts and ears, washed and seethed in equal parts of wine, vinegar and water. But it was a brilliant decoration, and they treated it almost like stained glass, colouring it rich ruby red and sapphire blue, golden yellow and emerald green, and setting it ingeniously in layers.

'Colour it with turnsole [sunflower] or with indigo, or with alkanet or

100 Nineteenth century brass-and-steel sugar nippers, used for breaking up large pieces of sugar broken off a sugar loaf. The handle is stamped 'I. Smith'. Length 13½ inches. *Sotheby & Co.*

sanders [sandalwood] or saffron. And if thou will make of it two manners of colours in a dish take and make a round of paste and lay it in the midward of the charger and pour in the jelly and when it is cold, take out the paste, and pour together of another colour and serve it forth cold.'[51]

When it was spooned from the charger, clear and richly coloured, it might have been a fragment from a cathedral window.

Medieval banquets usually consisted of three meat courses followed by three fish courses, with a confection, a 'doucety' or 'soteltie', at the end of each group of dishes. These were also called 'removes' and by a rather tortuous linguistic route, through the French *'desservir'*, came to be known as desserts. The interval for the 'remove' was probably extremely necessary for the butlers, pantlers and all the other servants to clear away the messy debris of fish, flesh and fowl dismembered by hand on the inadequate bread trenchers of the day. A brightly-coloured pretty dish would distract attention from all the mopping up activities around the table.

The first dishes which fall into the category of sweet or pudding are brose and frumenty – ancient grain-based dishes made from time immemorial. Brose was made from corn in the husk, soaked in water, stirred and set on a gentle fire in a skillet. The husks floated to the top and were skimmed off, leaving a brownish sediment which thickened as it boiled, like porridge. It was served with milk and honey or salt. Frumenty was made from wheat, cracked and hulled in a stone mortar, washed, and then boiled in water in a skillet till the grains burst. New milk was stirred in until it thickened, egg yolks were added, it was coloured with saffron and served well salted, with honey or sugar. Gruel was a poor version of these two, made with oats and water. All three are exactly the same as basic pottages, except that no meat or vegetables were added to them.

Under the more sophisticated rule of the Normans, custard mixtures made from milk and eggs were cooked till they were almost solid, then cut up in slices and eaten with fingers. 'Cream boiled' is such a dish.

'Take cream of cow milk and yolks of eggs and beat them well together in a pot and let it boil till it be standing and do thereto sugar and colour it with saffron and dress it forth in leaches [slices] and plant therein flowers of borage or violet.'[52]

Decoration, once again, was all-important. Wine, ale and cider were the only drinks for man, woman and child, almost without exception, until the nineteenth century. They were often enriched with egg yolks, gently heated and served as a drink or thickened with breadcrumbs, heated, left to cool, cut into slices and eaten with salt and honey. These mixtures were known as 'runnynge' and 'stondynge' caudles. 'Running' caudles were rather like egg nogs and were still being made in the eighteenth century, warmed in small rounded copper saucepans with turned wooden handles on the parlour fire.

One of the most ancient sweet dishes originated in Greece and travelled the familiar road up through Rome and Italy to France, Normandy, and eventually to England. It was known as egg sponge with milk, but it is more like an omelette than anything else. 'Mix together 4 eggs, $\frac{1}{2}$ pint milk, 1 oz oil, pour a little oil into a thin frying pan, bring to sizzling point and add the mixture. When it is cooked on one side turn out on to a round dish, pour honey over, sprinkle with pepper and serve.'[53] Later, the beaten whites of eggs were added, so that it became a soufflé omelette, served with melted fruit conserve. But these needed the quick heat of a copper pan, and though they may have been made in France and on the Continent long before, the English cook had only heavy iron pans until the seventeenth century.

The division between sweet and savoury was faint before sugar was freely available, and perhaps the dividing line is not as clear we think today. Some ingredients, like pepper, are neither sweet nor sour and only came to be associated with one or the other as cooking itself developed in a series of arbitrary rules, dictated in the main by the French chefs who were the founders of 'classical' French cuisine. 'Crustard Lombard' of the thirteenth century is an example of what today would be abhorrent to those who must classify dishes in neat ranks of sweet and savoury. Best beef bone-marrow was mixed with strained eggs, cream, sliced dates and prunes, and cooked slowly with frequent stirring, in an earthenware pot.

Like the Celtic apiarists who found that bees could be encouraged to make flavoured honey, thirteenth century experimentalists found that a whole variety of curds and junkets could be made by mixing herbs and spices with the milk before setting it to the rennet in a carefully-preserved calf's stomach bag:

'Then was the bag clean with warm milk, and put in a few streakings (the last of the milk drawn from a cow) a beaten egg or so; twelve cloves, and mace and tie up the bag and hang it in a pot. Then boil blackthorn and burnet and marjoram in half a pint of salted water, and when cool put some of this flavoured water into the bag and let the bag soak in it.'[54]

Almond paste and gingerbread are true confections, made from sugary mixtures, and both of them were made and eaten in great quantities all through the Middle Ages. Almond paste, marchpane or marzipan originated in Italy or the Near East and consisted simply of blanched almonds ground up with sugar. It was cut and coloured and made into all shape and sizes and used to decorate the 'sotelties' – green for trees and battlefields, red and blue for soldiers, brown for animals, which fought, hunted and were chased over landscapes of translucent flummery. Sometimes, if the master-cook was an artist, marchpane achieved something akin to sculpture in the carved and gilded eagles, swans and pelicans in piety on nests of green rushes.

The origins of gingerbread are obscure, but for centuries it was an uncooked mixture of breadcrumbs and honey, mixed to a paste and

101   Pastry or biscuit printer in carved olivewood, probably French eighteenth century. It is marked with a cross and was probably used to mark *panis domini* or paindemain, sacramental bread. Length 7½ inches.   *Sotheby & Co.*

flavoured with cinnamon and ginger, coloured red and decorated with box leaves impaled on cloves. On feast days the leaves were dipped in gold to add gilt to the gingerbread. By the seventeenth century there were two kinds of gingerbread, red and white. Red gingerbread was made with breadcrumbs, cinnamon, aniseed and ginger, darkened with liquorice and bound with red wine. The mixture was rolled out on to moulding boards carved with animals, leaves, flowers, and heraldic designs. Then it was dried in a cool oven, turned out, and decorated.

'White gingerbread' was not gingerbread at all, but marchpane flavoured with ginger. Sometimes red and white were alternated to make gingerbread chequerboards or a simple pattern, such as a rose, fleur-de-lys, star or crescent moon, was cut from each and the pieces exchanged and pressed in. As always in those dark winter castles and halls, colour was tremendously important and no opportunity was missed to decorate and brighten up every dish that came to the table.

This passionate love of colour led to some imaginative tree-grafting by fifteenth century gardeners, to produce highly coloured fruits for decoration. Vines were grafted on to cherry trees to grow red grapes, pears to hawthorn stock, apples to elms or alders to make red-fleshed apples. Dyes were even poured into holes in the tree-stock to make it bear coloured fruit. But though they took such trouble to grow fairybook apples and pears, they never ate raw fruit at all and only reluctantly started cooking it in the sixteenth century. The reason for this curious abstention from the fruits of the earth goes back to the quasi-scientific medical and dietary schools which flourished at the time. All foods had 'humours' and terrible consequences were predicted if the wrong food was eaten. 'All manner of fruit generally fill the blood with water, which boileth up in the body as new blood to putrefy and consequently bringeth in sickness.'

There may have been some topsy-turvy sense in this, for fruits were particularly forbidden during plague years, and since the plague was contagious and fruit was handled freely, disastrous consequences may have been caused by infections carried and transmitted by touch. When at last the Englishman was persuaded to eat fruit at all it was cooked. Who knows whether Adam in the Garden of Eden did not contribute to the superstition about the evils of raw fruit? By Tudor times the fear of fruit seems to have been largely forgotten, for Henry VIII was sending to France for special cherry stock to plant at Hampton Court, and half Kent was an orchard. The obsession with colour still persisted and can have done nothing to improve the reputation of apples, for they brought 'fine green apples' cooked to the table, coloured by stewing them gently in a brass or copper pan so that the acid in the fruit produced a solution of copper in the stewing water. Less poisonously, apples were roasted on spits or in the embers, stewed and pulped in mortars for tarts and pies, and filled the nave of roasting goose to cut the greasiness and add flavour to the festive bird. As 'sea cole' began to be shipped down from Newcastle to London, apples were sent back as a return load, and the North of England made apple pies long before the Midlands or the West Country.

Among the many exotic bags of spices which came into England at the beginning of the seventeenth century was a sticky, glutinous substance which looked like ambergris. This was 'gum tragacanth' or 'gum arabic', which was the basis for Arabic sweetmeats, flavoured with rosewater or

lemon, rolled in fine powdered sugar and eaten like slices of thick fruit
jelly. Gum arabic came from a certain species of acacia tree. After a
search for an English equivalent, a similar substance was soon found
oozing from the bark of damson trees and cherry trees. Once its use was
known, gum tragacanth took the place of crystallised sugar for preserving fruits and flowers to decorate sweets and desserts. In this recipe it is
rather charmingly called 'Gum Dragon':

'To Dry Flowers to keep their Shape and colour. Take Gum Dragon
steaped all night till it be difsolved than take some of it betwixt your
Thumb and finger and soo rub each leafe of every flower with the Gum
till the flower be wet and Stiffned with it then strew a little scarfed Sugar
upon that flower. Lay it upon Glafs to Dry and take another and after
the same manner you must doo them all.'[55]

Now at last, towards the end of the seventeenth century, the lady of the
house began to assume an important place, for it was to her that these
precious sugar-drenched sweetmeats were entrusted. 'In the dark
Closett in my Bed Chamber a Sweetmeat Cupboard large and high with
Six Shallow boxes therein . . .' With coals from her chamber grate, a
small brass skillet, a chafing dish, pewter dishes, silver bowls and
spoons, it was her task to make and keep these rich and rare confections.
She candied and dried flowers and fruits and supervised the wine and
mead making of the household.

'To Candy Cowflips or any other flowers: Take the weight of the flowers
you will Candy in Sugar – put so much water to the Sugar as will wett it
sett it upon a slow fire Stirr it continually lett it boyle till it be soo thick as
that you can but stirr in the flowers then having your flowers ready pickt
put them in and lett them boyle their Moiftnefs out Stirring them now
and then. Then pour them into a silver or pewter Difh sett them upon a
Chaffing difh of Embers Stirr them to and fro continually with a Spoon
till they be thoroughly dry and the Sugar well off them. In the Sugar that
is rubbed off them after the same manner you may doo more.'[56]

Down in the kitchen the first English puddings were beginning to
bubble. White breadcrumbs were still the basic thickener for sauces and
pudding mixtures, but apart from pastry coffins there were still no dishes
suitable to cook them in the oven. Earthenware cracked in the heat, iron
heated too slowly and copper too fast. The more refined appetites of

post-Elizabethan England were tiring of the paste coffin and all sorts of other receptacles were tried for cooking rich, sweet pudding mixtures, such as hollowed-out turnips and pumpkins, but they too failed. Pigs' bladders, which had been used for centuries for making hog's puddings and meat sausages, were not porous and therefore could not be used for boiling sweet puddings. Although it was probably used long before, the first mention of a pudding cloth was in 1617. The pudding itself was known as 'Cambridge pudding' or 'College pudding'. Breadcrumbs, flour, minced dates, currants, pepper, shredded suet, fine sugar and eggs were mixed with warm milk to a doughy consistency. 'Then take butter and put it in the midst of the pudding and the other half aloft. Let your liquor boil and throw your pudding in, being tied in a fair cloth. When it is boiled enough cut it in the midst and so serve it forth.'[57] It was a cross between a dumpling mixture and the old enriched bread or raston. The method, adopted immediately by all and sundry, resulted in some strange menus, for the 'ball' or pudding was dumped into the stewpot and boiled with the broth and the beef. Diners supped the broth first, then had a good helping of pudding. The meat was served last when the edge had been taken off their appetites. This treatment was even accorded to a far more subtle, dainty dish, Quaking pudding:

'Take a pint and somewhat more of thick cream, ten eggs, put aside the whites of three, beat them very well with two spoonfuls of rosewater, mingle with your cream three spoonfuls of fine flour, mingle it so well that there be no lumps in it, put it altogether and season it according to your taste; butter a cloth very well and let it be thick that it may not run out, and let it boil for half an hour as fast as you can, then take it up and make a sauce with butter, rosewater and sugar and serve it up. You may stick some blanched almonds upon it if you please. Elegant puddings are boiled where the mutton is boiled or in the beef pot . . .'[58]

Before the cities drained the countryside of produce, cream was used extravagantly for desserts. One of the most spectacular and unbearably rich dishes was 'cabbage cream', the skin of risen cream being skimmed in crinkly waves from the top of the cream pan with a scollop shell and built up in a dish, round and high, with sugar and rosewater sprinkled between the leaves. Syllabubs were also an old and well-loved dish. Milk straight from the cow's udder was squirted from a great height into a pan of cider, beer and cider or fruit juices. The result was a curdled froth and was simplicity itself to make, providing the house cow was good tempered. Running out to the cowstall had its disadvantages though, and by 1696 turners were making a special 'wooden cow' which squirted the milk and cream mixture into a punchbowl containing white wine, cider or fruit juice, sweetened with sugar and flavoured with lemon and nutmeg.

Other things had changed too. Gingerbread had metamorphosed from the medieval paste and crumb mixture to a cooked flat cake, made with flour, sugar, eggs and black treacle, flavoured with cinnamon and ginger, mixed with chopped dried fruits and made into biscakes which were baked in the oven. By the middle of the eighteenth century it was being cut with tin cutters into gingerbread men with currants for eyes and buttons all down their middles.

The most common desserts of the eighteenth century were whitepots, fools and trifles. Devonshire whitepot was flavoured cream thickened with eggs, baked in a pot with currants. Trifles were simply cream mixed with sugar, ginger and rosewater, stirred gently together and warmed in a chafing dish. 'Norfolk fool' was a rich creamy custard, gently boiled and left to set. Eighteenth century trifles had broken Naples biscuits, macaroons and ratafias wetted with sack or madeira at the bottom of the bowl, with boiled custard in the middle and syllabub on top. From France came meringues – white of egg beaten with fine sugar and baked in a cool oven, browned with a salamander heated in the fire. They were shaped with a cool wet spoon and baked on buttered paper until the nineteenth century, when forcing bags allowed artistic cooks to swirl and twirl them in fluted scrolls.

Fruit of all sorts, growing in glasshouses and greenhouses, orangeries and conservatories, was eaten fresh-sliced in season or dried. For centuries past, apple rings, cored and sliced, had been strung and hung in the warmth of cottage chimneys, with strings of onions and nets of drying mushrooms. But in the kitchens of the gentry, drying more exotic fruits was a lengthy business:

102   An eighteenth century beechwood strainer for negus, a hot wine and water drink, and a turned yew wood lemon squeezer. Strainer: length 8½ inches. Squeezer: length 6 inches. *Sotheby & Co.*

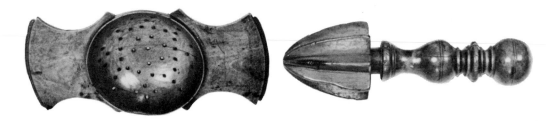

103 An eighteenth century mahogany rolling pin, made in eight segments like the very finest coopered work, with pewter handles. Length 18 inches. *Sotheby & Co.*

'To Dry Apricocks or Peaches: Stone and weigh your Apricocks and take half their weight in Sugar. Pare them and lay them in the sugar till it be difsolved then boyle them gently till they be tender lett them lye two or three days in Syrrop then lay them upon a sieve to Draine when they are well Drained lay them upon pye plates and cover them thin with double refined Sugar scarfed through a Tiffany sieve and put them into an Oven. Heat with a Bavin [bundle of brushwood] put them in an hour after the fire is out the lid [of the oven] having been kept up. After two houres turn them and scarf on Sugar as before keep them still in the Oven and every two hours turn them and Strow on Sugar till they begin to Dry then Strow on lefse sugar and only in the middle where they are moist. Every morning you must heat your Oven thus you may do peaches only you must take to every Pound of Sugar a Pint of Water and boyle them apace they will not come off of the Stone, therefore you must cut them as near to the Stone as you can in thin slices the Newington Peach is the best.'[59]

In this same eighteenth century recipe book there is a recipe for 'Orange Biscotts' which must have come down through generations of cooks, for it has all the original glitter and colour of pre-Tudor food.

'Take of the deepest coloured Oranges you can gett grate the yellow rind of them then dry it by the fire till it will rub to powder then scarfe it and take fine Sugar scarfed and leaf Gold with a little Musk and Ambergreese and soo much of the Orange powder as will give the Sugar

104 A brass and ebony pastry cutter with two stamps on the side arms for marking patterns on biscuits. Length 8½ inches. *Sotheby & Co.*

105 Copper moulds were used for cold puddings and sweet creams as well as for jellies from the late eighteenth century onwards. In the Victorian era many motifs were Scottish because of the Queen's passion for all things North of the Border – there was even a pudding called 'Balmoral'. Copper moulds and mousse rings were extremely popular in Edwardian kitchens too, and it is difficult to date individual moulds because the same designs were made year after year. Early copper moulds tend to be heavier than later ones which used a thinner metal as manufacturing technqiues improved. The one on the left is 5 inches, the rest to scale.   *Peter Nelson.*

a perfect tafte of the Orange then take Orange Peel boyled tender and scrape out all the White. Dry the Peels well in a Cloath then cut them small and crush it very fine in a Stone Mortar then put it to your powder of Sugar and Orange mingled with the Gold and Musk beat all together in your Mortar till it come to a paste then rowle it out and cut it into pieces what fafhion you pleafe lay it on paper and Dry it in a Stove many make it in the fafhion of little faggot sticks and lye it acrosse with some of the same.'[60]

Punched iron graters had been in use for a considerable time, mainly for grating breadcrumbs and hard cheese. Sheet brass graters were made when Dutch and Flemish brassmakers settled outside the walls of the City of London at the end of the sixteenth century, but it must be assumed that the grater used in this recipe was tinplate, for brass would have reacted fiercely with the acid juice of the oranges. It was in the eighteenth century that tinplate utensils became more and more common, and the cook who 'cut it into pieces what fafhion you please' probably used little tinplate cutting shapes as well. Glass, too, was now an everyday material, plain or cut, swirled or fluted. Glass rolling pins filled with cold water were used to roll the lightest of shortcrust and puff pastries. Wedgwood Queen's ware storage pots were replaced in many a kitchen by glass pots of every shape and size, their contents appetisingly visible on the larder shelf.

So there were jellies, more refined than their glutinous ancestors, clarified by running them through a jelly bag with whites of egg, but still as brightly coloured. The Georgians adored ribbon jelly made by running layer upon layer of red, green, yellow, blue and white jelly into little jelly glasses or cut glass bowls. There were cloth puddings of all sorts, and pies and pastries, all decorated with angelica and sugared violets, crystallised rose-leaves, nasturtium flowers, blanched almonds and walnuts, served in silver and glass, and on delicate China porcelain. Delectable dishes from the hands of the great chefs of France infiltrated England's plainer cuisine and, though it is only a guess, it must have been around this time that the first soufflés rose golden brown and glorious, in fluted dishes from the kilns of the Staffordshire potteries.

There was also ice-cream. It is to the East that one must look for the origin of these refreshing, pale-coloured frozen creams and fruit pulps. The Chinese made them for the refreshment of their khans and moguls, bringing the ice from distant mountain peaks to store in underground cellars lined with lead or zinc. The art of ice-storing and sorbet-making travelled West with the Arab traders, reached a pinnacle of development in Italy, and thereafter spread throughout Europe. Ice-houses in England date back as far as Queen Anne's reign – brick-built under-

106 (a) and (b)   Saltglazed stoneware jelly or mousse mould. By the middle of the eighteenth century many other English potteries were in competition with Josiah Wedgwood's famous range of Queen's ware, and glazed stoneware or earthenware moulds for mousses, creams and jellies were being made in considerable quantities. Designs varied from plain fluted moulds to beautifully-made reliefs of flowers, animals, fruit or shellfish depending on what the mould contained. Height 3¼ inches; length 6 inches. *Castle Museum, York.*

ground vaults where the ice was laid on a slatted floor between layers of straw sprinkled with salt, covered in sacking soaked in salt water. The salt in the ice would seem a bit of a drawback, but in a sorbet of rich fruit pulp it probably added savour and since sorbets were served between each of the fifteen to twenty courses of an eighteenth century banquet, they must have been more of a digestive than a sweet.

Ice-cream was originally made in pewter icing pots with tight-fitting lids which were buried in pails full of ice. Later, sieved fruit was liberally sweetened with sugar, the cream was scalded and added, then frozen in special sets of pewter basins which fitted one inside the other, specially made for the purpose. Although lead was known to be the best insulator for keeping food cold, the dangers of lead poisoning were also well-known and the lead content of pewter – an alloy of tin and lead – was rigorously controlled, so that it was the safest metal with the lowest melting point which best retained cold temperatures. Brown bread ice-cream, made with half a pint of brown breadcrumbs and one and a half pints of cream and sugar, was served in fruitless seasons of spring and winter, but on the whole fruit-flavoured ice-creams were most popular. The pewterers soon began making ice-cream moulds as fine and crisply modelled as the decorative metal casts for the elaborate plasterwork of the ceilings which canopied eighteenth century dining rooms. They made moulds for realistic fruits, heraldic animals, wheat-sheaves, fish and flowers to heap on sculpted ice-cream centrepieces.

107 Pewter chocolate moulds. Three dimensional chocolate animals were extremely popular during the nineteenth century, when raw chocolate was defatted in the big chocolate factories and sold in blocks. Length 4 to 4½ inches. *Peter Nelson.*

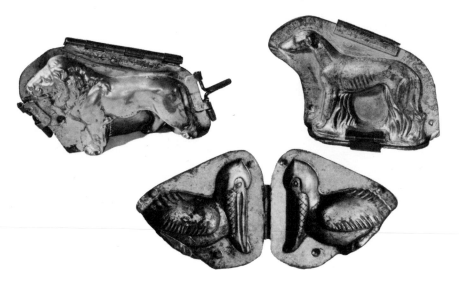

108 Tinplate pudding mould. Copper was unsuitable for cooked puddings, but tinplate was ideal since it neither tainted food nor bent or buckled at high temperatures. They were buttered, filled, wrapped in a floured cloth and lowered into a pan of boiling water to cook, and were extremely popular by the end of the nineteenth century. Length 6 inches; height 4 inches. *Jeremy Le Grice.*

109 Tinplate patty pans. Mainly used for sponge-based mixtures or rich biscuit-mixtures, these stamped tinplate patty pans could be found in their dozens in almost every kitchen by the mid-nineteenth century. Heart: $2\frac{3}{4}$ inches. Rectangle: $3\frac{5}{8}$ inches. *Jeremy Le Grice.*

But England never rivalled the heights of ice-cream sculpture attained by the Italians. According to Harold Acton:

Dr John Moore, who visited 'four of the principal nunneries' in the royal suite (at the Convent of San Gregorio Armeno) wrote that 'the company was surprised, on being led into a large parlour, to find a table covered, and every appearance of a most plentiful cold repast, consisting of several joints of meat, hams, fowl, fish and various other dishes. It seemed rather ill-judged to have prepared a feast of such a solid nature immediately after dinner; for those royal visits were made in the afternoon. The Lady Abbess, however, earnestly pressed their Majesties [Queen Maria Carolina, wife of Ferdinand I of Italy and IV of Spain 1759-1825] to sit down; with which they complied . . . The nuns stood behind, to serve the royal guests. The Queen chose a slice of cold turkey, which, on being cut up, turned out a large piece of lemon ice, of the shape and appearance of a roasted turkey. All the other dishes were ices of various kinds, disguised under the forms of joints of meat, fish, and fowl, as above mentioned.'[61]

The average consumption of sugar was still modest, but it had increased considerably from the parsimonious 1lb a head per year of the Elizabethans. By 1680 the amount had risen to 4lbs a year, which had doubled by 1720. At the end of the eighteenth century it was as much as

110 (a) and (b) White glazed earthenware mousse mould. By the end of the nineteenth century moulds were no longer made in small numbers, but mass-produced, the pattern being printed in relief on the inside of undecorated moulds. This one is made by 'Shelley' and was clearly intended for a fish or lobster mousse. With the increasing popularity of old-fashioned kitchen equipment in recent years some of these moulds are being made again. Height 3½ inches; length 5½ inches. *Castle Museum, York.*

111 A range of moulds spanning 150 years. In the centre, an early aluminium mould for a product called 'Lushas' creams. A Brown & Polson blanc mange mould. Two contemporary thermoplastic moulds and a pierced mould for making curds or Italian creams. Copper mould: height 7 inches. Aluminium mould 2 inches. Brown & Poulson mould: 4½ inches. Curd mould: 8 inches. Rabbit mould: Length 9¼ inches. *Castle Museum, York.*

11lbs to 13lbs per head per year. Taken by today's standards this amount was ridiculously small, but it must be remembered that there was a heavy tax on sugar, first imposed in 1751 and gradually increased to prohibitive proportions until it was finally abolished in 1846.

It was one commodity which was never in short supply in America, however, and cakes, puddings and sweets made up a large proportion of their diet, as well as all kinds of exotic and tropical fruits. For a time, eighteenth century English gardeners grew pineapples and melons in hotbeds and heated plant houses, but heating systems were expensive to install and run, and the special hot houses were costly to build. As sea trade improved and British possessions abroad expanded to include the islands of the West Indies, pineapples were imported. The Georgian gentry loved the prickly shape of this exotic fruit and moulded ice-cream pineapples were often the centrepiece of their showy dessert tables.

Of all the items made specially for the kitchen, mousse moulds, ice-cream moulds and jelly moulds were among the most attractive. The earliest moulds were made around 1730 in Staffordshire salt glaze, and may have developed from curd moulds for cream cheeses, which were pressed and drained in shaped, perforated containers. Josiah Wedg-

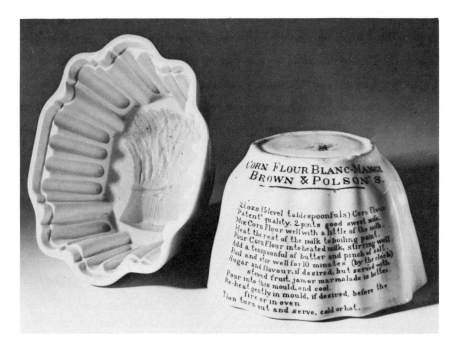

On the mould the recipe reads:

CORN FLOUR BLANC-MANGE
BROWN & POLSON'S.

2½ ozs (5 level tablespoonfuls) Corn Flour
"Patent" quality. 2 pints good sweet milk.
Mix Corn Flour well with a little of the milk.
Heat the rest of the milk to boiling point.
Pour Corn Flour into heated milk, stirring well.
Add a teaspoonful of butter and pinch of salt.
Boil and stir well for 10 minutes (by the clock)
Sugar and flavour, if desired, but served with
stewed fruit, jam or marmalade is better.
Pour into this mould, and cool.
Re-heat gently in mould, if desired, before the
fire or in oven.
Then turn out and serve, cold or hot.

112 Brown & Polson's Corn Flour blanc mange mould with an interior design of a wheatsheaf and the recipe printed on the outside. Arrowroot was first imported into England from America in the early 1820s and cornflour substituted as a homegrown product when supplies of arrowroot became difficult and expensive. Height: 6½ inches. *Castle Museum, York.*

wood, for ever seeking new opportunities to sell his pottery, began making his famous Queen's ware soon after, and before long there were moulds for galantines, meat and fish, and delicious cream mousses. 'Eggs in Moonshine', for instance, was made by beating cream and ground almonds together with rosewater, stiffly beaten eggs and concentrated jelly. The mixture was poured into crescent-shaped moulds, left to set, and served up surrounded by little jelly stars. Soon there were commemorative moulds and patriotic moulds, cones and pyramids, turban moulds and bombe moulds. By the beginning of the nineteenth century every household in the land could turn out a pretty jelly from a stoneware or white earthenware mould, while fine china moulds stood on shelves and in cupboards of the quality's kitchens.

There were tinned copper moulds too for Georgian desserts, matching their classical taste with temples and domes, scrolls and fluting. And by the nineteenth century a score of manufacturers were making plain common-or-garden tin moulds to make jelly lions and rabbits for the nursery and stepped pink and white blancmanges. Arrowroot was imported from America in the early 1820s and every child in Victorian England who wore frilled pantalettes and went to bed with a nightlight spooned it up obediently under Nanny's stony gaze. Queen Victoria's passion for Scotland and all things Scottish greatly increased the number of popular jelly mould designs, and thistles and stags joined the roses and lions, trembling and quivering on dark mahogany tables. And everywhere the people of England had abandoned ale and beer in favour of tea.

Tea came creeping into Europe through many different inlets. The Jesuits, with the grand intention of converting the whole of China to Catholicism, came home in ones and twos during the mid-seventeenth century, and some of them brought 'cha' or 'tcha', the Cantonese word for tea. Adventurous captains of Dutch East India Company ships almost simultaneously took 'tay', the Amoy word for it. They bartered it and tried chewing it and even smoking it. The merchants, who thought they had learned something from the traders who brought it from China to India (for tea was not grown in India until 1865), used the leaves like herbs and made it into cakes with boiled rice, nuts and spices.

The Jesuits knew better. Glad no doubt to have something other than ale or wine to drink, they commended the following treatment:

'To near a pint of the infusion take two yolks of newlaid eggs and beat them very well with as much fine sugar as is sufficient for this quantity of liquor; when they are very well incorporated pour your tea upon the eggs and sugar and stir them well together. So drink it hot. This is when you come home from attending business abroad and are very hungry and yet have not conveniency to eat presently a competent meal . . . the water is to remain upon the tea no longer than whilst you can say the Miserere psalm very leisurely.'[62]

The English, with customary aplomb, immediately adapted it as a new kind of beer and made China Ale, adding it to an ordinary brew with extra yeast and letting it ferment another ten days. But that was in the country, where they knew no better. One lady, according to Southey, served boiled tea leaves with salt and butter and, together with her afternoon guests, was astonished that the people in town saw any merit in it at all. In Queen Anne's London, however, the ladies drank tea with as much flourish as the gentlemen took snuff. It was served in little Chinese cups without handles, poured into saucers and sipped, green and hot. But apart from society ladies, tea did not really take hold as a national drink until the end of the eighteenth century.

The end of the eighteenth century was as bad as the beginning had been good, and the symbol of all the strife was tea. In 1773, in a desperate bid to make their point about the impossibly high taxes levied on America by the British, forty or fifty young men dressed up as Red Indians ambushed a fleet of British ships and dumped an entire shipment of tea into Boston harbour. King George III took the insult to heart and shortly after declared war on America. France, Spain and most of Europe took America's side and England suffered the dreadful consequences of being at war on both sides of the Atlantic. Taxes of all sorts were raised to pay for the war, for the loss of ships and damage to trade was immense. Tea coming into England carried an enormous duty and, along with 'brandy for the parson and 'baccy for the squire', it was smuggled into the country in prodigious quantities. In 1784 it was estimated that 13 million lbs of tea was consumed in Britain, of which duty was paid on only 5 million.

That year the harvest failed in England. Everywhere labourers rioted. Grain was so expensive and of such poor quality that they were denied their beer – their principal source of sustenance and comfort. William Pitt the Younger immediately abolished the duty payable on tea and encouraged the poor to drink it. A dozen years later it had become the national beverage. Sir Frederick Eden wrote 'Any person who will give himself the trouble of stepping into the cottages of Middlesex and Surrey at meal-times will find that in poor families tea is not only the usual beverage in the morning and evening, but is generally drank in large quantities at dinner.'[63] He did not add that the labourer's lot had been so reduced that he had little more than bread and cheese to sustain him. The price of food had risen prohibitively. After the costly battle with America and her allies came the monstrous Napoleonic wars, which dragged on for no less than twenty-two years and impoverished the whole nation.

The poor in the country had no choice but to sell what produce they could to the towns, where thousands of artisans had to be fed and clothed. Vegetables, poultry, eggs, butter and cheese were carried by canal to the industrial towns. The barges, so it is said, returned to the country with effluent and refuse cleared from the filthy city streets. The agricultural labourer could make neither broth nor soup – for fuel was scarce again, coal being largely reserved for the armament factories and industrial centres. So he boiled his water and drank tea, without milk.

Milk was too valuable to be drunk by countrymen, because it would

113 Two milk boilers, the 'Eddystone' and the 'Cascade'. With the advent of gas as a domestic fuel, problems arose over enamelled pans which did not perform well over the increased, concentrated heat. Milk in particular stuck to the bottom of the pan and burned, or boiled over. Ingenious gadgets were devised to prevent this from occurring. As the milk heated it was drawn up the funnel and kept moving in the pan so that it could not burn. Instructions on the 'Eddystone' are printed beneath the badge of Gourmet & Co. of London. 'Stand in Saucepan to prevent contents boiling over. The liquid should not cover holes nor be lower than the badge. Do not put on a fierce fire.' Height 5 inches and 4½ inches. *Peter Nelson.*

make cheese and butter to sell in the market. Only when every last ounce of solids had been churned, skimmed and pressed from it, did they drink the whey and buttermilk. The gentry never drank milk, for it harboured dangerous germs and carried infection. It did not travel well either, for the jolting of cart and waggon turned it to butter or soured it. There were cows which grazed the meadows of Mayfair and were milked on the doorstep, but their milk was scalded, boiled and used for cooking, never as a drink. In the eighteenth century there were dairies in towns which supplied 'blue milk', milk skimmed of cream and probably watered down and adulterated, which, once it had been scalded, was considered safer for human consumption than whole cream milk. The nineteenth century brought the milkman on his rounds with fresh milk transported by rail, but even then the artisans had to be persuaded to give it to their children to nourish them in the grimy back streets of London and the industrial cities.

Coffee, on the other hand, was always a fashionable drink and a manly one. It came into England from the Turkey merchants, traded for fine woollen cloth in Charles II's reign, and was almost immediately adopted by the fops and dandies as a welcome alternative to the heavy drinking habits of the day. Coffee became a social drink and a welcome change from gin, brandy, ale or wine. Water, it must be remembered, was unpurified and undrinkable unless it was boiled or came direct from a clear spring – an impossibility in the cities, where sewage and effluent ran in the streets and polluted the water supplies. Coffee houses became quite the thing. In Queen Anne's London there were nearly five hundred coffee houses where gentlemen of rank gathered and conducted the business of the day – noisy, sociable meeting places to which many of the great banks and insurance houses of the City owe their origin.

Coffee was also drunk at home, but to a lesser degree than tea, at least until the end of the eighteenth century. It was a serious business:

'Heat the berries in a fireshovel till they sweat a little; and then grind them and put the coffee pot over the fire with water; when hot, throw the water away and dry the pot by the fire, then put the powder into it, and boiling water immediately over the same; let it stand three or four minutes, and pour off the clear. By this means the hot water meets the spirit of the coffee; whereas if you boil coffee, as the common way is, the spirit goes away, so that it will not be so strong nor quick to the taste.'[64]

Convenient, efficient coffee grinders were not made in any quantity until the turn of the century, when steel spindles were mass-produced and fitted into wooden box-shaped coffee grinders equipped with a little drawer with a brass knob to catch the ground powder. The Americans had tin coffee roasters – cylindrical drums attached to a handle which were rolled to and fro in the hot embers. A few of these were made in England, but soon there were coffee merchants who sold beans ready-roasted. After the Boston tea party the Americans took to coffee as a national drink and Colombian and Brazilian coffee came into Europe, at last replacing the thick black Turkish brew from Mocha and

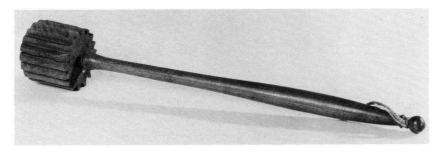

114 Notched wooden moliquet or chocolate mill, with a turned wooden handle which screws into the head. Before these simple instruments arrived in England at the end of the seventeenth century the only way of beating egg white was with a small bundle of twigs. One unhygienic alternative was to squeeze egg white repeatedly through a sponge. Chocolate mills were a boon to the kitchen for this reason. They were spun between the palms of the hands and quickly beat liquids to a froth. Length 13 inches; diameter 2 inches. *Castle Museum, York.*

115 Tinned wire balloon whisk. Early balloon whisks were in use at the end of the eighteenth century, and usually had a bound iron wire handle. Just as the manufacturers of patent pudding mixtures began making moulds and basins with their products' names on them, so the family firm of Bourneville made 'cocoa whisks' with their name prominently displayed on the handle. Length 9 inches. *Castle Museum, York.*

the Middle East.

There were chocolate houses too, which opened a little before coffee houses, for cocoa beans came to England from Jamaica soon after 1655. At first, with their single-minded attitude to drink of any kind, the English made chocolate as they had made wine caudles, with yolks of egg and wine. The preparation was fairly lengthy, but chocolate had many other uses, so it was considered well worth the trouble:

'Take cacao-nuts gently dried in an iron pan, then peel off the husks, powder them very small so as to be sifted; then to every pound so prepared, add of white sugar six ounces, cinnamon half an ounce, one nutmeg, one vanilla pod of the best; ambergris or musk each four grains, if for high price or Spanish chocolate, but in the English it is left out. All these ingredients worked together with an iron roller on an iron plate over a gentle heat and while it is warm it may be made into rolls or cakes, or cast into moulds, or what form thou pleasest.'[65]

Drinking chocolate was known as 'chaculato'. To make it 'Take half a pint of claret wine, boil it a little then scrape some chaculate very fine and put into it, and the yolks of two eggs, stir them well together over a slow fire till it be thick, and sweeten it with sugar according to your taste.'

Soon the recipe was adapted, the wine left out and milk substituted, still with eggs and still extremely rich. Silver and Sheffield plate chocolate pots graced the silver serving trays of Georgian England. Tall, elegant, usually silvered and not tinned inside if they were plated copper, they had lids with holes in the centre for the chocolate mill or 'moliquet', which twirled and frothed the mixture rich and thick. And, of course, chocolate was grated into creams and puffs – English meringues – but it was a while before it was realised that chocolate was fatty and needed extra flour or cornflour to balance the 'cocoa butter' in a recipe. By the mid-nineteenth century the great Quaker names of Bournville and Cadbury had founded their 'chocolate towns' to process raw cocoa-beans, extract the cocoa-butter and make blocks of ready-made defatted chocolate.

There is one other recipe which returns again and again in cookery books from its first mention in medieval times to the graceful Georgian era and, though it has nothing to do with sugar and could not be called sweet by any stretch of the imagination, it ought perhaps to be included. It is 'Cock Ale' and it has a flavour of ancient magic and ritual so strong and strange that it is almost unnatural to find it dispassionately copied out in fading ink between black cherry wine and candied flowers in an eighteenth century recipe book.

'Take a Cock Draw him and cut him in the middle wash out the blood and Dry it with a Cloath then beat it well in a Stone Mortar bones and all then taken 3 Nutmegs half a Dozen blades of Mace 3 roots of ginger beat these Grossely and mingle them with the flesh. Then take one Orange and one Lemon cut them in long slices put all these in a thin canvas bag and hang it in a firkin of new Ale that it may Work with it. When it hath done Working stop it up and in 12 days you drink it tis a great Restorative and good for Consumption.'[66]

——7 Carvers and—— Servers

116 An engraving after an illumination in the Louterell Psalter, 1340 showing the Carver with his huge flat-bladed knife and wearing his chaperon. Three servants and a page are filling individual salts. *Mansell Collection.*

EVEN THE MOST MEAGRE ANCIENT MEALS were not conducted without some nod at God, from whom all blessings flowed. Even if it was only a communal bowl of gruel, a formula of thanks was muttered over it before it was offered to the head of the house. Famine was all too frequent for men and women who scratched an existence from the jealous earth for them to ignore their good fortune at being able to keep body and soul together. There were communal feasts at harvest time, before the world slid into a fearful darkness from which it did not emerge for nearly six months. Feasts with bonfires and ritual killings kept up the spirits of communities whose daily diet contained fewer calories than today's dieticians consider essential to support human life.

Anglo-Saxon feasts had little in common with the banquets and orgies of the Roman Empire. The nearest one can come to the behaviour of pre-Norman England is probably in descriptions of the Gauls and their feasts. They sprawled on bundles of straw round a great fire on which a carcase roasted or small game seethed in a huge iron cauldron. 'Each man takes a whole joint and bites it; it is a lion's meal. Should the piece be too tough or too big, they use for cutting it a small knife, the sheath of which is attached to the scabbard of the sword.' A single drinking vessel, either earthenware or metal, was handed by the slaves and made its rounds as often as possible. Sometimes the drinking vessels were the skulls of enemies killed in battle or of their own dead parents, whose memory they thus honoured out of respect and filial piety:

'On special days a round table is set up and the guests sit around it in a circle. The middle place is given to the most distinguished or the most valiant; . . . Next to him sits the master of the house, then all the other guests in order of importance. Behind is the circle of 'clients' who accompany their masters in battle, some carrying shields, others lances. They eat as other guests . . . There was an ancient custom which decreed that the legs of the animals served should be allotted to the bravest, that is to those who were declared to be such. This was a source of quarrels and, often, fights to the death.'[67]

Table manners improved vastly as Gallo-Roman customs were grafted on to the Britons' uncouth behaviour. The newly-established barons were well aware that they risked their lives in breaking bread with their conquered tribal chiefs. Second only to the Carver or 'esquire tranchant' therefore, the most important member of the household was the Taster. He carried a linen cloth wrapped around pieces of bread or bread rolls and headed the procession of servers entering the banqueting hall, as like as not to a flourish of trumpets. Standing before his

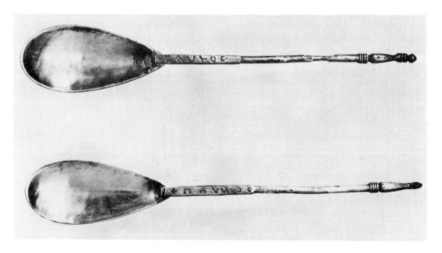

117 Two silver spoons with Greek engraving from the excavated site of the ship burial at Sutton Hoo, dating from the seventh century AD. Fine flatware was being used despite the popular image of uncouth Britons between the departure of the Romans and the invasion of the Normans. Length 10 inches.   *Reproduced by Courtesy of the Trustees of the British Museum.*

master, he dipped a piece of bread three times into the serving dish. Then he flourished the bread three times over the head of the server and put it to the lips of the chief officers. Each dish was thus tested and then covered, to thwart any further attempts at poisoning, while a 'panetier' kept a sharp look-out for anyone trying to tamper with the dishes.

Medieval feasts began with a ceremonial and extremely necessary washing of hands which, in due course, would be trawling for tasty morsels in the communal bowls and chargers. Pages carried ewers, basins and lavers – double-spouted brass or silver water jugs – round the table. Guests dipped their fingers in the scented water, then dried them on their own napkins, which they brought with them. The head of the household, either sitting alone or at a high table with people of equal rank, said grace and then ate the first mouthful, after which the rest of the guests plunged in. The Cup-Bearer began his rounds with a ceremonial fringed towel around his neck with which he wiped the rim of the cup after each guest had drunk from it. So, in exactly the same manner, does the priest offer the communion wine today.

In the thirteenth century the young sons of the high-born took over the duties of serving at table. Many books were written with strict rules of ceremonial behaviour for these little pages. The *Boke of Nurture*, a guide to the rearing of male children, instructs:

'Put the salt on the right hand of your lord; on its left a trencher or two. On their left a knife, then white rolls, and beside, a spoon folded in a napkin. Cover all up. At the other end set a salt and two trenchers; cut your loaves equal, take a towel $2\frac{1}{2}$ yards long by its ends, fold up a handful from each end, and in the middle of the folds lay eight loaves or buns, bottom to bottom; put a wrapper on the top, twist the ends of the towel together, smooth your wrapper, and open the end of it before your lord.'[68]

This was a 'cornet' of bread. Pages had to serve their lords on bended knee, bow when answering if spoken to, and remain standing until told to sit.

Napkins and towels played a vital part in the serving of food, both as part of the ritual of display and as essential equipment for reasons of hygiene. By the fifteenth century it seems that the duties of pages had been more or less taken over by the Carver, the Pantler and the Butler, for their instructions in a 'Courtesy Boke' of the period are almost the same as the page's a hundred years before. To the Carver: 'A towel must be layed on his shoulder when he shall bryng his lords brede.' And to the Pantler or Butler: 'Put a towel round your neck, for that is courtesy and put one end if it mannerly over your left arm. Take one end of the towel in your left hand . . . together with the salt cellar . . . and the other end in your right hand with the spoons.'[69]

As for the guests, they hardly seemed to deserve all this bowing and scraping, for they were a lewd and unmannerly lot: 'Thou must not put either thy fingers into thine ears, or thy hands to thy head. The man who is eating must not be cleaneing by scraping with his fingers at any foul part.'[70] They were not to blow their noses with their fingers nor go scratching at their 'codware'. Yet another 'Boke of Demeanour' severely condemns the diners for scrubbing or clawing their dogs' heads or backs. Diners were not to 'prowl round their heads' searching for lice, nor pick their noses, let them drip or blow them on the tablecloth or on their napkins, put their tongues into a dish, belch or hiccup. Nor must they use their napkins to wipe away perspiration or make such a mess of them that they were offensive. And that was not all. Some diners were in the habit of dipping their hands into dishes almost up to their elbows, poking about for the best pieces. Others thoughtlessly dropped their gnawed bones back into the serving dish. The right place for bones was the floor, liberally covered with rushes and strewn with sweet-smelling herbs.

In medieval banqueting halls, where the spits turned and hissed in full

118 A rare survival – a double-sided wooden trencher dating from the sixteenth or seventeenth century, with a separate hollow for salt at one side. Length 9¾ inches. *Sotheby & Co.*

view of the diners, obviously the Carver was an extremely important man – the focus of attention and distributor of correct cuts of meat according to rank. He also wielded an unsheathed knife in the presence of the assembled company – in those uncertain days when drunken fights could easily turn into blood feuds, a mark of highest confidence and trust. There were books written for him, too, for carving fish, flesh and fowl. The terms were clearly defined: a chubb was 'finned', a pike 'slatted', a hen 'spoiled', a mallard 'unbraced'. He must 'untache a curlew, barb a lobster, border a pasty, thigh small birds, dysfigure a peacoke'. As for the fair handling of his knife 'he should place on the knife only two fingers and a thumb and the same on the bird or animal to be carved' and he must wipe the knife on his napkin, not on the tablecloth.

The *Boke of Kervynge* describes how to 'displaye a crane': 'Take a crane, and unfolde his legges, and cut off his wynges and his legges, and sauce him with poudres of gynger, mustard, gyngre and salt. To dismembre a heron: take a heron and reyse his legges and his wynges as a crane, and sauce him with vynegre, poudre of gynger and salts.'[71] Elsewhere and with feeling an epicure remarks that 'a crab is a slutte to carve.'

Banqueting tables were called 'boordes' and were made from planks two to four inches thick split with an iron wedge from a straight tree and set on trestles. When the feasting was over, the fire had died down and the lords and ladies had retired to their bedchambers, the 'boordes' were taken down and laid on the floor for the servants to sleep on. Only in the darkest days of winter were flaming torches held aloft to light the procession of Carver, Taster, Cup-Bearer, Pantler, Butler and all the rest, for the gentlemen of England lived by the wheeling sun and ate their main meal in the middle of the day while there was light enough to see. In the evening they 'supped' ale and spiced cakes, often kept locked away in livery cupboards and bread hutches.

The Carver had a set of knives, varying from the largest, which was more like a murderous broadsword, with which he cut slices from whole roasting carcases, to smaller, more pointed ones to deal with capons and game. Sometimes he served the meat spiked on a long skewer like a kebab, sometimes on a broad-bladed serving knife, whose blade was a similar shape to a Victorian fish-slices, and sometimes on a charger. He had a flesh-fork for lifting cooked meat on to his carving block, and a slatted spoon for fishing round inside the cooking pot. There was a collection of small earthenware or pewter bowls for spice mixtures and cold pounded sauces and stoneglazed bottles of verjuice, vinegar and alegar. For the rest, he relied on his fingers to transfer the carved meat on to dishes and chargers which were presented to the master of the house by a little mob of pages, disciplined by the Chamberlain. The Carver's unique position in the household was marked by the privilege of wearing a 'chaperon' or cap. All the other servants went bareheaded in obeisance to those they served, all of whom wore headgear at table.

As manners improved, the high table was covered by an increasing number of cloths. There was an undercloth of white linen, then a table cover of coloured cloth, and then, down the centre, a runner of richly-coloured silk, damask, brocade or embroidered linen of the finest quality. Until the end of the sixteenth century only the highest ranking members of the household and their important guests had their own dishes, bowls and spoons. The rest of the company, numbering anything from fifty to two hundred or more, ate in pairs with one 'cover' between them consisting of a platter, a bowl and a drinking cup.

On feast days the high table would be decorated with leaves and flowers set around the 'nef' – a great gold, silver or silver-gilt salt-cellar, grandly made and exquisitely decorated. The 'nef' stood in front of the lord and lady, carrying spices to season their food, usually made in the shape of a ship to signify the origin of the spices it held. Very few of these fragile galleons have survived, but they often had hulls of nautilus shell or mother-of-pearl and rigging of such fine gold and silver strands they might have been spun from moonshine. If the grand drinking cup ever ceased its rounds, it too would be placed on the richly-coloured runner in the centre of the high table.

Feast days and celebrations meant good wine for all the assembled company. The wassail bowl would be filled and the pages would follow the Cup-Bearer who bore it, ladling spiced wine or mulled ale into every drinking cup and beaker round the hall. These wassail bowls were often called 'mazers', a corruption of the German word for maple wood, from which they were made. They were richly mounted in silver or silver-gilt and gradually evolved into the beautiful covered loving cups of the Tudors and Stuarts.

In the draughty passage between the banqueting hall and the kitchen was the buttery, where the wine was kept under the drooping eye of the butler or 'boutellier'. Opposite was the pantry, where the 'pain' or bread was kept, together with the salt, cups and platters. There were no drinking glasses, serving spoons, forks or plates. Food was eaten from trenchers, cut from four-day-old wholemeal loaves, squared and laid at each place. When the privileged had finished with their trencher-bread it was thrown to the dogs or passed down the table to the lowest orders. Ale, wine and cider was sipped from the communal cup at the high table – knights and squires shared a horn beaker, and the lowest of the low had to make do with rough wooden mugs.

Until the cooking hearth was moved from the main banqueting hall there was little necessity for serving bowls, dishes or plates. There were chargers – huge deep decorative plates on which the carver placed the remainder of the meat after every person had been served individually. There were slipglazed bowls for punches and caudles, perhaps a pewter dredger for flour or breadcrumbs, bowls to hold batter for basting, and small dishes for spices and seasonings. As paste coffins were used to contain both meat and sweet dishes, little else was needed but flat boards or wooden platters to display them and carry them on.

In Elizabethan days, however, when the cooking hearth had been removed from the central hall, the buttery and the pantry became more like rooms and less like closets for storing bread, wine, salt, cups and platters. The East India Company began to import precious porcelain

119 A beautiful example of blue-and-white Chinese porcelain mounted in silver, with a fruitwood handle. The beaker has fine hair-cracks, but was too valuable to throw away, and was mounted in silver. *c.* 1690–1710. Height 5½ inches. *Christopher Bangs.*

from the East and sweetmeat dishes in blue-and-white china could now be seen on the tables of wealthy households. It became the fashion to display the shining, polished surfaces of tables, sideboards and dressers. Furniture design had become more decorative, and dining tables had carved legs and shallow drawers for holding tapers and rushlights. Sometimes tables were covered with thick Turkey carpets during the daytime – those who could not obtain these symbols of status had their oak tables polished until they gleamed. At mealtimes table-tops were reversed and covered with a cloth so that the polished patina was not marked and stained by wine and food.

Porcelain was so highly prized at that time that if a footed sweetmeat dish was broken during its voyage from China, a silver mount was specially made to take the place of the broken foot. Blue-and-white pottery was all the rage, in imitation of this highly-prized Chinese porcelain. Bowls and serving dishes from the English potteries were no longer traditional streaked green glaze, but glazed white and painted in naive copies of Chinese designs. All these dishes were valuable and were kept in the pantry, safe from the clumsy kitchen servants. Pewter bowls, chargers and dishes could safely be entrusted to them, but not fragile chinaware. The butler, pantler and their assistants were carried away by their new important status, and took to wearing immensely long and voluminous gowns and cloaks.

Queen Elizabeth's tireless mind had turned to matters of expense and economy during England's isolation from the rest of Europe. She laid down an entire code of conduct for every household in the land. These Sumptuary Laws covered every aspect of English life, down to those very same flowing servants' clothes and she declared that 'it was not lawful for any man below the rank of gentleman to wear their gowns lower than the calves of their legs except they were above three score years of age.'[72] Enormous mandilions, garments which covered the entire body like 'bagges or sacks' were forbidden and, because of their shortened tunics, servants took to wearing scantily-cut breeches and hose. Thus appeared the recognisable figure of the footman, known in those days as 'indoor grooms'. The clothes of indoor grooms, outdoor grooms and kitchen staff were always grey or russet. When they were in the presence of guests they wore their master's insignia, a badge worked in silver, on the front or back of their outer tunic or on their sleeves.

There were all kinds of superstitions and myths about women, particularly with regard to the preparation and serving of food. It was said that they must not salt hams, touch meat, eggs or fish at certain times of the month, for then they were 'unclean' and would taint the food. One can only imagine that they were allowed to keep the dairy as their own province because cows behaved in the same manner and therefore there must be an affinity between them. Nevertheless, many country women were suspected of being able to turn milk sour and make cows barren and, particularly during the witch-hunts of the Reformation, many an innocent dairymaid was persecuted for her supposedly supernatural powers. Such maids as there were, were bought and sold like slaves and did the most menial of tasks around the house and on the estate.

'No servant, yeman ne yeman, jentilman ne Jentilman the Steward'[73] was allowed to cover his head in the presence of those guests he now served at table, but women and serving maids wore plain wimples or kerchiefs as a token of submission. Many poor unfortunate girls were indentured and sold off to the Virginia Company, for the new colonies needed servants, and most men who took passage across the Atlantic went in search of cheap land to farm so that they could improve their status and become 'gentlemen' of the New World. Female servants were far more common in Colonial America, waiting at table, cooking and preparing food in the separate buildings of kitchen, smoke-house and storehouse, where they taught black slaves what little they knew and, like them, worked at the hardest and heaviest tasks.

Once the architecture of England had become more comfortably proportioned and there were pewter plates, bowls and dishes for everyone, meals were less like a military mess, more select and certainly better-mannered. As Queen Elizabeth set about educating her people, she encouraged 'straungers' to come to England to teach their skills and crafts to the English. Glassmakers came from Normandy and Lorraine, and soon there were glassworks in the Weald of Kent, where the men followed behind the ironmasters 'lopping and topping' what was left of the timber for their small charcoal-fired hearths. Other glasshouses were set up in Hampshire, Staffordshire, and outside the walls of the City of London.

So there were delicate fluted glasses for the nobility to drink from and engraved glass bowls, large and small, for delicate cream desserts and fruit purées. Horn beakers, rimmed with silver to show their status, were still used by the rising merchant classes. Pewter, which almost passed for silver on all but the richest tables, was a very soft metal which was easily scored and marked, so the Elizabethans still used trenchers, laid upon the pewter to avoid marking it with their knives, and supped with

120 Steel and bone serving fork with brass inlay. This is a fine example of mid-seventeenth century English cutlery. The tines are tempered steel and the handle may well be deer's antler, which would be in keeping with the leaping stag inlay. Forks were not used as eating implements in England until the end of the seventeenth century, and were mainly used to spike slices of meat from dishes and chargers. Length 14 inches. *Rupert Gentle Antiques.*

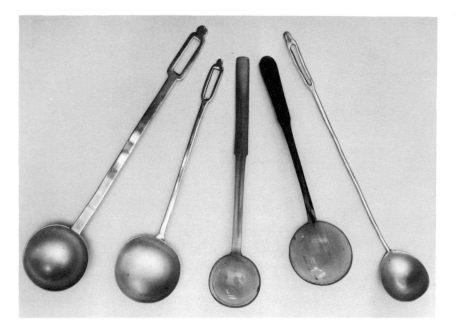

121 Horn and cast brass kitchen spoons. Polished horn was a great improvement on wooden spoons with their rough surfaces, particularly for stirring egg and cream mixtures and spooning syrups. It is doubtful if they were used in the general hurly-burly of the kitchen, but were almost certainly kept for special use. The slit-handled cast brass spoons were probably first imported through Flanders and not made by English brass-founders until the eighteenth century. The slit-handled design was then made continuously by a number of manufacturers until the turn of this century. Length 14 to 18 inches. *Ruper Gentle Antiques.*

horn spoons for the same reason. More often than not, though, they raised their bones and chewed the meat, using their fingers as they had always done. Their teeth were notoriously bad, and the carvers of the day frilled the meat away from the bone so that it was easier for loose and blackened teeth to bite. Even the Queen herself used her fingers for food which could not easily be reduced to decent mouthfuls with spoon and knife alone.

Silver ladles and long-handled spoons came in to the parlour, to dish out ragouts and stews, but in England at least, there were still no forks other than refined flesh-forks for carving and serving. Forks took a very long time indeed to penetrate to the Northern fastnesses of Europe from Byzantium, where they were used as early as the tenth century. With political shifts and changes, they travelled to Greece and from there to Italy, where they stayed for the best part of five centuries. Sucket forks, no more than a couple of sharp prongs at the other end of a thin spoon, appeared and disappeared in Northern Europe through all those years, to spear ginger and preserved fruit from glass or pottery jars. English travellers brought sucket forks home as curiosities from Renaissance Italy. They were most beautifully wrought, but hazardously sharp for anything but spiking delicacies from deep jars.

Catherine de Medici, so it is said, brought her own knives, forks and spoons with her when she came to France to marry the Dauphin in 1533. She also brought her entire retinue of servants and all the equipment from her royal kitchens. Over the succeeding years, foreign diplomats visited England with elegant knife-fork-and-spoon sets in silver-mounted shagreen cases, but the earliest known silver table-fork

122 Wooden porringer, butter bowls and horn, bone and steel cutlery. Small round bowls were often made by turners from burrwood (the tree-root), since the wood was dense and enduring. The smaller rimmed bowl may have been a butter bowl, the smallest a humble 'salt' for a farmhouse. The bone fork is too big to have been used for eating and was a kitchen implement. The carved horn spoon may have been a traditional 'wedding spoon'. Fork: length 14 inches. The rest to scale. *Private collection.*

made in England is dated 1632. If they were made in any quantity at that period, they were probably melted down along with other Royalist silver to pay the Cavalier troops. Restoration England, for all the foreign influence of Charles II's court, was still without forks, and as late as 1669 foreign visitors complained that English tables were devoid of them and that even at large supper parties the most they were offered was a basin and ewer to wash their hands.

There were roasting and toasting forks at that period, many of them as ornately scrolled and decorated as Scottish bar grate roasters, but it is hard to determine whether they were used for serving or were still basically a kitchen implement. They were made almost exclusively in wrought iron or steel, and brass toasting forks are rare before the eighteenth century.

By the end of the seventeenth century brass trivets for warming plates and dishes took their place in parlour grates, shining with the soft sheen of gold. Firedogs in chamber and parlour were topped with brass finials at the very least, and on side-tables and dressers there were silver bowls and dishes, candlesticks and richly decorated loving cups with ornamented covers. Food was no longer served up in the receptacle in which it had been cooked, but was transferred to brass and silver, pewter, gold or porcelain before it came to the table. There were

123   Turned lignum vitae spice mill. This strange living wood is immensely dense and resinated, so that before the introduction of steel and iron spindles it was possible to make grinding surfaces which would endure. This spice mill is turned, and the arrows indicate the position beyond which the cup-shaped reservoir should not be screwed in case of breaking the thread. *c.* 1720. Height 4¾ inches. *Rupert Gentle Antiques.*

individual shallow-footed salts and spice dishes, spice and pepper querns or grinders in lignum vitae, brass, pewter or silver, and tazzas piled high with fruits and sweetmeats.

Under the Puritans England lived plainly and simply – or covertly, with Royalist silver hidden away. Very little managed to escape the melting pot during the Civil War, but a number of richly repousséed and engraved pewter serving dishes and flagons have survived, a fine testament to the craftsmanship of the period. With the triumphal return of Charles II however, everything changed. Restoration banquets were gaudy, greedy affairs, running to as many as twenty separate dishes, with the ladies and gentlemen behaving like children let out of school. They hurled food at each other, played practical jokes, and wrapped what they could not eat in kerchiefs to take home with them. They gobbled and slurped, hiccupped and burped, while above them in the gallery the common folk looked on in amazement at the sight of their overdressed, bejewelled masters and mistresses eating and drinking. Minstrels, who had been silenced by the Puritans, returned to play sweet music and aid digestion. Tumblers and jugglers entertained the company and sometimes a mock hunt would gallop through the banqueting hall, blowing horns and shouting, in pursuit of an imaginary quarry.

Dressers and side-tables were heaped with riches: gold plates and goblets, silver branched candlesticks and candelabra, and whole dinner services in silver or gold. All glimmered in the light of flaming torches held by servants or sputtering in iron wall-sconces. There were mirrors everywhere and gilt gesso frames round great panoramic paintings of sea battles, under which there passed a procession of footmen and servants dressed in entirely new liveries, as gaudy as peacocks and as proud. After the Civil War the house dress of retainers diverged into two separate identities: one of them livery for the servants, the other uniform for the militia. Rich Royalists with Court connections had special suits made for all their indoor and outdoor servants. Every man had a trencher coat, for in those days a trencherman meant a servant who lived and ate under his master's roof. The lower grades of serving men wore 'gaberdines' – loose coats with hanging sleeves – clothes which had been the fashion for gentlemen half a century before.

Queen Anne England, expansive and prosperous, settled down a little as it grew accustomed to rich living and long lazy days of peace. Lord Derby's footmen in their theatrical livery of red feathers and flame-coloured stockings were toned down a bit, and in 1701 servants were forbidden to carry swords, which thereafter became the privilege of

124 Alder and sycamore coopered jug bound with withies, similar in design to 'stave mugs' mounted in pewter and originally made in Germany. Coopers often made important items of household equipment such as salt boxes, candle boxes and mead and ale jugs from alternating staves of different coloured woods to produce a striped design. This one probably comes from Scotland, and dates from the mid-eighteenth century. Height 11½ inches. *A. & E. Foster.*

gentlemen only. Swordsmiths found themselves going out of business. The weapons of war had changed to powder and shot, and swords were worn and used less and less except for ceremonial occasions. Some swordsmiths began to make tools for the houses and gardens of their patrons, and some of the most decorative implements ever made graced eighteenth century kitchens and pantries, orangeries and hothouses.

The routines and rituals of eating and drinking, living and sleeping, all needed special equipment. Silver teapots, cream jugs and sugar bowls adorned tea tables set with fine porcelain tea services. There were beautiful covered silver dishes to hold muffins, which the ladies toasted on elegant ivory-handled toasting forks, and engraved or repoussée chestnut roasters lay beside steel-and-brass fire-irons, trivets and four-legged pierced 'footmen' in parlour grates. The same plates and dishes were no longer permitted to be used for breakfast as well as dinner. Houses had breakfast rooms and parlours, dining rooms and halls, whose functions were no longer interchangeable.

In spite of all this new sophistication, mealtimes had hardly changed since medieval days. Gongs were a sonorous summons to breakfast at ten o'clock in the morning. Dinner was at four o'clock in the afternoon; tea was taken at around seven; and a little light supper was left out by early-rising servants to which the household helped themselves at about eleven o'clock, retiring just before midnight. The Englishman's day was still ruled by the sun, and he preferred to eat in daylight rather than under the fitful light of wavering candles and flambeaus. Only banquets were held after dark, and then the chandeliers were lit with a thousand candles, hanging from the ceiling like frozen fireworks.

The English potteries had at last discovered how to make 'hard paste'. As a result, earthenware and stoneware were relegated to the kitchen, as 'china' from Chelsea, Bow, Derby and Worcester competed with Meissen and Sèvres, which were imported from the Continent from about 1730 onwards. The French had set the fashion for matching dinner services, cutlery, drinking glasses and goblets. Now at last these replaced the hodge-podge of odd plates, knives and forks with which England's tables were still set – a habit surviving from the days when guests each brought their own 'covers' with them.

Gracious town houses and spacious country mansions needed dozens of domestic servants to make them run smoothly. Women servants were at last allowed to be visible about the house: as ladies' maids performing the long toilettes of their mistresses, and as maids cleaning and polishing the elegant furniture and sweeping the marble halls and passages. Delighted by such 'privileges', their heads were soon turned by the clothes provided by the master and mistress and there were complaints that 'they grow proud and for fear of soiling their gay garments avoid all manner of household business.'[74] Not so surprising, when for centuries they had worn nothing but drab grey kersey. They were so proud of their pretty printed linens and cottons and took such care of them that the mistress of the house was furious at the amount of soap and starch they used to wash their dresses, caps and aprons. Housemaids had the task of polishing the brass firedogs and fire-irons and all the gleaming *batterie de cuisine*, but they were not allowed to touch the silver or tableware. That was still in the hands of men, and was the sole preserve of the head steward or butler.

The bigger and grander the house, the more staff were needed to run

125 Brass dredger. Throughout the long history of spit-roasting, joints were 'dredged' with dry mixtures of breadcrumbs of flour and seasoning and spices, in order to make a crisp coating which held in the meat juices. These dredgers were frequently made in pewter as well as brass and, by the end of the eighteenth century, in tin. Height 5 inches. *Rupert Gentle Antiques.*

126 Three cast brass casters or shakers for sugar, spices or ground pepper. These are refined versions of the kitchen 'dredger' and were the forerunners of the matched salt-and-pepper cruet sets of the nineteenth century. *c.* 1765. Heights 3 inches, 3½ inches and 4½ inches. *Rupert Gentle Antiques.*

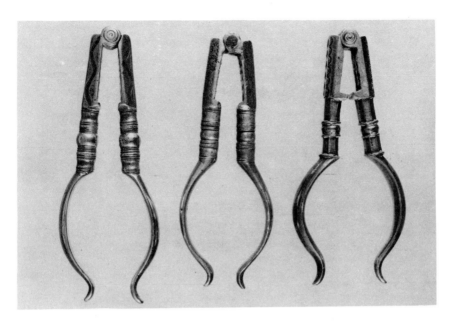

127 Three typically eighteenth century pairs of nutcrackers in cast brass. Once the art of making and casting brass had finally been mastered by English brass-founders, all kinds of household items were made for elegant eighteenth century houses. Similar pairs of nutcrackers were also made in steel at the same period. *c.* 1780. Length 4½ inches, 4 inches and 4 inches. *Rupert Gentle Antiques.*

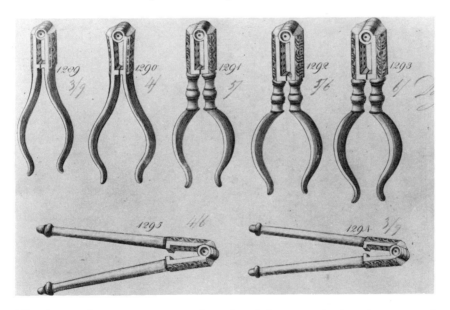

128 A page from a contemporary brass-founder's pattern book – forerunner of illustrated catalogues – showing designs similar to the nutcrackers in the previous illustration. The engraved decoration on the heads can be seen clearly. *c.* 1780. *Rupert Gentle Antiques.*

it. Country people were 'seduced by the appearance of coxcombs in livery' and swarmed to London in the hope of a luxurious life and fine clothes. Little negro boys were quite the fashion in the mid-eighteenth century, wearing exotic livery, feathered turbans and silver or brass collars engraved with their master's name and crest, symbol of their estate. They ran about the house with trays of hot chaculato, tea, coffee and sweetmeats. Not all the engraved brass collars made without hinges or fastenings were for dogs by any means.

It was still the custom to lay out every main course dish on the dining table in an immensely grand display. Thick and thin soups were served in urn-shaped tureens. Fish, game, poultry and meat was decorated and laid out on porcelain, silver, silvered brass or gold. It was a daunting sight – a display of *richesse* and rank equalled only by the astounding liveries of the servants. The desserts, equally fantastic, piled in quivering castles on the sideboard were, if anything, even more dazzling. But this ostentation gave way to mess and confusion when the guests seated themselves – a business which could take so long that the food was cold by the time the social niceties had been observed – and began to help themselves. There were long-handled spoons, ladles and fish-slices, but mostly it was a question of stretching across the table to reach a distant dish, spilling a great deal of everything on the fine linen napery.

129 Pewter vessels in lay or trifle. *Left:* Channel Islands measure *c.* 1740–1826. *Centre:* Late eighteenth century English flagon. *Right:* Scottish tappit hen *c.* 1780. A Scottish pint is three English pints. About 12 inches high. *Rupert Gentle Antiques.*

130 A cook in his kitchen around 1835. It was not *de rigeur* for another ten years for a cook to wear a chef's hat, but the large apron swathed around the gentleman's waist indicates that he is indeed a cook and not an 'upper servant'. *BBC Hulton Picture Library.*

131 An elegant round-bellied pint tankard in cast brass, intended perhaps for mulled ale or wine. Drinking vessels in brass are not common, for the metal interacts with acids, releasing minute quantities of poisonous elements and corroding the metal. *c.* 1760. Height 4⅝ inches. *Rupert Gentle Antiques.*

132 Cast brass sauce boat. The design has been taken from silver models of the same period. It is rare to find such an elegant piece of tableware in brass: originally it was silvered. *c.* 1740. Height 4¾ inches; length 8 inches. *Rupert Gentle Antiques.*

Georgian England, under the influence of a Hanoverian court, gratefully took to the practice of serving food *à l'Allemande* or *à la Russe* with footmen handing each dish, backed up by housemaids who scurried to and from the kitchen with replenishments. Warming plates stood on the endless expanse of sideboard or buffet and chafing dishes reappeared with modifications so that dishes could stand over their gentle warmth and be prevented from congealing or growing cold. Plate-warmers of all shapes and sizes, hooded, branched, ingeniuos and clumsy, stood near the hearth and brass dish-crosses kept hot dishes from marking the solid shine of serving tables. There were scalloped monteiths and raffraichisseurs to warm or cool wine glasses, wine coolers filled with ice to hold hock and champagne, decanters for elevating spirits, brandy and home-made wines, silver goblets, silvered brass, silver or gold tankards for ale and, now that the dining table was not cluttered with dishes, huge solid silver centrepieces of classical mythology or patriotic sentiment.

In the evening the ladies gathered to gossip in the withdrawing room. Beside the mistress of the house stood a tea-kettle on a tall three-legged

133 Brass chafing dish with turned wooden handle. Early chafing dishes were used directly on the fire, and often had wrought iron frames. More refined versions such as this one stood on side-tables in late seventeenth and early eighteenth century dining rooms, filled with hot charcoal to keep dishes warm while waiting to be served. Height 6 inches; diameter 7¼ inches. *Colonial Williamsburg Foundation.*

strand, often with a little brazier set into it. They were often made of brass, frequently identical in design to silverware, and were often silvered outside as well as being tinned or silvered within. Japanned trays swirling with blush roses, cake baskets with 'barley-sugar' handles and pierced sides, rosewood tea caddies and silver tea strainers stood among the cups and saucers on fragile tea tables in the twilight. Tea bells

134 A superb cast brass coffee pot with carved ebonised pearwood handle. Many coffee pots were made to be used in coffee houses and, later, in early restaurants and hotels. They were sometimes quite grand in design and were made in silvered copper, tinned inside. This one was made for the Bostock-Huddleston family, whose coat of arms it bears, and it still retains some of its original silvering. *c.* 1755. Height 9½ inches; diameter of base 4¼ inches. *Rupert Gentle Antiques.*

135 An intricately-pierced Georgian brass cake basket. Once it had become the fashion to take 'tay' or tea, and times of meals had altered, there were teapots and kettles, trays and cake baskets and covered muffin dishes for the lady of the house. Many tea things were in silver, some in porcelain, and some in silvered brass. *c.* 1755. Length 14 inches. *Rupert Gentle Antiques.*

summoned the parlour maid for more hot water, muffins or macaroons and the little negro servant sat at his mistress's feet like a pet dog.

By the end of the eighteenth century the nation had been called to arms and servant girls ran away to London to seek their fortunes. Social climbing hostesses lured them away from the country with promises of sprigged muslin aprons, frilled cambric, and fine lawn mob caps. Cook-generals, indomitable women who ruled the kitchen and struck fear into the hearts of the young mistress, replaced the master cooks of the previous century. The wheels of industry had begun to turn, and when the war was over men went into business in the city. The social hub of life was the gentleman's club, which had grown out of the coffee houses of the eighteenth century. Grand dinner parties grew a little less grand and a little more solid, the rituals less elaborate. Now it was the master's responsibility to carve the joint or fowl on the sideboard with ivory-handled carving sets, sharpening his knife meaningfully and teaching his son the art of slicing beef and shaving wafers of white meat from chicken breasts.

In the nineteenth century the times of meals changed at last, now that there were acrid gas lamps to see by after dark. The day was divided into four quarters, marked by a meal at each quarter. Breakfast was at eight, with enormous plates of kidney and mushroom, kippers, eggs and porridge kept hot for reluctant children on water-plates. Lunch, which was now a social meal, was at midday, tea at four and supper at eight. The men kept business hours: trade had become respectable and food a little more solid and stodgy. If there was to be a grand dinner it was held at ten o'clock, with carriages at the door and much formality. The banquet no longer consisted of two endless main courses, but was divided into soup, fish, game, meat and dessert, usually all laid out in the room where the dancing and socialising were going to take place.

These nineteenth century banquets were strange affairs, not really intended to be eaten at all. They were an essential part of a rout, or noisy social gathering, and were still laid out as food had been displayed a century ago. But though there were chairs set round the long 'cold table' people came and went, picking and pecking at a little cold salmon here, a little potted brawn there, a slice or two of ham and a spoonful of dessert. After all, the guests had come to be seen and not to eat. To that end they danced and drank and observed the rules of rank, introducing themselves and being introduced, snapping their fingers at the footmen who stood like sentries with silver salvers tucked under one arm, waiting to be called to serve. Every indoor servant wore white, washable 'Berlin' gloves and the stripes on their vests or waistcoats were horizontal. When the carriages crunched on the gravel sweep or clattered up the cobbled street, the outside servants, in breeches, cutaway coats and top hats, could be distinguished at a glance by the vertical stripes on their waistcoats.

It was an era of self-indulgence. England's Empire was growing, there were no taxes to speak of, investments yielded splendid percentages, gentlemen lived on their incomes while their capital increased by leaps and bounds. Yet there seemed to be a stagnation of imagination and a lack of joy in living which brought plainer food to the table on plainer dishes. The mistress of the house was busy about her social affairs and housekeepers took over the management of the household with a consequent decline in imaginative, festive food. It was the age of lazy-tongs and bell-pulls, bottled milk and bought pies, of commercial bakeries and patisseries, boiled mutton and steamed sponge puddings.

Flamboyance died and ostentation was born, with mass-produced nickel-plate and chrome, and coarsely cast brass ornament. Fortunes were spent in maintaining huge estates, but it seemed to be more of a business than a pleasure. Industrial barons tore down gracious Queen Anne and Georgian houses or erected façades of horrendous Gothic design to obscure them, and certainly in towns and sometimes in the country too cooking went underground. The kitchen was finally relegated to the basement, along with the servants, who carried coal and hot water and answered the bells which jangled down underground stone corridors. The practical consequence of this significant social change was a plethora of serving hatches and service lifts to bring the food up from the nether regions into the light of day.

In stately homes, grown unmanageably large, there were ugly steel trollies which looked as if they had been made for hospitals, to sterilise unspeakable instruments. They were kept hot with a water-jacket, and into their surgical surfaces slotted containers of soups, vegetables, sauces and hot puddings. They were hauled down passages and corridors, and through the green baize door which separated the servants' quarters from the rest of the house. Outside in the passage the food was dished up on ornate Victorian china and carried in to be served. Housemaids and parlour maids were no longer frivolous but severe in high-necked dark dresses, white aprons and plain white caps which tied under the chin. Afternoon tea came rattling down the passage on a wooden trolley, and every dish had a cover to keep in the heat during the long journey from kitchen to dining or drawing room.

The steam engine and the railways had arrived, and everywhere hotels rose like sooty wedding cakes, the best of them vying with each other to attract 'the carriage trade'. In these unlikely, phantasmagoric monuments to commercialism there was still a certain reverence for food, a certain delicacy in serving the top-hatted gentlemen and plumed ladies, and a certain pride in their cuisine. But the origins of most of the panoply of ornate silver-plated serving dishes were Continental. The elegance of English eighteenth century design had been abandoned in favour of ostentatious German Gothic, French Empire or bizarre *art nouveau*. Only in certain old-established and exclusive gentlemen's clubs, distant country houses and in America did English excellence still linger on.

Nineteenth century America had almost the same time-lag as English provincial country estates. The newest fashions in London usually took two decades or more to percolate through to traditional establishments in the shires and the North and West of England, so that provincial craftsmen only began to make copies of designs as they were about to be superseded by the latest fashion in the capital. After the War of Independence, when the ban on manufacture was finally lifted, American craftsmen slowly broke away from making the necessities of life and ventured into making furniture, silverware, copper, brass and ironware which were decorative as well as functional. They had many trading connections with Catholic Europe, but for a while they severed their connections with England after 1776 and drew on the talents of their own newly-settled Dutch and German communities.

At the end of the eighteenth century, America had established a considerable trading connection with China, and in the last twenty-five years of the eighteenth century almost a quarter of all the fine furnishings, porcelain, carpets, fabrics, pewter and silver which graced post-Colonial America originated in China.

It is well-known that English crests and cyphers had a distinctly Oriental look about them when the finished articles were delivered. What is less well-known is that the Americans imported a great deal of silver made to their own design in China. And since they were quite a while catching up with the latest fashions in Europe, much of the silver made in the first quarter of the nineteenth century still had the sweet lines of English Regency design. By the middle of the century the designs had a far more Oriental flavour and were much more ornate, covered with writhing dragons and serpents. But early nineteenth century silver flatware, trays, teapots and cream jugs, cutlery and serving utensils made to American designs by Chinese silversmiths had the slim grace and elegance that English silver was beginning to lose. There was also a considerable amount of pewter and brass, also made in China to traditional English-American design, so close to the originals that they are almost impossible to distinguish. The silver and pewter sweetmeat dishes, soup tureens, sugar bowls and flatware which gleamed on the dressers and dining tables of the First Families are today most inscrutable in their origins, not least because they are often marked with facsimile assay marks and touch marks copied faithfully – and illegally – by Chinese craftsmen.[75]

8 Preserving

136 Wooden icing mould, probably in fruitwood. This mould was used by the confectionery firm of Terry's of York for the christening cake of Edward VIII in 1894, though the style belongs to the first quarter of the century. Length 9 inches; width 5½ inches. *Castle Museum, York.*

WIND, SALT AND SMOKE – these were the primeval elements which dried and preserved meat killed in the bountiful flush of the year to feed the empty-handed hunters and their tribes throughout the winter, when the hours of daylight diminished and a grudging sun wheeled lower and lower in the dark grey sky, until the Ancient Britons believed the world would end. On the shortest day of the year they lit towering bonfires to propitiate the gods and festooned trees with skulls and bones and haunches of dried meat to stir the limbs and loins of the fertility gods, who had apparently abandoned them. If a manchild was born in those black and bitter days, it was surely a sign that somehow life would continue and they offered him up to the gods as a reminder of their existence.

The islands of Ancient Britain had a kinder climate, swept as they were by currents of drier air as the earth spun out of its frozen Ice Age sleep. Neolithic man was blessed by light salt-laden breezes from the rolling North Sea, and he dried and preserved his meat and fish by hanging it from beams and branches, leaving nature to dry and salt it. The busy Celts began winning salt from the sea in the early Iron Age on the East coast marshlands of Lincolnshire, Norfolk, Essex and Kent. But the world turned, glaciers melted and the skies filled with clouds. Mist rose from sodden ground, seeping into huts and hovels, causing grain to sprout pale unhealthy shoots and preserved meat to take on a new and putrefying life of its own.

The hearth became the centre of life. In winter fire was a man-made god which drove the blood faster through bodies chilled to the marrow and brought dry warmth to huddled families. Haunches of meat were hung from rough beams inside smoky huts to dry. After the Romans had gone, wave after wave of northern invaders clawed footholds on the fertile hills of Britain and colonised the rich green valleys. From them the Britons learned to cure wild pig-meat. They rubbed it with salt, steeped it in its own juices in earthen or clay pots and let it lie from the

137 Slip-glazed earthenware salt jar. Traditional slipglazed jars and shallow pie dishes were made and used all over the British Isles. Earthenware salt jars were the successors of the wooden 'salt kits' built into the mantelpiece of the chimney, and were in common use by the end of the eighteenth century. Height 10 inches. *Castle Museum, York.*

138 A fine salt box in sheet brass, repoussée with chased decoration. A rare example of fine English craftsmanship, possibly from Bristol, the first major brass centre in England and the principal port of the East India Company, which might account for the two whales on the backplate. *c.* 1700. Height 12¼ inches to top of backplate; width 9¼ inches. *Michael Wakelin.*

new moon to the full. Then they drained it on a cradle of branches, left it to dry, and rubbed it with rape oil and soured beer or alegar. Finally they hung it in smoke for two more days. There have been few changes in curing methods since those lean hams swung from the roof beams of pre-Christian Britain.

As salt-winning became more and more difficult with the changing climate, salty little fish were often substituted for dried salt grains to

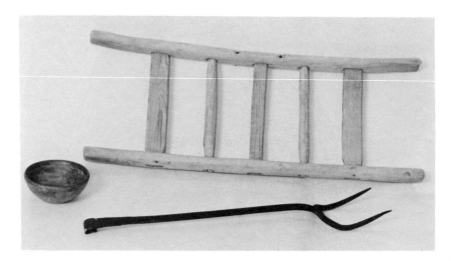

139 Ham rack, flesh-fork and wooden dish. These curved ladder-shaped racks were often made from the spokes of broken cartwheels. Hams which had been soaked in brine were lifted on to them to drain. The flesh-fork is wrought iron and of a traditional pattern, dating probably from the late eighteenth century. Ham rack: length 37 inches. Flesh-fork: 22½ inches. *Private collection.*

make brine. Liquamen or garum was made and stored in earthenware amphorae both as a preservative and a seasoning for broths and pottages. There were shoals of anchovy, sprats, herring fry and mackerel to be caught by wading into the sea and casting jute nets into the surf. Roughly coopered barrels bound with withies were made and filled with little fishes, layered with bay leaves and hedgerow herbs and turned every three days. Each time the top was uppermost the barrel was opened and more fish added as those in the barrel shrank and the level of the brine rose. Bigger fish were speared on green sticks through their gills and hung like necklaces round the fire, turning copper-coloured in the smoke as they kippered.

The Norman invaders continued to buy their salt from the Bay of Bourgneuf, central trading port for salt made all along the Atlantic coast from Brittany to Northern Portugal. 'Bay salt' was crude, with large crystals. To make it fine enough to stand in rich, ornamented dishes on the High Table, it was boiled in sea water in huge iron cauldrons, dried and pounded to a fine powder known as 'salt-upon-salt'. Bay salt, though too crude to be sent to the table, had great advantages over salt-upon-salt for curing and preserving. It had a sharper, sweeter taste and penetrated raw meat far more completely than salt-upon-salt, which drew the juices, wrinkled the skins of meat and fish, and only sealed the surface tissue so that the inner flesh putrefied inside a briny, hardened coat.

Dried and salted cod or stockfish came across the North Sea to Britain in Viking ships from the ninth century onwards, until the English built their own fishing fleets. Elsewhere, where Roman fleets had once sailed, trading as far as the south-east coast of India, where pepper grew wild, the Arabs now dominated the spice trade. Their slant-sailed feluccas brought pepper, ginger, cinnamon, cassium and spikenard to Alexandria from the East. There it was traded for copper and lead, iron and bronze in such great quantities that spices were one of the principal trading currencies of the age.

The Normans, setting law and order over the undisciplined people of the British Isles, introduced protective guilds for almost every commodity. Among them were the Guild of Pepperers, or 'grossarii', bulk dealers in this precious commodity. From here descend the grocers of all the ages since. It took the supermarkets less than three decades to kill off the ancient name and put those canny dealers out of business. The pepper that the guildsmen sold in medieval days was green – sweeter and less pungent than the black and white dried peppercorns of today – and pepper was used in huge quantities, both as a seasoning for sweet dishes, meat and fish and as an ingredient for preserving.

The other main preservative of medieval England was 'vinaigre' or sour wine which broke down tough fibres with its strong acid content. It was particularly effective with venison, which was steeped in a mixture of vinegar and oil before being spitted and roasted. This mixture came to be known as a 'marinade', though the original marinade was a brine solution – a corruption of Latin and Spanish *marinare* or *marinade*, which simply means sea water. In England, as the Roman vineyards were largely abandoned and left to die, cider and beer were substituted for wine, and alegar and cider vinegar became the basis for sousing and pickling mixtures used by farmers and fishermen, husbandmen and their goodwives.

Mutton fat, beef dripping, 'sweet suet' or beeswax was melted down in an iron grisset pan for making rushlights and candles. Rushes or twists of cotton were dipped, dried and dipped again until there was enough thickness to the coating for it to burn for as long as possible. Pure beeswax made fine fat candles for important houses, churches and monasteries. They were impaled on pricket sticks on altars, on high tables and in bedchambers. In the houses of the poor rushlights would burn for an hour or more, but gave out precious little light. Elizabethan

England was better lit after dark, for the Merchant Adventurers, seeking new trade routes while Spain usurped the English Channel, ventured north through icy seas to trade woollen cloth with Russia in return for timber, furs and tallow. Instead of dipping candles repeatedly in evil-smelling wax, the Elizabethans began to make moulded candles from imported tallow, which dripped less and gave a clearer, brighter light.

Apples were sliced in rings and hung from the rafters to dry, with onions, mushrooms, thick sausages and black puddings. Animal gut was used for all manner of things: stuffed with the smoked remains of ham and bacon, stretched over pots and jars to keep out the air, filled with boiled cereal grains soaked in animal blood – usually pig's – to make black puddings, or with offal from a freshly-slaughtered beast and hung in the smoke to preserve them. Wild plums and sloes were steeped in crocks of honey syrup and stored in sealed jars, as were cherries and damsons. Cries of delight must have greeted the discovery that if the fruit was kept too long the juice fermented and made thick, heady wine.

The bloody pilgrim Crusaders, returning from their battles with the Infidel, visited ancient shrines and holy places in Spain and Portugal, tasted delicious foreign fruit preserves and confections and with excitement brought them back to England, where they began a new and peculiarly English life. There is a charming little story that 'marmelade' came to England from France to soothe the sickness from poor Mary Queen of Scots, and that the name is a corruption of *'Marie est malade'*. Charming, but quite untrue. The origins of marmalade lie thousands of miles from Scotland and hundreds of years from Mary's imprisonment, in twelfth century Portugal. It was here that quinces grew in great profusion and were made into a thick confection called 'marmelado' from the Portuguese word for quince – *marmelo*. There is a fourteenth century English recipe for 'marmelado' which uses almost the same ingredients: thirty quinces are brayed in a mortar with ten warden pears, mixed with wine, boiled thick with honey, then spiced with powdered ginger, galingale and cinnamon.

However, other bands of Crusaders took a different route home, passing through southern Europe, where they also found a delicious confection, made from oranges and lemons and called 'citronade'. They could not pronounce this word too well, and called it 'succade'. This was made by boiling orange or lemon peels in water to take off the bitterness, then boiling them again in honey or sugar syrup and sealing the confection in stoneware pots or little barrels. Some Crusaders brought home a name, others brought a confection, and the two were indissolubly wedded for evermore as marmalade.

Arabic sweetmeats were greatly prized and there were all sorts of adaptations of these perfumed jelly confections. The original quince 'marmelado' was made so thick that it could be printed with decorative moulds. Stiff jellies were made from soft fruits crushed in a mortar with sugar, then boiled with rosewater and 'huysenblas' (isinglass), sieved and left to set. Sealed in small airtight wooden boxes, these sweetmeats would keep for a year or more.

Once the English fleet had swept the Channel clear of Spanish galleons, the Merchant Adventurers set out doggedly to recapture their lost trading grounds and, though they failed to win back the nutmeg and mace trade from Portugal, they sailed into incredibly distant waters and returned home with prizes of their own. Tripoli, Syria, Aleppo, Babylon, Bakara and even Goa. 'What English ship did heretofore ever anchor in the mighty river of Plate, the Straits of Magellan, the coast of Chili, Peru and the backside of Nova Hispania, the South Seas, enter into alliance, amity and traffic with Princes of Malluccas, the Isle of Java, double the Cape of Good Hope, St. Helena, and return home richly laden with commodities of China?'[76]

To the North and East, English fishing fleets sailed into the teeth of

140 An early wrought iron and brass chafing dish (or 'chaffing dish'), used directly over the fire, for making sugar preserves and confections as well as for heating pewter dishes when filled with charcoal and set upon a table. This one dates from the seventeenth century. *c.* 1670. Height 5¾ inches; length 13¼ inches; diameter 8¾ inches. *Mac Humble Antiques.*

Dutch opposition and returned with huge catches of fresh herring, cod and haddock. Thomas Nash in *Lenten Stuffe*, written in 1599, goes into raptures over smoked herrings, which were shipped in barrels from Yarmouth, Grimsby and further north down to London. 'Their goodnesse consists in their being large, fresh, fat, soft and pliable, well salted and barrelled; their roes safe within them and their outside of a yellow gold colour.' They were a great improvement on 'green fish', which were barrelled in salt on board the fishing boats and left in their own brine until the boats came home and they could be smoked. The fishermen's wives of Findon made an enduring contribution to food in Britain by smoking haddock over peat or seaweed fires on the beach and calling the pale yellow fish 'Finnan haddies'.

Freshwater fish were seldom kept, except alive in stew-ponds and fish ponds, to be fished out on the day they were to be eaten. Carp, though, that strange monastic fish, could be kept alive if it was wrapped in wet moss and hung in a net in a cool place. In this suspended state it was fattened up on bread and milk to rid the flesh of its muddy taste before it came to the table. There was, of course, a regular traffic in salmon down the East coast at certain times of the year. It was an oily fish which smoked well and kept relatively well unsmoked too, wrapped in seaweed and doused periodically during the voyage with salt water.

Other preserved food sounds less appetising. 'Venison and frumenty' was declared to be 'a gay pleasure', but scarcely sounds it. Venison which was not fresh-killed but had already begun to stiffen was buried in the ground for three days and nights. Then 'Take it up and spot it well with great saltpetre, there where the resting is, and after let it hang in rain water all night or more . . .'[77] If the deer was fresh-killed the treatment sounds more appetising. The meat was soaked for half a day in clean water, dried, salted, boiled in brine, left to soak for three days, then salted again and barrelled up for store.

Large households could easily consume whole carcases of beef, sheep or deer, but apart from pig-meat, which could be smoked for bacon and ham, an average-sized family had to find a way of preserving some of the meat from a fresh-killed animal for a short time, or it would go bad before it could be eaten. Left-over cuts and joints were dipped in brine and vinegar pickle, then dry-salted with saltpetre, and would keep for several weeks. Beef was green-salted by steeping it in brine for one night, and would keep for several days in summer and a week or more in winter. It was boiled in a pot with roots and pot-herbs and called 'silverside', because of the curious silvery surface the pickling gave it.

Traditionally, cattle were slaughtered on November 11th, the Feast of St Martin, and carcase meat was laid down during the days that followed, to keep as best it could through the winter. Known as 'Martinmas beef' or 'hanged beef', it was cut in strips, steeped in brine, then hung to dry from smoke-blackened beams above the fire. By the time it came to be eaten, it had to be soaked and then simmered with hay or bran to get rid of some of the salt. It was of such a leathery consistency that it was known as 'jerkin beef' or 'jerky' and was still known by this affectionate name in America long after it had died out in England.

Under the rigorous regime of the Commonwealth, not only were the English deprived of their puddings and pies, but a heavy salt tax was levied – presumably because of Cromwell's general policy of ceasing to trade with Catholic countries. The cost of preserving fish and meat became alarmingly high, and all over England salt was treasured and used as sparingly as possible. Every house and home had a salt box which hung near the fire to dry out small quantities of salt for the table,

141 Two ingenious mousetraps, an essential part of preservation in most households down the centuries. The one on the left when triggered drops the wooden block on the unfortunate marauder – the one on the right slips a running noose round the mouse's neck. In some parts of the country, notably in Wales, great wooden cradles were hoisted up to the ceiling on pulleys to keep bread and grain out of reach of mice and rats. Length 8¼ inches *(left)*; 6¼ inches *(right)*. *Private collection.*

142 (a) Welsh oak high dresser with two delft racks, spoon rack and spice cupboard. This form of dresser was peculiar to Wales; low ones with two tiers are known as 'duedarns' and were a regional variation on the 'buffetier' once cooking and eating activities separated into different rooms. This one dates from the first quarter of the eighteenth century. Height 74 inches; width 55 inches. *Cedar Antiques.*

but salt could no longer be bought by the sackful and stored in the rafters, because it cost too much. Housewives scrutinised the meat to be preserved and judged whether it was worth its salt or not. If not, it was pickled.

Although by the end of the seventeenth century most households had some brass and copper cooking pans, the pots and pans which were used for preserving and pickling remained much the same as they had been centuries earlier. The pickling mixture was more or less the old recipe for verjuice diluted with water and seasoned with bay leaves, hedgerow

142 (b) Detail of false cupboard door concealing the drawers which held precious and costly spices. *Cedar Antiques.*

herbs and whole peppercorns. Brine could not stand in brass or copper without producing verdigris, and pickling mixtures with their high acid content were even worse. Stoneware or earthenware ham soakers and crocks stood in cool stone-flagged larders and store rooms; meat that was being dry-salted lay on slate shelves. In farmhouses there were wooden troughs with a plugged hole at the bottom to let out the changes of water and brine, and in well-equipped sculleries there were lead-lined tubs and sinks in which meat or fish could be steeped in brine or pickled.

Big estates which had their own stands of wood kept coopers to make jugs, salt boxes, tubs and barrels of all sizes in which they kept their salted and pickled produce and stored their wines and cordials. Coopering is one of the oldest crafts of all and barrels and casks were the earliest form of enduring container which could survive rough handling in ports and ships, keep the goods they contained relatively well-protected against damp and damage, and return knocked down into their basic bundles of staves, to be set up again, refilled with goods of quite a different sort and shipped back. The names of different-sized barrels come from every quarter of the medieval trading world: a hogshead, a pin, a firkin, a kilderkin, a barrel, a tun. Wines and spirits were shipped in casks – ale and cider stored in barrels.

In the rich days of the Restoration, a new way of preserving meat and fish was discovered. Brawn would keep for months if it was packed in a pot and sealed with melted butter. Lampreys and eels, shrimps and prawns were also 'potted'. Soon all sorts of 'potted meats' were stored in stoneware jars, and by the early eighteenth century the cooks of the day were chopping cooked meat as fine as possible, beating it with butter and herbs, combining white meat with brown, potting it in deep dishes and sealing it with butter. When the dish was dipped in hot water the potted meat turned out easily and looked so deliciously marbled and pretty that the cooks took to using shaped moulds to make them prettier still.

The passion for colour in the kitchen persisted even with preserved food. Samphire was greened by boiling it in a brass pan in vinegar. Red cabbage was boiled with beetroot and turnips, pickled in claret wine

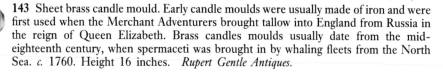

143 Sheet brass candle mould. Early candle moulds were usually made of iron and were first used when the Merchant Adventurers brought tallow into England from Russia in the reign of Queen Elizabeth. Brass candles moulds usually date from the mid-eighteenth century, when spermaceti was brought in by whaling fleets from the North Sea. *c.* 1760. Height 16 inches. *Rupert Gentle Antiques.*

144 Sheet brass candle box with raised and chased decoration of a crown and thistles. The Union of Scotland with England took place in 1707 and this is possibly a commemorative piece of the period. Candle boxes were hung in the hall or parlour to hold candles for the table. *c.* 1700–1720. Height 8½ inches to top of backplate; length 12½ inches. *Michael Wakelin.*

vinegar when 'it will also serve both for garnishing and salad; for your turnips thereby shall be dyed into a crimson colour, a handsome garnishing to the eye.'[78] Nasturtiums from the West Indies were a triple delight. Their leaves were peppery and added zest to salads, the unopened buds and young seed pods were pickled and used like mild pepper, and the flowers themselves were such bright scarlet, orange and yellow that they were irresistible as decoration.

The eighteenth century country gentleman owned a fowling piece, and no longer had to depend on hawking for his wild game. Inevitably, carried away by his own skill and marksmanship he shot too many birds, or brought home game when there was already enough food waiting to be eaten in the house. The custom of hanging game until the rigor had gone out of it and it was tender became almost an obsession and the results were often an acquired taste. An extremely strong sauce was served with pheasant, partridge and other game birds, consisting of pepper, lovage, thyme, mint, filberts, dates, honey vinegar, wine,

145 Cast iron candle holder. While the rooms and tables of the gentry were furnished with elegant candlesticks with new-fangled 'bobeches' or detachable drip pans, the servants were still equipped with iron candle holders. In country cottages and farmhouses candle holders such as this one were the best that could be afforded. *c.* 1737. Height 22 inches. *Rupert Gentle Antiques.*

146 Wrought iron rushlight and candle holder on three feet. These were made over
centuries with little change in design, in iron and (rarely) in brass. This one is probably
dated towards the end of the eighteenth century because of the high standard of the
metalwork and the fine finishing. Height 14½ inches.   *Christopher Bangs.*

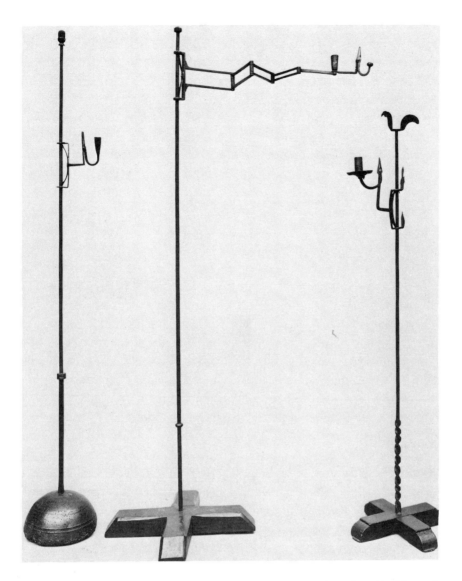

147 Three standing wrought iron candle and rushlight holders from the mid-eighteenth century. Although the workmanship was excellent, these clumsy objects were the only way of providing freestanding lighting in kitchens, sculleries and pantries until well into the nineteenth century. *Victoria & Albert Museum.*

liquamen, oil, wine lees and mustard, and game larders were added to the growing number of special outhouses, in which steel and iron game-hooks hung festooned with festering birds.

Little birds could not escape the pathetic destiny of being laid out on toast and during the netting season, when far too many were caught to be eaten before they putrefied, they too were committed to pickle.

Plucked, dressed and boiled, they were put into a strong liquor of Rhenish wine, white wine vinegar, herbs, spices and plenty of salt. 'Once in a month, new boil the pickle and when the bones are dissolved they are fit to eat: put them in china saucers and mix with your pickles.'[79] Mushrooms were pickled, and eggs, and onions and 'pickalilli'. Lila was an Indian pickle and thus the name was adopted for a mixture of shredded cabbage, cauliflower, celery, onions, raisins and pepper boiled in vinegar and herbs and put up in bottles in its own liquor.

As the comfort and equipment of kitchens and their staff improved, more elaborate ways of preserving meat, particularly for the cold table, became fashionable. Collaring and sousing belong to that indulgent era when the entire carcase of a small pig or lamb was boned and tied up 'in collars' rolled up tight, bound with tape and boiled in heavily salted water. It was left to cool in its own juice and served on the side-table. Often it was scored and filled with chopped parsley, fat pork and spiced breadcrumbs so that when it was cut each slice was chequered pink, white and green like a Battenburg cake. Sousing was a method of preserving fish which had been cooked, as opposed to raw pickled fish. The pickling mixture, consisting of fish stock, vinegar, bay leaves, juniper berries, peppercorns and cloves, was poured boiling hot over the fish, which was then left to cool in the liquid.

There were funnels of pewter, copper and untainting tin with which to fill sausages less messily, and tongue and brawn presses to turn out neat cylindrical shapes for the butlers and footmen to slice thinly for the guests. Fresh salmon, brought by sea from Newcastle to London packed in ice, lay on specially-designed fish dishes. Smoked salmon was drearily commonplace, since previously there had been no other way of preserving salmon on its long journey south. But at the end of the eighteenth century a member of the East India Company, returning from a visit to China, told of the way the Chinese transported fish packed in ice from the coast to inland towns. He had seen it with his own eyes and verified the freshness of the fish at the end of its long journey. Scottish fishmongers took up the idea and a brisk trade developed, first with salmon and then with fresh sea fish of all kinds.

But it was the abundance of fruit, grown in the orchards and gardens of those lovely eighteenth century houses that was the epicentre of all the preserving and conserving of that age. Stoned fruits had been successfully preserved for many years, but soft fruits had so far proved difficult. In the late seventeenth century soft fruit was stored in stoneware bottles, but it neither kept nor tasted very nice. Around the

148 Cast brass toaster trivet, too small and elegant to be in daily kitchen use. Trivets like this one may have been used on chamber grates for making warm drinks in small round-bottomed posnets or early saucepans. They may also have been used for keeping hot dishes of muffins, crumpets and scones from marking the table. Length 15¾ inches; width 6⅜ inches. *Mac Humble Antiques.*

149 Kitchen spice box in the grand manner in sheet copper. The compartments are for salt, black and white pepper, white and Vienna flour and spices. It belonged in the Duke of Devonshire's kitchen at Chiswick House. *c.* 1830. Overall width: 15 inches. *Christopher Clarke Antiques.*

1720s soft fruits were bruised to release the juice, boiled quickly in sugar syrup and, without sieving or straining, used as a filling for open fruit tarts. Vulgarly, in the servants' quarters, this mess when bottled up for later use was known as 'jam'.

As essential piece of equipment for fruit preserving and sweetmeat-making was a 'stove' built like a tall shallow cupboard with no doors. Its shelves were often lined with tin or lead, on which crystallised, dried, candied and preserved fruits and flowers were laid. The stove was set fairly close to the cooking fire so that warm air circulated around the shelves and dried out the last of the moisture, preventing the confectionery from getting sticky. If the bake oven had recently been used for baking and there was still some warmth in it, then the drying could be done in the last of its heat. Otherwise, the stove was used so that sweetmeat-making did not have to depend on baking hours. Recipes of the time sometimes suggest one and sometimes the other. Here, for instance, are those unfortunate soft fruits put to as good a use as

150 A country kitchen in 1830. Hams hang from slats near the warmth of the chimney, while strings of onions and cheeses tied in cloths hang in the cool draught above the door. Here is proof, if any were needed, that many cooking methods were still being used long after kitchen hob grates and ranges were in common use. Compare Figure 74, where raised brick hearths were being used in the same year. Many kitchen utensils and items of equipment continued to be made long after the date when many present-day collectors believe they were superseded. *BBC Hulton Picture Library.*

151 Pollard oak settle with bacon cupboard in the seat. Oak settles were usually placed between the door and the hearth to keep out the draught. High-backed chairs also sometimes had a lifting seat which concealed a cupboard. As well as bacon and hams, sacks of salt and grain were often kept in these warm, dry, convenient storage spaces. *c.* 1750. Height 56 inches; width 54 inches. *Cedar Antiques.*

possible, though the resulting 'Rafberry Pafte' was probably not eaten, but only used as a colourful decoration.

'Take ripe Rafberrys and pommell them small set them upon a quick fire and boyle them as fast as you can till the juice be all boyled away you must stirr them conftantly to keep them from burning. To them take

their weight in Sugar. Stirr in the Sugar while the Pulp is hott and as
soon as you have put in the sugar it will make it have a quicker Colour
mingle them very well together sett them in an easy Stove to Dry for one
hour or more then put it into a broad earthen pan set it in a luke warm
Stove or Oven till they be Stiffe enough to lay out. As soon as they will
lye without spreading lay them upon Glafse. Shape them with tin
moulds and Stove them till they be Dry turning them upon Cleane
Glafse as often as they need.'[80]

'Marmalott of Apricocks' is neither jam nor preserve, and most certainly
is not marmalade.

'Take ripe Apricocks and half their weight in Sugar finely beaten. Pare
and slice them into a Bafon put to them 7 or 8 spoonfulls of Water lett
them Stand till the Sugar is melted then set them on the fire boyle them
till they are cleare and the Syrrop thick keep them as whole as you can
put them into Glafses and Stove them till they are Jelley.'[81]

152 Sheet brass strainer or sieve, dating from the early eighteenth century. The absence
of handles indicates that it was probably used for sieving crystallised and preserved
confections, and was not in common kitchen use as a colander. Diameter 11½
inches. *Rupert Gentle Antiques.*

153 'Ideal' fruit bottler. Fruit bottling became a national pastime in England during World War I when food was scarce. This one uses an early version of the 'Kilner' jar principal, with rubber sealing ring and tinplate-and-glass screw-tops. The fruit was packed in jars and lowered into the container and boiled in the same way as commercial vacuum-packing. Height 12 inches. *Castle Museum, York.*

By the middle of the eighteenth century the equipment in kitchens was a wonderful mixture of the old and the new. Side by side in one recipe book is an antique skillet and a sophisticated glass preserving jar. 'To make Syrrop of Lemons Take half a pint of the juice of lemons 3 quarters of a pound of double refined Sugar and put it into a Deep preserving Glasse and set it into a Skillet of Sand over the fire and soo lett it stand till it be of a good thicknefse it must never boyle but as the Scum arifeth take it off and when it is of a good thicknefse put it into a Viall Glafse and keep it clofe Stopt.'[82]

To make another variation on 'Marmelott':

'Take some good White Sharp Plumbs before they be too ripe and put them to boyle in a Double Pott, often pouring away the liquor and when you have got as much as will come pour them out and take a pretty quantity of Apricocks pare and slice them and sett them to doo in a Double Pott then draw it and bruife it and to every pound of your Pulp put half a pound of your Plumb Juice and to every pound of the Pulp and juice put a pound of Double refined Sugar soo boyle it well and scum it and put it in your glafses.'[83]

Sliced fruits captured in glowing amber jelly, pulped fruits and fruit juices, were visible in all their glory in glass jars of every shape and size. Small wonder that often when the ladies left the gentlemen to their port and pisspots after dinner the lady of the house took her guests on a tour of her larders and still rooms. They must have been a pretty sight as well as proof of good household and estate management, for everything stored, preserved and conserved was produce from the well-tended grounds of the house.

There were wines and cordials too, ranked on those dark delicious shelves or laid in racks on brick or stone-flagged floors. There might have been a grooved wooden bottling rack which held bottles of indeterminate capacity for private consumption, with a cork press. There would certainly have been some tubs and small barrels in the process of fermentation, for almost all through the year, from the first cowslip to the last sloe, wine was working, fermenting and settling in still rooms everywhere, from labourer's cottage to royal palace. One recipe is enough, for they were all made in much the same way, and this one for 'Spirrit of Black Cherry' has something special about it:

'Take Black Cherrys full and Ripe beat them in a Stone Mortar be sure to break the Stones put them in a Wooden Vefsell that is some tub standing upright put to them Ale Yeast according to the quantity if 3 or 4 Dozen of Cherries a quart of Yeast lett it stand eight Days Stirring them for 3 or 4 days twice a Day then lett them Stand till they have a Venomous Smell and have done Rifsing then Still them off in a Limbeck.'[84]

A limbeck was a distilling apparatus, the word being properly 'alembic', which has ancient roots in alchemy.

As the eighteenth century tipped over into the nineteenth, the ugly offspring of the industrial revolution were already cutting their first teeth. In 1795 a Frenchman called Louis Appert had invented vacuum-packed canning as a method of preserving meat. In 1807 Thomas Saddington took out a patent for preserving fruit in cans. Shortly after, Bryan Donkin began to manufacture tinned metal containers at the Dartford Iron Works, but there was no great enthusiasm for the process beyond considering it a suitable way for keeping food in the Quarter-master's store on board naval ships. The first canned food duly made its maiden voyage across the Atlantic to America, where the idea was at once seized upon by the salmon merchants of the East coast who could

154 Brightly-painted late-Victorian tinplate sweet tins and biscuit tins. By the mid-nineteenth century all manner of foodstuffs were sold ready packed in tinplate containers often painted with scenes or motifs to indicate the region they came from: shortbread in tartan boxes, tea in tins with mock-lacquer designs and so on. Considered of no account at the time, or for years after, these early examples of commercial packing are now much sought-after items for collectors of ephemera. Large box: height 6 inches. *Dodo.*

not sell their fish fast enough to make their very seasonal business profitable. In the space of a decade preserving ceased to be an artistic and ingenious domestic activity and became commercial. Gone were the tall glass jars and the pressed brawns and tongues, gone the dough rising in the hearth, the golden raised game pies with sculptured sides and decorated lids. As the steam trains chugged from London to Inverness, Bristol, Cardiff and Penzance and everyone had more time for everything, gadgets appeared to save everyone time.

9 Gadgets

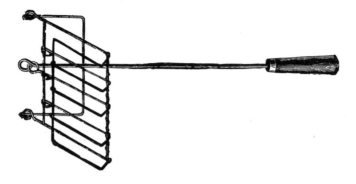

155 Tinned iron toasting fork, with a wooden handle, from a catalogue of 'Kitchen Requisites', 1914. *Mansell Collection.*

A HUNDRED YEARS before the first steam locomotive chugged from Liverpool to Manchester at the terrifying speed of eight miles an hour, the links were being forged in the chain which was simultaneously to bind and free the people of Britain. Pretty little girls in Gainsborough dresses, taking a second or third cake from the flowered, latticed cake basket under Mama's disapproving gaze would live to see gas lights flaring down the Mall, steam ploughs raking deep furrows across the face of the English countryside, and would breathe the sooty air of a London grimed and stained with progress.

In the spacious kitchens of town and country young girls in sprigged muslin mob caps and wooden shoes would probably not live long enough to see mechanical graters clamped to kitchen tables, saving the finger-ends and knuckles of their successors, nor watch the miracle of minced meat swirling into a dish at the turn of a handle. But if Cook thought she was a responsible girl, she would be allowed to wind up the bottle-jack and watch the joint twist in the fierce glow of the kitchen fire without any help from her or anyone else.

Bottle-jacks were the first real mechanical aid made specially for cook and her underlings. They were a combination of the traditions of the clockmaker and the skill of John Hanbury, Richard Ford and John Pickering, three men who between them made it possible for sheet metal to be rolled, raised and stamped into thousands of identical shapes, including the cogs inside the bottle-jack and the shining brass cylinder which contained them. Weight-driven spit-engines, it is true, were highly sophisticated mechanically, but they were made by hand and not by machine. The smoke-jack was a further development of the basic principle of the spit-engine which owed more to engineering than gadget-making. When smoke-jacks were introduced in the 1840s, the industrial revolution was in full swing and engineers and physicists were grappling with steam power and the principles of convection and conduction. There is a strong whiff of engine oil about them and the shining steel shafts and brass cogs and gear-wheels belong more to locomotion and the age of the railway than to the domestic scene.

From 1770 onwards clockwork toys of all kinds began to be mass-produced, now that each part could be stamped out identically by machine. Now that musical boxes were no longer the province of the quirky clockmaker, little feathered birds in gilded cages turned their heads and sang at the turn of a key. Other little birds in less gilded cages wound up the products of Messrs Linwood and Messrs Salter, two of the main manufacturers of bottle-jacks, and, if they were made in sheet brass, polished them until they shone like the best gold plate.

It was quickly apparent that tinplate had other advantages apart from being easily worked by machine. It was far lighter than cast iron and cheaper than brass or copper, and it did not taint food, corrode or rust. The manufacturers searched eagerly for more ways of using this admirably utilitarian metal. Cylindrical shapes were the most suitable, for there were problems in joining edges, and seaming was the most satisfactory way of sealing tinplate to tinplate. Coach lamps and gig lamps, tins for tea which could be lacquered and painted (early examples of packaged food), decorated boxes, pen trays, ink standishes and many other items poured from the tinplate mills, some pretty, some much less so. At first tinplate was used as a decorative material, but as techniques improved and the price of manufacturing came tumbling down, manufacturers began to look for new markets.

In America, where tin was almost the only metal available apart from cast iron, there was practically nothing which was not made of tin at one time or another, under the name 'toleware'. Sometimes the results are endearingly angular and strange to the eye, such as tin chandeliers. Nineteenth century American jugs and vessels have more in common with English canal-boat buckets and jugs than items for parlour and dining room. But at the time they must have been greatly prized, for Colonial America had little enough in the way of utensils of any kind.

From this distance in time they are naively attractive, with the same innocent primary-colour freshness found in paintings and portraits of the early American period.

In Britain by the turn of the century, steam power was harnessed to the great rolling and stamping machines, power which had hitherto been supplied by teams of horses. The industrial revolution had really begun. For a few brief years men still hand-finished every object which was stamped mechanically from sheet tinplate or brass and craftsmanship lingered on. Stamped brass frames for pictures and mirrors were by no means as beautifully made or designed as early repoussée work, but there was a certain style to them which still echoed the perfection and elegance of the century just past. But new markets all over the world

156 Cylindrical tinplate tongue press with folded seams and reinforced iron wire rim. The base is perforated, and the iron screw and handle fit into a cast iron crossbar held by two lugs. As with so many items of kitchen equipment, tongue presses like this one were made continuously throughout the nineteenth century and well into the twentieth with virtually no alteration. The tongue was boiled and skinned, then pressed down into a thick round which was easy to carve and serve. Height $6\frac{3}{4}$ inches; diameter 6 inches. *Castle Museum, York.*

were opening up, and no man with machines capable of turning out by the thousand what craftsmen had once turned out by the dozen could be expected to ignore the ever-widening horizons of trade. The kitchen was an obvious place for tinware, and soon there were nests of patty-pans and pastry cutters in little tin cases, jelly moulds, mousse moulds and biscuit cutters, which all came rolling out as run-of-the-mill items. Tongue presses, which had been made on the old cheese-press principle, of wood, with a steel spindle, were ideally shaped for tinplate, and soon the manufacturers of traditional hollow ware joined the race to improve the working conditions below stairs.

The impetus for making machines which could do the work of skivvies and scullery-maids was threefold. The Great Exhibition in 1851 was a showcase for Victorian invention, ingenuity and technical achievement. At last the hitherto ignored and socially despised captains of industry were acknowledged and admired in a glare of publicity, under the patronage of Queen Victoria herself. Prince Albert was deeply interested in the architectural and artistic possibilities of industry and engineering and did more for their reputation than anyone else. All the same, many of the exhibits at the Crystal Palace were in the most appalling taste and showed to what depths design could sink for the sake of mass production.

Machines could not do what craftsmen could. Ornament was coarse and ugly, finish was poor, and many of the materials themselves were of low quality. But in the world of heavy industry, of cast iron and stamped metal, machine-turning and finishing, the first of the artefacts made by sweating foundrymen and engineers still had that quality which had been lost by so many other manufacturers: pride in craftsmanship and determination to make their products admirable as well as efficient.

As if the acknowledgement of their existence and the patronage of their Queen was all they had been waiting for, manufacturers in the iron and allied industries blossomed like an ugly child which has been praised for being clever. Cast iron had at last been acknowledged as a decorative metal: rustic seats and tables, pagodas, balconies, trellisses, gates and railings writhed with artistic invention. Designs were Gothic, Oriental, Egyptian, Grecian, Byzantine – nothing was safe from imitation. Trade and industry had become socially acceptable – at least in concept, though the *nouveaux riches* who made their fortunes from the results were not yet admitted into the best drawing rooms.

The second reason for improving conditions below stairs was the great reforming zeal of the solid middle classes, who had begun to exercise their power over slavery and who by the mid-nineteenth century had turned the searchlight of their attention on servants as a whole. The American Civil War, which was fought over the question of the 'Peculiar Institution', as southern Americans euphemistically called slavery, gave a further boost to the whale-boned morality of the reformers. Though none of them could bring themselves to dismiss their servants, for they could not live without them, it was universally agreed that the lot of the serving girl should be improved.

The third cause, and probably the most important, for all the wider

157 (a) 'Spong' sausage-making machine with black enamelled cast steel body and wooden turning handle. The meat was chopped by a series of blades in the barrel and fed into a sausage skin stretched over the nozzle at the front. Sausage-making machines only enjoyed a brief popularity, for local butchers soon began producing ready-made linked sausages from left-over scraps of pork and beef. Height 6½ inches; length 8¼ inches. *Castle Museum, York.*

157 (b) Sausage-maker opened to show cutting blades. *Castle Museum, York.*

social implications of the first two, was purely technical. In 1865 the Bessemer and Siemens-Martin processes made it possible to cast a lighter, cleaner metal which, though it was still called cast iron, was in fact mild steel. Thinner castings were possible, and soon the metal could be run into moulds and impressed with decoration. Though mild steel still had to be tinned to prevent it from rusting, the new processes brought about a revolution in the thinking of ironfounders, and many manufacturers began to make articles using a combination of tinned cast iron and tinplate.

The hardest, longest and most time-consuming tasks in kitchens at that time were peeling, chopping and slicing. Home made 'potted meats' looked delicious and splendid, but the chore of chopping cooked meat to such a fine consistency was long and arduous. Grating on hand-graters was another soul-destroying task. One of the first mechanical gadgets which combined cast iron and tinplate was a sausage-maker, but it was a bad first choice. It came on the market at almost the same time that the local family butcher began to make linked sausages at the back of his shop and sell them to his customers. If they could be bought ready-made, there was little point in going to all the trouble of making sausages at home and the sausage-maker had a very brief life as a desirable addition to the kitchen cupboard.

Graters were another matter. Soon after the sausage-maker came on

158 Cast iron bean slicer with steel blades. A fine example of early ornate casting which reflects the Victorian passion for decorative cast iron after the Great Exhibition of 1851. Height 7 inches. *Peter Nelson.*

159 Vertical marmalade cutter with screw-clamp to bolt it to the edge of the kitchen table. The double-edged knife has a cast iron handle, painted black and gold and inscribed 'Follows & Bate Ltd/Patent/Marmalade Cutter/Manchester.' The turned wood feeding ram pressed the fruit against the knife, which was raised and dropped by hand, and the sliced fruit dropped into a bowl held underneath. Height 17½ inches. *Castle Museum, York.*

the market, a rotary grater also appeared, consisting of a cylinder and stand in cast iron which could be bolted to the table and an inner punched tinplate cylinder which rotated and grated the food which was fed into the opening at the top. Sausage-makers were not entirely abandoned, however, and the principal of a spiral feeding screw was

160 Late Georgian model of a butcher's shop. The butcher is waving a butcher's knife in the air, and he and his two assistants have sharpening steels tied round their waists. There is a marked absence of 'traditional' strings of linked sausages, which corroborates the early date of this delightful child's toy. *Rupert Gentle Antiques.*

slowly developed into a recognisable meat mincing machine by the late nineteenth century. The familiar flat metal cutting discs which screwed into the casing with a greasy butterfly nut became as much a part of every kitchen as a rolling pin or a chopping board.

The other basic piece of equipment in those early days of gadgetry was a marmalade cutter or orange slicer, for shiploads of Seville oranges were now coming into England and had to be made the most of while they were available. Early orange cutters were wood with a brass cutting blade, but once the kitchen revolution was in full swing, they were superseded by more efficient ones in cast iron and tinplate which, like meat mincers, screwed to the table and could be taken apart for cleaning.

The fertile and inventive mind of mechanical man, in his newfound world of sprockets and spindles, drive-shafts and transferred power, began to deluge the housekeeper and cook-general with weird and wonderful machines designed to reduce the hours of toil in the kitchen. Hand-choppers were mechanised in a marvellous machine which looked like a Lilliputian steam beam-engine, with crank-handle, rocker arm and flywheel. The blades laboriously chopped the contents of a tinplate drum, but, like many of man's inventions for domestic use, it was not very practical. The only way of removing the wood-bottomed bowl was to disconnect the bolted rocker arm – cleaning it must have been a nightmare.

In all this excitement and invention, only the brass-founders seem to have lost their way. Inundated as they were with demands for all sorts and sizes of valve, cock, screw and pipe, their sense of design faltered and then failed altogether. Manufacturers of sheet brass suffered less, but their reign in the kitchen had been brief even at the height of their skill. At the end of the eighteenth century James Emerson perfected the technique of direct fusion of zinc and copper, and brass-making was a mystery no longer. As long as brass was difficult to make and needed the experience and ancient knowledge of smelting it, it was a golden metal with a silky sheen the colour of old brocade. For a very short time after 1781 stamped brass was used with great taste and effect for door plates and door handles, backplates and lock plates, with the same exquisite simple lines as the furniture it decorated. And then it fell from grace.

It was not the craftsmanship of the makers of brass knobs and embellishments which made nineteenth century kitchen ranges look like Black Knights straight out of the pages of storybook chivalry, but the relentless rule of Cook, whose minions rubbed and scrubbed every item of brass and copper in the kitchen until they acquired the worn, pale patina of eighteenth century elegance. Copper was queen of the kitchen – brass was just a trimming, used for round domes of coffee grinders, stewpot taps and kettle trivets, locks, doorknobs and hinges for black enamelled coal scuttles, and shaving-water jugs for the master of the house.

In 1866 Samuel Timmins puffed out his chest and wrote:

'Our colonies, carrying with them the wants and habits of their native land, spread the demand for our manufacturers over the whole world. The frying pan, tea kettle and coal scuttle are to be found in every cottage as well as in the Royal Kitchens. The soldier and sailor look to us for various cooking appliances . . . our coffee must be roasted in iron coffee roasters. Our emigrants depend upon portable ovens, and gold-seekers wash the ore in pans . . .'[85]

He was not thinking, of course, of America, for America was no longer the hungry market it had once been for English wares. She had cut her ties with her mother country and begun to experiment with new ways of manufacuturing. By the turn of the century there were iron foundries and tinplate mills to manufacture enough basic goods to satisfy the American home market and, as more and more immigrants paid their passage to a new life on the other side of the Atlantic, more skills and crafts were available for her struggling industries and many inventive

161 (a) and (b) 'Perplex' rotary-drum grater for making breadcrumbs and grating cheese and vegetables. The first of these graters was made in the second half of the nineteenth century and they continued unchanged until 1935, when this one was purchased. The stand and face are cast in one piece in aluminium alloy, painted grey with the maker's name in gold. The drum and barrel are tinplate; the wooden feeding ram is beech. Height 10 inches. *Castle Museum, York.*

men at last found an outlet for ideas which had been ignored in their own homelands. When trade restrictions ended in 1865, America began to catch up on England and the rest of Europe, and by the end of the century they had overtaken the tradition-bound manufacturers of the Old World with new methods and materials which were to change the domestic scene beyond all recognition.

The cause of this dramatic leap was alumina ore, which American metallurgists and scientists were experimenting with as early as 1844, using electricity to provide the high temperatures for smelting which coal-fired furnaces could not attain. Aluminium was vastly superior in every respect to pressed steel or any of the iron-based metals. The problem was that it was extremely costly and difficult to make, and for a while progress was slow. Then the first giant electricity generators were built, harnessing the water-power of America's vast rivers. In 1886 the electrolytic process was applied to aluminium smelting, with spectacular success. The price of expensive aluminium tumbled to a twentieth of its cost, and in the space of a few years cast aluminium had replaced iron and steel in kitchens all over America.

English manufacturers went on making graters and mincers in tinned pressed steel and tinplate, but glanced uneasily across the Atlantic and bowed to the superior qualities of aluminium, which was now so cheap and easy to manufacture that it was being cast as well as pressed. The Chicago World Fair in 1893 gave another competitive boost to manufacturers in Europe, who travelled over in transatlantic steamers and saw to their dismay that American technology had far outstripped them. There were gadgets by the hundred, with cast aluminium casings which did not need to be tinned and did not mark or rust. Admittedly some of them were as extravagant in their concept as some of the early English cast iron and tinplate ones had been. The Bonanza apple peeler looked as though it could machine-stitch, print visiting cards and wind wool all at the same time. All it did was pare, core and slice even-sized round apples. The London Aluminium Company was founded four years after the Chicago World Fair, and British manufacturers began to make a whole new range of mincers, choppers, slicers and grinders from cast aluminium.

Among the innovations which British manufacturers introduced at the end of the nineteenth century was the 'digester'. This was a renaissance of Papin's famous seventeenth century invention exhibited and demons-

162 'Bonanza' apple peeler, corer and slicer of immense complexity, inscribed with the maker's name 'Goodell Co./Antrim/NH' (presumably New Hampshire, USA). Other, more simplified, models were made throughout the latter part of the nineteenth century until the early 1920s. Length 24½ inches; height 13¼ inches. *Castle Museum, York.*

163 Cast iron 'digester'. This forerunner of today's pressure cooker was first made in the 1860s when imports of chilled Argentine beef needed lengthy cooking to break down the toughness. It has a central pressure valve and three wedge-shaped clamp-catches around the rim to secure the lid. Similar models were available in Kenrick's catalogue in 1926. One gallon capacity. Height 9½ inches; diameter 8½ inches. *Private collection.*

trated at the Royal Society and witnessed by John Evelyn. It came back into the lives of British people for a specific reason. England was no longer self-sufficient and could not feed her steadily growing population with home-produced beef. Imports of chilled Argentinian beef supplemented English beef, but it was tough and fibrous and needed specially long cooking. On the coal-devouring kitchen ranges of the day this was an expensive business. The 'digester' reduced the cooking time to a fraction and was, even in its early cast iron form, extremely efficient in rendering tough meat into a tender, appetising stew. It had a conical weight in the centre of the lid which acted as a safety valve when pressure inside the digester exceeded three pounds per square inch. Recognisably, it was the first pressure cooker made and used in Britain.

164 Cast aluminium alloy 'Health Cooker', with pressure gauge and spring-loaded whistle. The lid is held down by an arched clamp, inscribed 'Easiwork. London'. The makers won a gold medal for the design of this patent cooker at the 1932 International Exhibition of Inventions. The pressure gauge has the address of the firm: '242 Tottenham Court Road, London W.l.' Height 9½ inches; diameter 7¼ inches. *Castle Museum, York.*

On a humbler level, though perhaps for the same reason, knife sharpeners and cleaners belong to the earliest group of mechanical aids in the kitchen. They were a vital piece of equipment, for knives were forged from steel which rusted and blunted quickly. In the kitchen, choppers, cleavers and kitchen knives were sharpened on a sharpening stone. In the dining room, sharpening steels joined the carving knife and fork in handsome silk-lined cases at the end of the nineteenth century, but with the proliferation of different knives for every course, the problem of sharpening them became intense. Rotary sharpening stones in stout wooden frames were made to put an edge on all but the best knives, which were still sharpened by hand by the butler. When the level of domestic staff rose to include a boot-boy, there was a knife cleaner whose cast iron case enclosed a bewildering mechanism of felt pads and bristles. Knife cleaners were standard equipment in large Victorian households, and were still being made and used right up to the 1920s, when stainless steel put an end to this monotonous business.

But while Britain chewed its way through tough imported beef, Americans sat down to pan-fried steaks, fresh from the railhead, transported direct from ranch to city slaughterhouse. They also developed a very sweet tooth. Immigrants from Bavaria, Austria, Italy and

165 Knife-sharpening stone in tin-lined wooden box with two handles and cast iron cog-wheels. Without exception all knives were made of tempered steel until the 1920s when stainless steel put an end to the irksome chore of cleaning the stained blades. Pedlars went from house to house sharpening scissors, knives and tools with knife-grinders on the backs of carts. Later, they attached them to bicycles so that the pedals supplied the power to turn the stone. But in households of any size knife-cleaners and sharpeners were an essential piece of equipment. The most common models which survive are the nineteenth century drum-shaped knife-cleaners. This one is an early model for kitchen knives, and probably dates from the last decade of the eighteenth century. Height 10½ inches width 17½ inches. *Private collection.*

Poland all had a tradition of rich cream cakes and desserts, and home-baked cakes and pies became part of the American way of life. Even when baking powder and self-raising flour were available commercially, frothy sponge mixtures needed the extra lightness from whisked egg-white. In 1873 a hand-held egg-beater was patented in America, with a cast iron frame and tinned pressed steel beating hoops, and its design has barely changed since.

The Americans also marketed an enormous variety of cake-mixers and bread-dough mixers, ranging from iron and tinplate models with tinned iron wire beaters to enclosed ceramic bowls with the instructions printed on the lid. Cocoa manufacturers and pudding-makers produced appropriate containers, moulds, whisks and cookie-cutters which they sold with their names prominently displayed to make sure that the housewives would remember to order their brand next time. Now the tide had turned and what America did today, Britain did tomorrow. Bourneville contracted a manufacturer to make a cocoa-whisk for them. Brown & Poulson made moulds for blancmange – another import from

166 Tinplate cake mixer with two iron wire mixers which rotate round each other. A great variety of cake mixers and dough mixers were made by the Americans, whose appetite for sweet things was almost insatiable. This model was almost certainly made in the USA around 1904 and imported into England at a slightly later date. It takes to pieces to clean – a great advance on earlier mixers and choppers. Height 4½ inches; diameter of bowl 8½ inches. *Castle Museum, York.*

167 Cast steel or iron rotary egg whisk with a pierced gear wheel bearing the inscription 'Pat April 14/ 1903/ Made in USA'. The first rotary egg-beater was patented in America in 1873 and had a cast iron frame and tinned pressed steel beating hoops. It was one of the first gadgets to come into the kitchen since the invention of the spit-engine. Length 8¾ inches. *Castle Museum, York.*

168 Cast iron and tinplate chopping machine on a wooden base, operating on the same principal as a steam beam-engine, the rocker arm lifting and dropping two cutting blades into the bowl. The base of the bowl is wood and is fixed on a cogged wheel so that the bowl rotates, driven by the complicated mechanism. Length of wooden base 15¾ inches; width 7 inches. *Castle Museum, York.*

America, made with arrowroot and owing nothing but its colour to the blancmanger of medieval days. Britain imported egg-beaters from America, and then manufactured her own.

And still inventions were being pushed aside in Britain, ignored or undeveloped, only to be snapped up by Americans with an eye to the future. In 1904 a minute electric motor went on sale in London, only three inches wide. Nobody took much notice of it, except as a clever novelty. It took time for the Americans to exploit it to its fullest advantage, but in 1912 the first electric egg-beater went on the market – made in the USA.

The folk image of America would not be complete without the long, cool drinks and ice chinking in tall glasses, ice-creams and milk shakes and ice-cream sodas with straws and wafers – strawberry, raspberry, blueberry, pecan and banana split. The Americans were so besotted and insistent that their drinks should be iced and their food kept cool that by 1882 New York alone was consuming no less than 1,450 tons of ice per head each year. It should be added that some of this stupendous quantity was used to cool the air in lobbies and lounges of hotels, theatres and public places. But as they built up their own trading patterns, the Americans proselytised the virtues of ice, even going to the lengths of shipping it to the West Indies to show the inhabitants how the

169 'Reliance' ice-cream freezer and pewter ice-cream moulds. The handle turns an inner metal drum in the ice-filled pine pail. The metal alloy crossbar is inscribed 'Reliance Swedish 2 qts' and this was one of the ice-cream freezers listed in London store-catalogues from 1908 to 1939. With the exception of individual fruit moulds, the ice-cream moulds are far larger than moulds for chocolate figures or icing sugar shapes. Freezer: height 9½ inches; diameter 8½ inches. Wheatsheaf mould: height 7½ inches. Cucumber mould: length 12 inches. *Castle Museum, York.*

heat could be made tolerable with ice in their sundowners. Ice was made commercially in huge ice plants which used steam to pump an ammonia-based refrigerant round the the ice-making compartments. Daily deliveries of ice to houses and apartments were kept in wooden ice boxes lined with zinc or slate, packed with cork, ash, charcoal or seaweed between the inner and outer skins.

Ice-cream freezers, at first identical to the simple containers used in England, had an inner drum with a crank-handle which turned inside a wooden barrel filled with a mixture of salt and ice. The Cincinnati Gooch Freezer Company, among many others, advertised and sold four models – the Peerless, the Zero, the Pet and the Boss. No American home was complete without one. As early as 1888 Westinghouse produced a rather unwieldy electric motor which could circulate a refrigerant solution in commercial refrigerator rooms, but they did not succeed in making a domestic model until 1913.

Many of the first refrigerator plants used steam power to circulate the refrigerant solution and manufacturers competed furiously to improve both the method and the refrigerant, which was still based on ammonia. At the World Fair in Detroit in 1914 Kelvinator exhibited the first truly domestic refrigerator, but since they had changed the refrigerant solution from ammonia to a sulphur-dioxide base, the company had to admit the best place for it was the cellar. Any leakage of the refrigerant solution was stomach-turning and quite unacceptable. Meanwhile, Britain remained largely ignorant of the bliss of ice-cold drinks until the American invasion of Europe after World War I. Soldiers who shared trenches with American troops learned the blues, while at home their girlfriends danced alone to the music of His Master's Voice, learning the Black Bottom, the Bunny Hug and the Charleston. When they returned home the smartest place for a soldier to take his girl was a milk bar, while Society toasted their victory with iced martinis and shook their heads at the very idea of iced beer.

After World War I, with all its sadly inevitable advances in technology, the *Daily Mail* staged its first post-war Ideal Home Exhibition. In the ten hideous years which had passed since they held their first exhibition, electricity had been harnessed to a welter of gadgets. Many of them were still recognisable adaptations of old, hand-turned implements – the Kenwood electric cake-mixer was still virtually the same as the hand-cranked nineteenth century originally, the electric egg-beater was streamlined, but little had changed in the basic principles of their mechanisms. Domestic refrigerators did not make their debut until

1925, and then the motors were still so clumsy that they had to be
housed outside the sleek white enamelled shells of the food compartments, and shuddered and whirred so noisily that the best place for a
refrigerator was anywhere but in the kitchen itself.

The oddest tailpiece to the history of kitchen gadgets is the tale of the

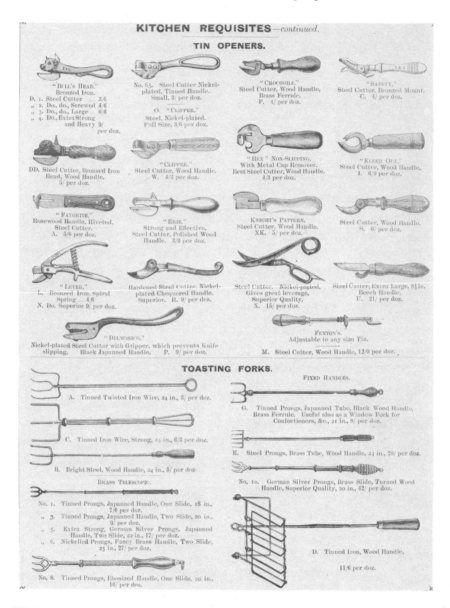

170 A page from a catalogue of 'Kitchen Requisites' showing a variety of lethal
tin-openers – whose main requisite was brute force and a thick cloth to cover the hand
holding the tin in case the wicked implement should slip. *Mansell Collection.*

can-opener. Louis Appert's invention of vacuum-sealed glass bottles won the prize of 12,000 francs offered by Napoleon to the man who could devise a way of provisioning his armies. That was in 1795. In 1812, the year of Napoleon's retreat with the remains of his butchered, frost-bitten army from Moscow, an English patent was taken out for Appert's process. Tinplate was substituted for glass bottles, and the first cannery opened in Bermondsey, London. After a hesitant beginning, when the British Navy was supplied with food in cans, the canning process reached America. There was taken up and exploited to the full, and tinned pink salmon and cling peaches became Sunday treats the length and breadth of Britain.

It was nearly fifty years before anyone invented a satisfactory gadget to open these lovely cans. And even then, they were dangerous weapons, with a spike like a marline-spike and a cast iron bull's head comp-lemented by curly cast iron tails or wooden handles, which were first put on the market in 1860 by the manufacturers of bully beef. Until then, amazingly, the instructions on the label read 'cut round the top near the outer edge with a chisel and hammer.'

—— *Places to Visit* ——

BARRINGTON COURT, SOMERSET Tudor kitchen.

BELGRAVE HALL, LEICESTER Eighteenth century house and kitchen.

BRADLEY MANOR, DEVONSHIRE Fifteenth century kitchen.

BUCKLAND ABBEY, DEVONSHIRE The Grenville kitchen, built in 1576.

BURGHLEY HOUSE, LINCOLNSHIRE Fifteenth century manorial kitchen.

CARLYLE'S HOUSE, CHELSEA, LONDON Basement kitchen.

CASTLE WENHAM, SUFFOLK Medieval kitchens.

CHARLECOTE, WARWICKSHIRE Victorian kitchen.

CLANDON PARK, SURREY Country kitchen.

CLAVERTON, BATH American museum with kitchens.

CLEVEDON COURT, SOMERSET Old kitchen with a collection of Elton ware from the Victorian Sunflower Pottery.

COMPTON CASTLE, DEVONSHIRE Great kitchen.

COTEHELE, CORNWALL Tudor kitchens with later additions including nineteenth century ranges.

ERDDIG, WREXHAM, CLWYD Kitchen quarters and outbuildings from the eighteenth century.

GEORGIAN HOUSE, EDINBURGH Eighteenth century town kitchen.

GLADSTONE'S LAND, EDINBURGH Eighteenth century 'close' house with kitchens.

GLASTONBURY ABBEY, SOMERSET Abbot's kitchen, fifteenth century.

HADDON HALL, DERBYSHIRE Medieval kitchens.

HARDWICK HALL, DERBYSHIRE Reconstructed kitchens.

LANHYDROCK HOUSE, CORNWALL Rebuilt 1883 to refectory-style design and louvred roof.

LONGLEAT HOUSE, WILTSHIRE Renovated Victorian kitchen.

OSBORNE HOUSE, ISLE OF WIGHT Royal children's kitchen in the Swiss Cottage. Victorian.

ROYAL PAVILION, BRIGHTON Victorian kitchens.

SALTRAM HOUSE, DEVONSHIRE Eighteenth century kitchen with nineteenth century ranges.

SNOWSHILL MANOR, BROADWAY, WORCESTERSHIRE Collection of early kitchen equipment of all kinds.

SULGRAVE MANOR, NORTHAMPTONSHIRE Eighteenth century kitchens in George Washington's family house.

TATTON PARK, CHESHIRE Early nineteenth century kitchens.

OLD HALL, TATTON PARK Medieval Great Hall.

UPPARK, WEST SUSSEX Eighteenth century kitchen.

WELSH FOLK MUSEUM, ST FAGANS, CARDIFF Castle kitchen. Numerous reconstructed dwellings with kitchens dating from medieval times.

Museums:

AMERICAN MUSEUM, CLAVERTON, BATH.

CASTLE MUSEUM, YORK.

COALBROOKDALE MUSEUM OF IRON, TELFORD, SHROPSHIRE.

GEFFRYE MUSEUM, SHOREDITCH, LONDON.

MUSEUM OF LONDON, THE BARBICAN.

SCIENCE MUSEUM, SOUTH KENSINGTON, LONDON.

Most rural and folk museums have some space devoted to domestic life and cooking.

Glossary

ARC WELD	A method of welding used over the past fifty years. An electric current heats the metal (see *Metals and Techniques*).
ALEGAR	Soured beer 'viegar'.
ALKANET	Red food-dye, obtained from the roots of a South European borage plant.
ALEMBIC	Distilling apparatus. More commonly known in England as 'limbeck'.
ALMS BREAD	Dispensed to the poor of the parish at certain times of the year.
AMBERGREESE	Ambergris, wax-like ash-grey substance with strong perfume. Used to scent sweet dishes and drinks in the seventeenth and eighteenth centuries. Bears no relation to amber.
AMULUM	Wheat starch, used like cornflour to thicken broths. Also known as 'amidon'.
ANDIRON	Wrought iron firedog. See BRAND-IRON. (Figure 29).
APIARIST	Bee-keeper.
AQUA VITAE	Strong spirit of alcohol – often brandy.
ARROWROOT	Starch made from the tubers of a West Indian plant.
BACALAO	Strongly spiced Portuguese fish dish, similar to *bouillabaisse*.
BAKING HOOP	Circular band to contain batter, pastry or cake mixtures baked on a baking iron or baking sheet. Made of wood, iron or tinplate.
BAKING IRON	Cast iron plate of considerable thickness, usually with one or two handles. (Figures 73, 88 and 90).
BAKING TRAP	Similar to baking hoop. Sometimes deeper, made

of wood bound with iron for baking standing pies and pastries.

BAR GRATE	Intermediate method of enclosing a fire before the manufacture of hob grates and ranges. (Figure 32).
BARRELL	Measure of liquid contained in a standard-sized cask.
BASTABLE	Heavy iron cooking pot (Irish).
BASTE	To spoon hot fat over roasting meat.
BATTERIE DE CUISINE	Full range of kitchen equipment.
BAY SALT	Large, sweet crystals from the Bay of Bourgneuf – equivalent to 'sea salt'.
BEEVES	Old English plural for beef cattle.
BEDSTRAW	Weed used as a cooking herb.
BEER BARM	Yeast from beer.
BELGAE	Pre-Roman Iron Age invaders of the British Isles from the Seine, Marne and Rhine.
BELL METAL	An alloy of copper and tin in varying proportions – generally in the ratio of 80 parts copper to 20 parts tin (see *Metals and Techniques).*
BESSEMER PROCESS	Method introduced by Henry Bessemer in 1856 for making steel by reducing carbon content in crude iron (see *Metals and Techniques).*
BISCOCTUS	Twice-cooked.
BISCOTTE	Corruption of medieval Latin *biscoctus,* applied to small crisp confections.
BISCUIT	Originally French corruption of *biscoctus.*
BLANC DESSORE	Pounded or shredded white meat combined with ground almonds, milk and rice flour, eaten with brightly coloured sauce.
BLANC MANGER	Bland medieval dish of poultry meat, whole rice and almond milk heavily sweetened with sugar and sometimes jellied.
BLANC MANGE	Meatless Elizabethan version of above, made with cream, sugar and rosewater, thickened with egg yolks or beaten egg whites. Both versions co-existed during the seventeenth century.
BLANC MANGE	Eighteenth century version: a jelly stiffened with isinglass or hartshorn, flavoured with almonds.
BLANCMANGE	Nineteenth century version made with milk

flavoured with lemon peel and cinnamon, thick-ened with arrowroot from the 1820s and later with commercially manufactured cornflour.

'BLUE MILK'   Skimmed milk sold in towns in the eighteenth century.

BOMBE   Ice-cream originally made in a spherical mould – hence its name.

BOON WORKER   Worker who did not live on an estate who came in as a 'boon' or favour – usually during harvest-time.

BOUTELLIER   Keeper of wine in large households. From the French *'bouteille'*. Hence 'butler'.

BRAISE   To cook in a closed pan – originally with charcoal heaped above and below it.

BRAZE   Method of joining two pieces of metal together with a flux of molten brass.

BRAND-IRON   Origin of 'andiron'. Originally to hold 'brands' or pieces of burning wood (Figure 29).

BRANDRETH   Small iron frame to support cooking pots on the hearth (Figure 52).

BRASS   An alloy of copper and zinc in variable propor-tions and a range of colour from reddish-gold to pinkish grey. After 1781 the proportion became more or less fixed at 70 parts copper to 30 parts zinc to make the recognisable yellow metal of the late eighteenth century onwards (see *Metals and Techniques*).

BRAWN   Originally a cold dish made from the foreparts of a wild boar. Pig meat was substituted in the seventeenth century, and by the eighteenth cen-tury the term applied loosely to cold meat dishes of all kinds.

BRAY   To pound or crush small.

BRAZIER   Metal container to hold charcoal – widely used on the Continent (Figure 26).

BREDE   Bread.

BREWE   A snipe.

BRINE   Solution of salt and water.

BROIL   To grill over or under a naked flame.

BRONZE   An alloy of copper and tin, usually to the propor-tions of 90 parts copper to ten parts tin (see *Metals and Techniques*).

BROSE	A dish made by pouring boiling water on to crushed oatmeal.
BURNET	A hedgerow plant used as a cooking herb.
BURRWOOD	Dense wood from the roots of trees, with the special advantage that it has no running grain and therefore does not split or crack easily.
BUTTERMILK	Residue of milk left over after butter-making.
CAMBRIC	Fine white linen.
CAMP OVEN	Heavy iron cooking pot on three short feet, with lid and bail handle.
CAPON	Castrated cockerel, specially bred for the table. Fatter and more tender than laying hens, which were too valuable to kill for the table.
CASE-HARDENED	Steel which has been tempered to produce a harder surface, used particularly for knives, swords, blades, etc.
CASSIUM	Spice of the cinnamon family.
CAST IRON	Description of artefacts made by pouring molten iron into a mould (see *Metals and Techniques*).
CAUDLE	Wine or ale mixed with eggs and gently heated.
CHAFING DISH	Brass or brass-and-iron dish filled with charcoal, used to heat pewter or silver dishes for drying and candying or for keeping dishes warm on sideboards and dining tables (Figures 133 and 140).
CHAMBER GRATE	Horizontal bars and stocky firedogs cast in one piece.
CHAPERON	Hood-shaped cap to protect the head. Hence 'chaperone', a protector.
CHARGER	Large ornamented silver, pewter or brass dish, charged or filled with meats to be served at table.
CHESSEL	Coopered drum-shaped wooden container with heavy lid for draining soft cheeses (Figure 13).
CHOCOLATE MILL	Instrument with a small, cylindrical notched head on a turned wooden handle for frothing rich drinking chocolate. Also known as 'moliquet' (Figure 114).
CIDER OWL	Squat stoneware jug with handles, traditionally used for cider.
CLOME OVEN	Heavy iron pot inverted over a bakestone or baking iron.

CIVEY	Hare stew, from the French *civet* (hare).
CODWARE	Seed shell or husk, as in 'peascod'. Hence its anatomical application to men's clothes.
COFFIN	Box, chest, coffer or container. Hence 'pastry coffins'.
COLLAR	To tie up meat in a tight roll like a band, ring or collar.
CONEY, CONY	A full-grown rabbit. Originally 'rabbit' applied only to the young animals.
COOPER	Maker of containers and vessels of wooden staves bound with iron or withy hoops. A 'wet' cooper or 'white' cooper made butter-churns and other items for the dairy.
CORN PONE	Bread made with maize flour, USA.
COVER	All the necessary items for one person's place at table.
CRACKNEL	Light, crisp biscuit.
CRUSTARD	An open pie with a crust or shell, often with egg and cream filling. Hence 'custard'.
CURE	To preserve raw meat by salting and drying or smoking. Additional ingredients in the curing liquor often included sugar, vinegar, pepper and alcohol in the form of beer, wine or spirit.
DANGLE-SPIT	Anchor-shaped meat hook with two weights on the arms, hung on a chain or rope and twisted so that the meat rotated (Figures 31 and 47).
DELFT	Originally blue-and-white glazed pottery from the Low Countries, the term was loosely applied to all glazed blue-and-white pottery during the seventeenth century.
DESSERT	Fruit course at the end of dinner. From the French *desservir*, to remove or clear the table of dishes. Originally desserts or 'removes' were served at the end of each main course.
DIGESTER	Heavy cast iron cooking pot with a tightly-fitting lid and pressure vent to allow the steam to escape (Figure 163).
DORSAR	A fireback (Figure 27).
DOUBLE-REFINED SUGAR	Loaf sugar which has been refined a second time to rid it of impurities.

DOUCETIE	Sweet confection. Sometimes they were spectacular set-pieces decorated with coloured sugar-paste scenes in honour of the principal guest.
DREDGE	To sprinkle roasting meat liberally with a dry mixture of fine breadcrumbs or flour mixed with herbs and seasonings to make a crisp coating.
DRESS	To prepare, usually of meat and fowl. So dressing board, dressing knife.
DUTCH OVEN	1 An earthenware screen to prevent the fat from spitting while a joint was roasting. Not used until mid-eighteenth century, when joints were often baked on a spit in front of a partly enclosed fire.
	2 Large metal hood, inside which meat was suspended to roast, usually on a bottle-jack. Used from the late eighteenth century until well into living memory (Figure 46).
	3 A heavy cast iron pot with closely-fitting lid which was buried in charcoal in a open hearth. Used for baking meat, bread, buns and biscuits, USA (Figure 28).
EGERDOUCE	A sweet-sour dish of coney (rabbit), young kid or sliced brawn in a sauce of vinegar or sour red wine and sugar or honey and dried fruits.
EQUISETUM	A rough-leaved plant containing considerable amounts of silica used for cleaning pewter. Hence 'pewterwort'.
EWER	A wide-mouthed vessel in cast brass or bronze, also called an aquamanile or laver (Figure 54).
FILBERT	A cultivated hazel-nut.
FILLET	A narrow band or strip of metal.
FINIAL	Terminal ornament on a piece of metalwork or furniture.
FIRE WELD	General term for all early joining of wrought iron (see *Metals and Techniques*).
FIRKIN	A cask containing quarter of the contents of a 'barrel'.
FLAMBEAU	A torch or flaming brand, usually pine or fir because of its high resinous content.
FLANC	A flan or open tart in a pastry shell. Originally such dishes 'flanked' the main dish in the centre of the table.

FLATHON	Similar to flans or crustards with a curd filling.
FLATWARE	Cutlery.
FLESH-FORK	English flesh-forks were wrought iron two-pronged instruments similar to a small pitchfork or hayfork. Continental ones were more elaborate, with claws. Used for spit-roasting or for retrieving meat from the depths of a large cauldron or preserving vessel (Figures 59 and 139).
FLESH-HOOK	Wrought iron hook for suspending meat directly over a cooking fire.
FLUMMERY	1 From the Welsh *llymru*, a dish of oatmeal boiled in milk. 2 Opaque and transparent jelly, eighteenth century.
FLUX	A substance facilitating the fusion of two metals.
FOOL	Originally a dish of clotted cream, now made with fruit pulp and cream.
FOOTMAN	A four-legged trivet used in the parlour as kettle stands or muffin stands.
FOWLING PIECE	A gun for shooting wild fowl.
FRUMENTY	A dish of hulled wheat boiled in milk (see also HOMINY).
GALANTINE	Originally a sauce made from the blood of game birds and wild fowl mixed with breadcrumbs or stewed prunes and spices. The term was first applied to jellied meats in the eighteenth century.
GALINGALE	Plant of the ginger family.
GALLEYPOT, GALLIPOT	A small earthenware pot.
GAMMON	A joint of bacon.
GAS WELD	Joining two pieces of metal edge to edge by heating them with an oxyacetylene blowtorch using a flux (see *Metals and Techniques*).
GATE	Opening in a mould into which molten metal was poured.
GAUFFRE	A thin batter biscuit which gets its name because it frills as it cooks.
GLASSES	In eighteenth century recipes refers to glass jars.
GLAZE	To coat with a vitreous substance (see also LEADGLAZE, SALTGLAZE, SLIPGLAZE).

GOBBET	A piece or portion of meat.
GRATE	See under individual entries: BAR GRATE, CHAMBER GRATE, HOB GRATE.
GREEN-SMOKED	Lightly cured to preserve for a short time.
GRIDDLE PAN	A circular plate for baking (Figures 73, 88 and 90). See BAKING IRON.
GRIDIRON	A metal frame with decorative or plain bars for broiling fish or meat or toasting bread (Figure 86).
GRILL	To broil or cook over or under a naked flame.
GRIND	To shred finely or mince, USA.
GRISSET PAN	Cast iron boat-shaped utensil with three legs and handle, for melting fat and wax for dipping rushlights. Home candle-making was declared illegal with the introduction of the Candle Tax in 1709 and implements connected with candle-making were hidden or destroyed (Figure 22).
GRUEL	Thick liquid broth made from crushed oatmeal.
GUM ARABIC, GUM DRAGON, GUM TRAGACANTH	Sweet sticky substance secreted by some species of acacia tree. A similar substance is also found oozing from the bark of plum and damson trees. The gum was used for candying leaves and flowers for decorating cakes, sweets and puddings.
HAMSTRING	To cut the tendons at the back of the leg joints of an animal.
HARNEN	A freestanding wrought iron toasting stand for drying out baked hearth-cakes. Also known as a 'cake stool' (Figure 87).
HASTENER	Large metal hood which stood in front of a cooking fire, in which the joint of meat was suspended to cook. See also DUTCH OVEN 2 (Figure 46).
HAUT GOUT	High or gamey taste of hung meat.
HOB GRATE	Cast iron grate with flat surfaces on either side of a bar grate fire.
HOGSHEAD	Large cask for liquids containing $52\frac{1}{2}$ Imperial gallons.
HOLLOW WARE	Manufactured domestic metal cooking pots.
HOMINY	Maize boiled with water or milk. American version of frumenty.
HOO GOO	See HAUT GOUT.

HUYSENBLAS	Swimbladder of a sturgeon (Dutch). Hence the gelatin obtained from them, known as isinglass.
IRON	See under CAST IRON, PIG IRON, WROUGHT IRON. See also *Metals and Techniques*.
ISINGLASS	Gelatin-like substance obtained by boiling the swim-bladders of certain fish, notably sturgeon. From the Dutch *huysenblas*.
JAPANNED	Coated with an exceptionally hard varnish, a process which came originally from Japan.
JENTILMAN	Gentleman.
JIB	The projecting arm of a pot crane.
JOHNNY CAKES	Small buns or biscuits made from maize meal and water. A corruption of 'journey cakes', USA.
JUNKET	Originally a curd or cream dish laid on rushes. Later adapted to a dish made from milk coagulated with essence of rennet flavoured with nutmeg.
KEROSENE	Paraffin oil – distilled petroleum.
KERSEY	A kind of coarse woollen cloth.
KETTLE	Vessel for boiling water. Originally 'cetel', a cooking pot (Figures 72 and 75).
KILDERKIN	Cask equal to twice the capacity of a firkin.
KITTLE	Northern and Scottish pronunciation of kettle.
KNEAD	To work up bread dough for baking.
LAMPREY	Freshwater fish with a sucker-like mouth, considered a delicacy.
LATTEN	Cast sheets of brass which were beaten into thin sheet brass. Also an adulterated alloy similar to brass (see *Metals and Techniques*).
LAVER	Cast bronze, bell metal or brass pot holding water for washing hands and fingers at table. Sometimes specifically used to indicate a double-spouted water-carrier with wide mouth.
LEADGLAZE	Method of coating pottery with a vitreous finish (see *Metals and Techniques*).
LECHE-MEAT, LEACH-MEAT	Cream, curd or jelly-based confections which were cut into slices and eaten with the fingers.

White leach was very popular in Tudor and Stuart times, also known as 'flummery'.

LIGNUM VITAE	An extremely dense living wood from the West Indies. Elizabethans believed it had great healing properties, hence its name: wood or tree of life.
LIMBECK	See ALEMBIC.
LIQUAMEN	Salty liquid seasoning made by steeping small, oily fish and fish entrails in water and leaving it to evaporate. The resultant concentrated juices were similar to a fishy Soy sauce.
LLYMRU	Welsh word for frumenty, a grain-based cereal dish. The two words were confusingly combined into 'flummery'. Later distinguished from jelly desserts as 'oatmeal flummery'.
LUGS	Ears or small handles on metal pots.
MACE	Outer husk of nutmeg used as a spice.
MANCHET	Medieval small loaf or large bread bun made from fine white flour.
MANDILION	Loose coat similar to a gaberdine worn by servants.
MARINADE	Liquor for steeping fish and meat before cooking.
MAWMENY	Cooked meat pounded to a pulp in a mortar, mixed with breadcrumbs, egg yolks, heavily seasoned and spiced. Similar to a coarse paté in texture and concept.
MAZER	Bowl or goblet made originally in mazer wood – veined and variegated like maple wood.
MEAD	Intoxicating drink made from fermented honey and water.
MILD STEEL	Iron which has had some of its high carbon content removed by firing (see *Metals and Techniques*).
MINCE	To grind up.
MOLIQUET	See CHOCOLATE MILL.
MONTEITH	A vessel with scalloped rim, usually in silver, silver-gilt or silvered brass, used for cooling wine glasses.
MORTREW	Pork or chicken meat ground to a pulp in a mortar – similar to a mawmeny.
'MYSTERY'	Medieval word for craft.

'NEALING	Annealing. To fuse, fire or temper.
NEF	A vessel for holding salt or spices on a grand High Table.
ORANGERY	Glasshouse for growing oranges. Very popular in Georgian times, when their design was extremely elegant.
OSIER	Species of willow used for basket-making and binding coopered vessels.
OVEN	See under individual entries: CAMP OVEN, CLOME OVEN, DUTCH OVEN.
OVEN–STONE	A stone set in the brickwork of a built-in baking oven which could be partially or wholly removed to regulate the heat.
OWL	See CIDER OWL.
PAIN PERDUE	White bread dipped in beaten egg yolk, fried in butter and sprinkled with sugar.
PANDEMAIN	White bread made from finest white flour, probably a corruption of *panis domini*, sacramental bread.
PANETIER, PANTER, PANTLER	Servant in charge of the bread. Hence 'pantry'.
PANIS BISCOCTUS	Twice-cooked bread dough, originally hard ship's biscuits.
PANIS DOMINI	Sacramental bread.
PARAFFIN	Kerosene, distilled petroleum.
PASTE	Mixture of flour and oil used for making paste coffins.
PEARLASH	*Sal aeratus*, bicarbonate of soda. Raising agent for cake mixtures.
PEEL	Flat shovel of wood or iron, for loading uncooked loaves into a baking oven (Figure 77).
PENNYROYAL	A species of mint.
PEWTER	Alloy of tin and lead (see *Metals and Techniques*).
PIG IRON	Cast ingots of raw metal (see *Metals and Techniques*).
PIN	A small cask.
PIPKIN	A small pot-bellied earthenware vessel, originally cast metal.

PLANC	Welsh baking iron. Hence 'plank bread'.
POMMELL	To pound or knead.
PORRAY	A stew of green leaves of plants and vegetables boiled, pressed and boiled again in good broth. From the Latin *porrum*, leek.
POSNET	Small round-bottomed saucepan with turned wooden handle, taking its shape from early cast metal skillets (Figure 62).
POT-CRANE, POT-SWAY	Device for manipulating a pot over the cooking fire (Figures 60 and 69).
POT-HANGER	Detachable pot handle (Figure 58).
POT-HOOK	Plain or adjustable hooks for suspending pots over the fire (Figures 59 and 71).
POTTAGE	Cereal-based stew of vegetables, meat or fish. 'Running' pottages were like thick soups, 'standing' pottages were thickened with amulum to make a solid spoonmeat.
PRESSED STEEL	Steel impressed mechanically into shapes (see *Metals and Techniques*).
PUG WELD	Early method of joining two pieces of pure iron by heating it over a charcoal fire until it fused, the join leaving a mark like a thumb-print (see *Metals and Techniques*).
PULSE	Seeds of leguminous plants such as peas, beans, lentils, etc.
PUNCH	Rich, heady drink made with wine or spirits and hot milk or water, often spiced or flavoured with citrus fruits, mint, etc.
QUERN	A rotary hand-mill for grain or spices.
RAFRAICHISSEUR	Vessel for chilling glases and bottles.
RAPE (OIL)	Species of brassica plant which produces oil-seed.
RASTON	Loaf of enriched bread dough, baked, hollowed out and the crumb mixed with butter, refilled and returned briefly to the oven.
RATCHET	Set of teeth on the edge of a wheel on which a cog may catch.
RATCHYNGCROKE	Saw-edged flat iron upright with adjustable hook which notches into the teeth (Figure 59).
REMOVE	Intermediate sweet dishes interspersing main courses of a banquet.

REPOUSSÉE	Sheet metal beaten into a pattern in relief (see *Metals and Techniques*).
REREDOS	Fireback (Figure 27).
RUSHLIGHT	Rushes dipped in animal fat or tallow, or soaked in oil.
RYEANINJUN	Coarse meal made of a mixture of rye and maize flour, USA.
SALAMANDER	Wrought iron disc on a long handle, heated and used to brown the tops of pastries and pies in large establishments, bakeries, pie shops and confectioners (Figure 59).
SALT	Small bowl to hold salt for each diner individually – later salt cellar in pewter, silver or brass for general use at dining table.
SALTGLAZE	Pottery coated with transparent vitreous finish (see *Metals and Techniques*).
SALT-UPON-SALT	Bay salt boiled in brine and evaporated to make a fine powder.
SALT-WINNING	Evaporating sea water to obtain salt.
SAMP	Thin cereal-based gruel, USA.
SAMPHIRE	Thin-leaved estuary plant considered a delicacy.
SANDER	Sandalwood used for food colouring.
SCARFED	Sieved.
SCARF WELD	An early fire weld (see *Metals and Techniques*).
SEA COLE	Coal which came by sea from Newcastle to East coast ports and the Port of London.
SEETHE	To boil slowly.
SHRUFF	Scrap brass and other allied metals.
SIEMENS-MARTIN	Steel-making process (see *Metals and Techniques*).
SIMNEL	Bread made from fine flour, usually small flat buns.
SKILLET	Three-legged cast bronze, brass or bell metal cooking pot with a tail handle. Saucepan, USA. (Figures 55, 56 and 62).
SKIVVY	Literally a slave, an unconsidered servant, usually a girl.
SLIP GLAZE	Method of decorating and coating pottery with a clay-and-water emulsion (see *Metals and Techniques*).

SMALLAGE	Variety of celery, also fennel.
SODDEN	Boiled.
SOTELTIE	Similar to a 'doucetie', often a grand banquet set-piece.
SOUSE	To steep or pickle cooked meats and fish.
SPIDER PAN	Shallow pan on three legs peculiar to Colonial America (Figure 89).
SPIKENARD	Aromatic substance from an Eastern plant, used to perfume dishes.
SPIT-DOG	Firedog with hooks to support a spit (Figures 29 and 32).
SPITTLE	Bat-shaped wooden board (Figure 77).
SPRUE	Opening in a mould into which molten metal was poured.
SQUAB	Young bird, especially pigeons.
STEEL	Crude iron from which carbon has been removed (see *Metals and Techniques*. See also under individual entries: CASE-HARDENED STEEL, MILD STEEL, PRESSED STEEL, TEMPERED STEEL.
STELEYARD	Steelyard, balance consisting of a lever with unequal arms moving on a fulcrum.
STOVE	Metal-lined open cupboard for drying confectionery etc. in front of the fire.
SUGAR-PASTE	Hard fondant mixture made by boiling sugar with water and working it while hot into shapes.
SUGAR-PLATE	Clarified sheets of 'white toffee'.
SWAY	Scottish term for pot-crane.
SWEDGE, SWAGE	Tool for bending cold metal.
TALLOW	Harder kinds of fat used for making candles.
TAMMY CLOTH	Straining cloth of fine worsted.
TAPER	Thin wax candle.
TEMPERED STEEL	Steel with extra hardness imparted by firing.
TIFFANY SIEVE	Thin transparent silk sieve.
TIN KITCHEN	Small reflector oven used in front of an open fire, USA.
TINNING	Coating the inside of vessels made of brass or copper with a thin layer of tin to prevent poisons being released into food.

TINPLATE	Rolled sheet iron or steel with a coating of tin to prevent corrosion (see *Metals and Techniques*).
TITHE	Tax or duty levied by manors and monasteries, originally one tenth of annual produce.
TOLEWARE	Tinware, USA.
TOSTE	Pieces of white bread browned on a gridiron, soaked in wine, reheated and crisped.
TRAMMEL	Pot hook with device for controlling the height of the pot (Figure 59).
TRAP	Wooden hoop bound with iron, later tinplate, which held the shape of pastries, pies, cookies, muffins and biscuits when baking in an oven on a baking sheet, or on a baking iron.
TREEN	Artefacts made from wood, 'from trees'.
TRENCHER	Thick piece of stale bread or specially baked coarse wholemeal bread which served first as an eating plate, and then as a protection for pewter plates.
TRENCHERMAN	A servant who lived in his master's house.
TRIFLE	Originally a cream-based dish. Made with broken biscuits soaked in sherry or Madeira, from the mid-eighteenth century.
TUN	Large cask equivalent to four hogsheads.
TURNBUCKLE	Catch or knob which fastens by being turned.
TURNSOLE	Violet-blue or purple colouring obtained from a plant which always turns its face to the sun.
VERDIGRIS	Green copper 'rust'.
VERJUICE	Juice of unripe fruit with high acid content, used in cookery and preserving meat and fish.
VETCH	Species of small creeping weed.
VIALL GLASS	Glass jar.
WAFER	Sacramental bread.
WAFER IRON	Originally for baking wafers, later adapted to make decorative crisp batter-mixing biscuits. Shaped like a waffle iron with cast decoration on the inner surfaces to imprint the wafers.
WAFFLE	Corruption of 'gauffre' or wafer.
WASSAIL	To drink a toast, hence wassail bowl.

WATTLE-AND-DAUB	Building material of stakes and brushwood packed with rough mortar or plaster.
WAX	To grow, as in 'waxing moon'.
WELD	See under individual entries: ARC WELD, FIRE WELD, GAS WELD, PUG WELD, SCARF WELD. (See also *Metals and Techniques*).
WHEY	Watery liquid remaining when curds have been removed from milk.
WITHY	Willow, pliant switches used for binding coopered items or for basket-making.
WROUGHT IRON	Iron which has been forged or wrought (see *Metals and Techniques*).
WROUGHT-IRON	Metal conforming to patterns of wrought iron but made after 1850 in cast mild steel (see *Metals and Techniques*).
YEMAN	Yeoman.
YETLING	Heavy cast iron baking pot (Figure 28).
ZEDOARY	Spice similar to turmeric.

Metals and Techniques

BELL METAL   Bell metal is an alloy of copper and tin with a ratio of 80 parts copper to 20 parts tin, though proportions vary. As well as being used for casting bells, it was used for making cauldrons, skillets, candlesticks and other domestic items, at least until the beginning of the eighteenth century. Bell-founders were among the few English craftsmen who were able to cast metal before large numbers of Dutch and German workers came into the country in the seventeenth century to teach the art of mining, metalworking and brass founding. In colour bell metal varies from pinkish bronze to dull grey, depending on the proportions of copper and tin. A slight variation in the alloy produces 'gun metal' which was originally used for casting cannon. It should be mentioned that bell-founders were not above adding scrap metal to the melting pot and traces of lead and zinc may also be found in the alloy.

BRASS   Brass is an alloy of copper and zinc in varying proportions, ranging from a low zinc content of 15% or less, with a reddish-gold colour, through yellow-gold with a 30% zinc 70% copper ratio to a high zinc content producing 'pink brass' and, eventually, an almost lead-coloured alloy of 70% zinc and 30% copper. Zinc is highly volatile and easily departs from an alloy if the heat of the furnace is incorrect. High zinc content brass is relatively rare, and was probably only achieved after 1738 when William Champion discovered a method of distilling pure zinc metal.

Brass was widely made all over the Continent from earliest times, but little or none was manufactured as a raw metal in England until after the beginning of the seventeenth century, when German and Dutch metalworkers came into the country to teach the English the 'mystery' of making brass. Artefacts made in England before that date were mostly scientific instruments, clocks, etc. and were made of brass imported in 'billet' or 'plate'.

Latten   Some latten was made in England, from imported thick plate brass which was 'battered' into thin sheets, and some cast brass made from melted-down 'shruff' or scrap brass and allied metals. Today's scientific methods of analysis may only confuse rather than enlighten: traces of tin and lead in brass may mean only that scrap metal was added to the melting pot.

Origin of design   Production of raw English brass was erratic throughout the seventeenth and eighteenth centuries, and considerable quantities of 'plate', 'billet' and brass wire were imported from Sweden and elsewhere on the Continent. Dutch and German brass-workers in considerable numbers were employed in brass foundries and brassworks all over the country. In many cases designs of articles made in England at this period are identical to those being made in other parts of Europe and may have been imported, or made by foreign workers in England from raw imported brass.

Cast brass   Cast brass was used for making cauldrons and skillets in England from the beginning of the seventeenth century, when these utensils had almost ceased to be used on the Continent, where raised brick-built hearths had been introduced and cooking was done in copper pans. Where cauldrons were still in use, they were made with the 'lost wax' or *cire perdue* method of casting which produced a thinner, smooth-surfaced metal. English brass-founders experienced considerable difficulty in casting cauldrons in one piece until they had perfected the technique of core-casting over a clay mould. Many cauldrons and skillets made in England were cast in two halves and then brazed together, though bell-founders, who also made domestic items, were expert in casting metals in one piece. It is by no means an absolute rule that a seam is the only genuine mark of age in a cast brass cooking vessel.

Raw brass intended for casting often contained a small quantity of lead in the alloy to make it pour more easily in its molten state.

Sheet brass   Sheet brass was more difficult to manufacture than cast brass, since it had to withstand battering into thin gauge with water-powered hammers. English sheet brass in the seventeenth century was an unsatisfactory material, since the brass-workers found that the metal cracked easily under the hammer owing to the English brass-founders' inexpertise in making raw brass. Consequently brass was imported in 'plate' and then beaten out in English battery works, until the English had mastered the art of producing the correct alloy. Sheet brass cauldrons and other early utensils which were simple to make were manufactured in brass battery works, but few have survived.

Early sheet brass with raised decoration, such as alms dishes, chargers, candle boxes and salt boxes were embossed or repoussée – the sheet metal was laid on a block of pitch and the decoration was hammered into the reverse side – a technique still employed in the Middle East and Asia. The designs were often chased with punches, chisels and hammers. to add a finish to the raised design.

Stamped brass   Brass was mechanically embossed with raised designs in England after 1769. The first dished articles, such as scale pans, warming pans, basins and ladles, were made from machine-rolled stamped brass in 1770. Frying pans, saucepans and other cooking utensils made of brass mostly date from after that date.

Use of brass for domestic articles   Brass has a very high melting point. It was an extremely suitable metal for cooking equipment which had to be handled when hot, for its poor conductivity meant that handles remained cool enough to touch while the contents of the skillet or cauldron were boiling hot. It was not suitable for use with acids such as vinegar, alegar, lemon juice or fruit juices, since the chemical action on the copper in the alloy was toxic, nor was it suitable for standing food containing acids in, for the same reason. But, particularly for such vital preparation processes as clarifying sugar, which has a very high boiling point, it was ideal. It was also used for handles of copper pans, and to reinforce copper vessels which were subjected to heat. It was rarely tinned when used for cooking pots, because the tin melted at a much lower temperature.

Silvered brass   A small range of articles made in fine cast brass were silvered to prevent the corrosive action of acids. Silver is reduced to a powder with the addition of various chemicals and then applied to the wetted brass surface and rubbed on in several coats. When the technique of silver-plating copper was perfected, it could not be used with brass because of the extreme difference in melting points of the two metals.

Direct fusion   In 1781 James Emerson discovered a method of making brass by direct fusion and the proportions of copper and zinc became fixed at 30% zince to 70% copper which still had some sheen to it. In France, brass for gilding was made with a more reddish colour and a higher copper content, but English gilt brass and ormolu seems to have been made with a yellower alloy. By the nineteenth century, as alloying and manufacturing techniques improved, it became the 'brassy' colour of Victorian ornament, except when old brass was melted down and re-used for casting.

BRONZE   Bronze is an alloy of copper and tin in varying ratios, but usually composed of 90 parts copper to 10 parts tin which gives bronze a redder colour than brass. Bronze is friable and cannot be worked in sheet form. It can only be cast and is a difficult metal to pour in its molten state. In England bronze casting was mainly confined to statues, busts and larger ornaments until the end of the eighteenth century when Matthew Boulton went into partnership with James Watt and set up the Birmingham Brass Company, making large numbers of bronze and brass articles. Bronze was not much used for domestic equipment until the nineteenth century, when it was used for making cast handles for copper stewpans, stockpots and shallow entrée dishes, largely for the fast-growing catering trade.

COPPER   Copper is a ubiquitous ore which has been smelted and used for all manner of domestic equipment since time immemorial. In England, however, where down-hearth cookery took place over uncontrolled heat, copper was not used in any but the grandest kitchens until the eighteenth century. On the Continent kitchens were equipped with flat brick-topped raised hearths and cooking took place over small charcoal fires or on braziers, where the heat could be controlled. In England copper was an unsuitable metal for cooking pots and pans until the eighteenth century and the advent of the enclosed cooking fire. Copper has a low melting point and bends and buckles if allowed to become too hot. It is rarely if ever found in cast form, but only in sheet, though the giant drip-pans of large kitchens were extremely thick and often contained a small amount of tin or lead.

Copper-mining in England Very little copper was mined in England in comparison with the rest of Europe until the end of the eighteenth century, because mining techniques were still relatively primitive and finance was lacking for such large enterprises. Because of England's unstable economic situation, copper was expensive to import. Until the discovery of the famous Parys Mine in Anglesea in 1768, copper utensils were largely reserved for the more wealthy classes and only small items such as bowls and ladles were made in any quantity. Once copper was cheap, however, many manor houses and country houses installed Continental brick-topped hearths for wood-burning cooking fires. In towns, where coal was in good supply, the first hob grates and early cast iron ranges replaced bar grate cooking fires. In both cases heat was controlled and copper pans could at last be used. Handles of copper saucepans and frying pans were made of brass, bronze or iron for strength and insulation. Some eighteenth century copper posnet saucepans had turned wood handles on an iron tail.

Iron heated quickly and became too hot to touch, but at the turn of the nineteenth century hollow iron handles which dispersed the heat were fitted into a copper neck on saucepans and frying pans. But they were cumbersome and tended to overbalance, and on the whole cast brass or bronze handles riveted to the pans were preferred. With the availability of cheap copper, scoops, dippers, jam pans, preserving pans and many other kitchens utensils became commonplace.

Design Most designs were strictly functional, and had no need for modification until changes occurred in the cooking fires and stoves. Identical utensils were made over a period of a hundred years from the 1760s to the 1860s with very minor changes. In 1840 M. Alexis Soyer equipped his revolutionary kitchens at the Reform Club and at Brighton Pavilion with a Continental-style *batterie de cuisine* manufactured in England. With virtually no alteration the same designs are being made in England today by manufacturers of catering equipment for hotel and restaurant kitchens.

Tinning Copper pots and pans are tinned in order to prevent poisons being released from the metal into the food. Tinning is an ancient art, practised by the Romans and the Greeks. A small billet of pure tin is melted directly in the pan to be tinned, and the molten metal is either swirled round or spread with a rough cloth over the inside surface. Because it has such a low melting point, however, tinning can be melted off if the pan is held over a high flame for any length of time. It can also be worn off with over-zealous scouring, in which case the pan must be retinned. Old-established manufacturers of kitchen equipment still use the same methods for tinning and retinning, but many modern copper pots and pans are electroplated or nickel-plated. Some are even made of copper-plated pressed steel – inside out, as it were.

Silvering and Sheffield Plate   Copper was also silvered for decorative and table ware. In 1742 Thomas Boulsover discovered a method of fusing a thin sheet of silver together with a thicker sheet of copper. It became known as 'Sheffield plate' and was used for making chocolate pots and coffee pots, among many other things. Such elegant articles were silvered inside instead of being tinned, the process being much the same. Many coffee and chocolate pots were made in copper and silvered inside – a luxury which was more economical than it might appear, for these pots were not subjected to a great degree of heat and the silvering, with much the same melting point as tin, did not melt off.

Electroplating   Electroplating copper with silver came into use on a commercial scale around 1840, and such was the vogue for it that many items of copper which dated from before that date were silvered by the ostentatious Victorians.

IRON   Cast iron   Iron ores vary considerably, depending on where they are mined. However, there are some generalisations which are helpful and concern the processes of smelting and working. Iron ore which is smelted with charcoal has a high carbon content and in this supersaturated form it is very ductile and easy to pour. Bar iron for forging with a high carbon content is easy to work, but it tends to become malleable when exposed to heat and therefore was not entirely suitable for items such as andirons which were subjected to constant contact with the fire. Articles made of cast iron withstand heat better, although they shatter easily on impact, leaving an almost crystalline break. When raw iron is heated to a sufficiently high temperature, much of the carbon can be removed and the resulting metal can be strengthened and tempered until, with all impurities removed, it becomes steel.

Pure high-carbon cast iron was used in England by Elizabethan ironmasters for firebacks, cannon, andirons, chenets and creepers, cooking pots, pot hooks and chimney and outdoor fittings. As casting and smelting techniques improved, cast iron was used for more elaborate work, such as door hinges and knobs, bell pulls, door knockers, latches and hinges, as well as the rough castings for much ornamental metalwork, whch was then worked and finished by hand. By the end of the eighteenth century cast iron was used extensively for frying pans and cooking pots, saucepans, grog pots, glue pots and spittoons. In the second half of the nineteenth century new methods of manufacture changed the whole cast iron industry, which began to make stamped, pressed or moulded hollow ware and ornamental ironwork from cast mild steel. In contrast to high-carbon cast iron, the forms and shapes into which this less malleable metal could be worked were more rigid than the early plastic examples of fine scrollwork and detail. This later work is recognisable from earlier pure cast iron work because it rusts and even when it has been cleaned still shows signs of pitting.

Wrought iron   The term 'wrought iron' properly applied should only be used for ingots or pigs of pure iron, but this terminology is generally considered archaic and the term 'wrought iron' in England is commonly applied to iron which has been forged and worked. Early wrought iron was smelted with charcoal and made into bars which were then forged and wrought in open hearths of charcoal which did not attain a very high temperature so that the metal retained a considerable amount of carbon. It is easily recognisable by the expert for its bloom and sheen and the fact that it does not rust. When high-carbon iron is repeatedly heated and forged, the carbon content is considerably reduced, so that in its final form it is a much harder, tougher metal. The more carbon that is removed, the less malleable the metal becomes.

Once Abraham Darby began to use coke on a commercial scale for smelting at Coalbrookdale in the late eighteenth century, much of the metal supplied to blacksmiths and forges in sheet, rod and bar was closer to steel in composition than pure cast iron. For this reason bar iron smelted with charcoal was imported from Russia and Sweden for a long time after English coke-fired furnaces successfully smelted iron for casting. In the 1780s problems with impurities in coal when smelting iron were overcome by John Wilkinson's blast furnaces and methods of 'puddling' to produce a strong, workable metal which feels less sympathetic to the touch and rusts more easily than coke-smelted iron. In 1851 Henry Bessemer discovered that crude iron could be smelted to remove most of the carbon content and the product of his new furnaces was a uniform quality of all-purpose mild steel. Confusingly, in America it is this metal which is known as 'wrought-iron' and not the supersaturated English metal. Between 1861 and 1865 William Siemens and the French Martin brothers discovered an improved method of smelting crude iron to remove the carbon content and reduce other impurities. This produced a metal which could accept a higher quantity of scrap than that produced by the Bessemer process. It was more ductile and poured more easily to make thinner castings – an ideal metal for the fast-growing hollow ware industry.

Differences between 'wrought-iron' and mild steel   To all intents and purposes, after the commercial application of the Bessemer and Siemens-Martin processes, all cast and worked iron was no longer pure iron but mild steel. Although this metal has obvious advantages in heavy industry, it was a far less amenable metal for blacksmiths and forges. It cannot be worked like soft supersaturated iron, because it is far less malleable and more rigid, even when heated. However, it was soon discovered that the original forms of worked 'wrought-iron' could be copied by casting mild steel in the new thinner castings. Virtually all ironwork of intricate design or variable thickness, from 'wrought-iron' gates to kitchen knives and cleavers, was cast in mild steel after 1865. Unlike pure iron, mild steel rusts and consequently many articles for domestic use were tinned or case-hardened. However, some pure iron in bar form was (and still is) imported from Sweden. As 'Best Crown Wrought', it is used by blacksmiths and metalworkers today – sometimes to reproduce old objects. With the revival of popularity for old-fashioned objects, many items such as ornate door furniture are made of black-enamelled cast aluminium.

Joins and welds   Early charcoal-smelted bar iron was wrought and joined or welded together by a fire weld – the two pieces of metal were simply heated and forged together. High-carbon iron is malleable and fuses easily. If necessary, a simple V-join was cut, or a stepped join, so that the two pieces of metal fitted roughly together before being heated. The former is known as a pug weld because the molten metal leaves a mark like a thumb print. the latter is a scarf weld. Scarf welds were used more and more frequently, as the iron became harder and less easy to fuse, at the end of the eighteenth century.

After 1860–65, when mild steel was in general use, new methods were needed for welding at a higher temperature. Fire welding was much more difficult with the newer, less tractable metal and 'wrought-iron' was joined by gas welding. The metal was simply joined edge to edge by heating with an oxyacetyline flame and the joint was brazed with molten steel, brass or bronze. The American terminology for this weld is a butt weld. Gas welding is still common in small forges where pieces of decorative metal are made. However, the blacksmith's hearth was soon fuelled with coke – which attained the high temperature necessary for welding mild steel – and fire welding was again possible, though because the metal was less ductile, pug welding was replaced by cleft welding. Before being forged, one piece of metal is split and the shaped second piece of metal is inserted into the 'open mouth' of the split piece before heating and forging to form the join.

A new technique of welding with an electric current was introduced at the beginning of this century. An electric current is made to arc or jump a small distance, thus creating a spark. A metal rod of flux is melted directly onto the metal to be joined, which has previously been shaped to take the 'filler'. The two pieces of metal are then forged.

Whereas gas welding is easy to detect because of its edge-to-edge technique, arc welding may look like fire welding to the uninitiated. The joint may be bumpy, and there may be traces of weld splatter around the joint which has not been cleaned off – particularly with right-angle joins. Weld splatter is quite distinctive from molten iron both in colour and texture – pure iron melts but does not run. On the other hand, where an arc weld has been painstakingly finished, the join may be suspiciously clean and free from millscale where it has been ground off. The faintly raised surface of an arc weld is the reverse of a fire weld which, if not perfect, tends to be infinitesimally concave where the two pieces of metal have fused together at the join. But these are only the most general indicators; the one test which is almost infallible is whether 'wrought-iron' bears any trace of pitting or roughness due to rust. Pure high-carbon wrought iron does not rust easily, if at all.

Riveting   Iron is often joined together with rivets or flat-headed nails. With pure wrought iron, the two pieces to be joined are punched and a separate rivet holds them together. Pure wrought iron rivets have a smudgy look and are seldom perfectly round, owing to the soft nature of the metal, unlike tenon heads or mild steel rivets. A common method of joining mild steel 'wrought-iron' is with a simple mortise and tenon joint similar to a carpenter's join. The tenons are shaped in a swage block, then fitted into a punched hole in the piece of metal to be joined. Finally, the tenons are hammered flat to resemble rivet heads. Pure iron rivets were used to join handles to copper ladles and saucepans; the smudgy shape of early rivets is easily distinguishable from the regular shape of later mild steel rivets. Brass rivets were also used, for joining handles and for scissor-joins on tools and rushlight holders where a more durable metal was necessary. Once forging was done at a higher temperature and gas welding techniques were common, scissor-joins were often riveted and then cleaned off so that no rivet head was visible. This technique was also used with fire welding on early high-carbon iron, though in the latter case the join is still faintly discernible because cleaning off was not so efficient.

LEAD AND ZINC   Both these metals were used as insulators for ice-boxes and for lining wooden wine coolers, though lead was more common until the turn of the nineteenth century when commercial methods of distilling pure zinc metal had been perfected and zinc manufactories were established in England and on the Continent.

PEWTER   Pewter originated in England, when the Romans combined Cornish tin with lead from the Mendip hills. It is an alloy of approximately 90% tin and 10% lead, and is an easy alloy to make, both components having a low melting point. However, the manufacture of pewter ceased when the Romans left Britain and was not revived until the end of the fourteenth century. By the sixteenth century almost every family possessed at least a few pewter spoons and perhaps a small salt for the table. In more wealthy households it became the custom to eat from pewter platters and display pewter objects of all kinds on buffetiers and dressers. Throughout the next two centuries pewter plates, tankards, dishes and chargers were increasingly made and used, until glazed 'delft' and pottery replaced it. The Victorians revived many traditional old shapes when fashion reflected a yearning for the romantic, and much of the pewter now found dates from that period.

Pewter collecting is fraught with dangers and pitfalls and a close study of the subject is essential, together with a knowledge of the 'touch marks' and their dates. Touch marks are the pewter equivalent of silver hallmarks and serve as a guide to dating.

Lead content   There was a keen awareness of the dangers of lead poisoning from earliest times, and by the eighteenth century there were three grades of pewter in common use: lay, trifle and plate. Lay often contained a high proportion of lead and was used for liquid and dry measures of all kinds. Plate contained up to 2% copper and could be polished to look like silver. Trifle contained no copper and was used for tankards and beer-drinking vessels. The powerful Pewterers Company secured the privilege of making all official liquid measures for beer, wine and spirits and for grain measures, when the rims were reinforced with brass to prevent the softer pewter metal from wearing out through constant friction.

Britannia Metal or 'hard pewter' In 1770 a Dutch version of lead-free pewter challenged the older, softer metal. It is known as 'hard pewter' or Britannia Metal and is an alloy of 90 parts tin, 8 parts antimony and 2 parts copper. Pewter and Britannia Metal dishes were used in the making of sugar confections and candies over a gentle fire, but it was not a suitable metal for more general use in the kitchen because of its low melting point. However, it was discovered that pewter was an excellent insulator and retained the cold, and it was used extensively for ice-cream moulds and confectionery moulds of all sorts from the end of the eighteenth century onwards.

SPELTER A term originally used for ingots of pure distilled zinc metal after 1781 and occasionally before that date for imported zinc metal and possibly also for billets of paktong, an alloy of copper, zinc and nickel imported from China. From the end of the nineteenth century and the beginning of the twentieth statuettes, light fittings and ornaments made of an almost pure cast zinc and finished to look like bronze or gilt metal were mass-produced. The term spelter is generally more commonly applied to these objects.

STEEL Steel is pure iron heated to remove the high carbon content and render the metal less liable to fracture. In earliest times this process was done in open hearths and the metal was heated repeatedly before the desired state of hardness and flexibility could be achieved. Birmingham and Sheffield were among the early centres for iron and steel in England, and both sites were originally used by the Romans. Unlike most centres of commerce and industry, which were sited near rivers or the sea to supply power and transport, early metal-working centres were built on hills in order to make the best use of wind currents to 'blow' the furnaces.

Steel-making was well-known throughout the Mediterranean, where it was brought to a high art by the Spaniards. The Spaniards in turn had learned the art of steel-making from the Moorish and Arab cultures and from as far east as Turkey, Asia and the Orient. Cutting blades of all sorts were made in Spain, as well as armour, often chased, inlaid or 'damascened' – an art which originated in Damascus.

Intricate locks and boxes, bits and buckles, horse harnesses, nails, tools and instruments were made to a high standard of craftsmanship in England in the fifteenth and sixteenth centuries. But until English metalworkers learned to smelt metals with coke and coal, only small objects could be made, and many English cutting tools were still made of case-hardened iron up to the middle of the seventeenth century. Knife blades in large quantities were imported into Sheffield from Solingen as blanks, and shaped and finished as 'Sheffield steel' right up to the end of the eighteenth century.

Case-hardening and tempering Iron blades were heated to a high temperature, giving the metal a hard outer skin akin to the 'blueing' on a gun barrel, which made it less liable to fracture or rust. The blades were also tempered –

the iron was heated, thrust into powdered carbon, cooled, heated again and then cooled. This imparted extra strength and flexibility to the metal. In general, however, the use of steel was confined to specialist trades until the second half of the eighteenth century, and even then Sheffield and other 'steel towns' continued to import bar iron from Russia and Sweden for making steel.

Cast steel After the Bessemer-Siemens-Martin processes (see under Iron) had changed the nature of iron to mild steel in the mid-nineteenth century, knives, choppers and all kinds of small domestic implements were cast in mild steel, then shaped and sharpened. Blades were cast with an integral 'shoulder', instead of being secured to the handle with a band of steel which held the metal tail between two plates or 'scales' of bone, ivory or wood.

Close-plating Flatware, scissors, spoons and early forks were close-plated during the seventeenth century. Tin was used as a flux to marry thin silver foil to steel, thus protecting it from rust, the great enemy of steel in damp climates. Close-plating went out of fashion in the eighteenth century with the advent of Sheffield Plate, but was revived for a short time in the 1800s, particularly for fish-knives, forks and slices, before being superseded by electroplating in the mid-nineteenth century.

Use of steel Articles which were exposed to constant and considerable heat, such as roasters and toasters, grills, griddles, gridirons and baking irons, flesh forks and fire tools were made of steel in increasing quantities after the English Civil War of 1642-49, when the art of steel-making greatly improved due to the work of the armourers and swordsmiths. Steel tools improved out of all recognition after 1701, when the wearing of swords except by gentlemen was declared illegal and swordsmiths began to make domestic and garden tools and implements.

TINPLATE Thin sheets of iron coated with tin to prevent rust and corrosion. The method was pioneered by John Hanbury in 1720 at his iron works at Pontypool, where the iron plates were hammered into thin sheets and brushed with molten tin.

Pontypool Objects made of tinplate and then painted with black enamel and decorated with designs in bright colours are sometimes referred to as 'Pontypool'. In 1728 John Payne of Bridgwater, near Bristol, took out a patent for rolling heated plates of iron into sheet and that same year John Hanbury began using the same method for manufacturing tinplate. By 1750 there was a large tinplate works at Kidwelly and by 1850 out of 35 tinplate works in Britain, 22 were in Wales.

Japanning In its early years, tinplate was used for tableware and decorative metalwork, being painted and then japanned or enamelled. The quality of this work varies enormously, but some of the fine pierced basketwork of trays and cake baskets is of a very high standard and is much sought-after. Coal boxes and plate warmers were frequently made in japanned tinplate, as well as more humble everyday objects. Tinplate was widely used for making hoops and traps from the mid-eighteenth century.

Stamped tinplate   Once sheet metal could be raised and stamped mechanically in one operation, at the end of the eighteenth century, biscuit cutters, patty pans and all manner of baking and cooking equipment was made from tinplate. Inevitably though, the tinning wore off with constant exposure to heat, and then the sheet iron was exposed and rusted quickly. Edges and joins of tinplate were rolled, often with an iron wire core for extra strength.

Hot dip tinning   In the second half of the nineteenth century, when mild steel replaced sheet iron, the 'hot dip' method of tinning was used. Sheets of metal were coated by passing them through a bath of molten tin. This was the metal used by Bryan Donkin at the Dartford Iron Works for making containers for vacuum-canning meat and fruit. From the 1930s onwards the electrolytic process was applied to tinplate, producing a thinner coating of tin and making it possible to manufacture fine-gauge tinplate and to coat articles of uneven or irregular shape evenly.

TOLEWARE   Properly speaking, this term should only be used for articles made of sheet tin, decorated or plain. It is primarily an American term and today it is generally applied to all tinware, whether of sheet tin or tinplate, in the USA. In recent years the description has been creeping into the specialist dealers' vocabulary in this country, where it is often applied at random to anything from rare sheet tin candlesticks to recently made highly-coloured bargeware.

POTTERY   Until the eighteenth century the only pottery which was used extensively in the kitchen was the cruder kind of crock and cooking pot, often glazed on the inside only, and white glazed pottery for mousse and jelly moulds.

Glazes   The earliest form of glazing was obtained by throwing a shovelful of salt into the firing kiln at high temperature. The composition of the salt divides, with the sodium combining with the silica in clay to form a vitreous coating while the chlorine escapes as a gas.

Smear glaze   Early glazing was uneven and often streaky, and is often known as 'smear glaze'.

Lead glaze   The traditional 'green glaze' of Tudor pottery was obtained by adding powdered red lead to the salt. In the firing, copper oxide was released to produce an unevenly-deposited greenish-yellow glaze.

Salt glaze   A more controlled technique of glazing, developed by John Dwight of Fulham in 1671, using rock salt which, when thrown into the kiln, volatilised, combining with minerals in the clay to produce a pitted look, like orange peel, because of the distribution of silica in the clay. Later, pots were fired once, rubbed with a strong salt mixture on the inside surface and then fired again to achieve a more even, colourless glaze. Saltglaze pottery was fragile and not ideal for kitchen use, though thicker, moulded saltglaze pottery was used for making meat moulds and jelly moulds. They are much lighter in weight than later stoneware moulds and relatively rare because of their fragility.

Slip glaze, slipware   White clay, found mainly in Dorset and Devon, was mixed to an emulsion with water and trailed like icing sugar over the surface of once-fired pottery. It was then returned to the kiln and saltglazed so that the decoration was fired into the glaze. Decorative motifs were primitive, and included trailed, combed and crisscross patterns. Jugs and pitchers, serving dishes and pie plates were made in slipglazed pottery.

Stoneware   With the addition of crushed stone or flint, the old porous earthenware was fired at a higher temperature to produce a harder, non-porous pottery, of which brown stoneware was probably the most common in kitchens, a result of the clay burning in the kiln to a colour ranging from a dirty yellow to a dark brown.

White stoneware   Developed around 1730 in Staffordshire, using crushed flint and a whiter clay to produce a dull, cream-coloured pottery, which was then saltglazed. In its undecorated state, it is often referred to as 'saltglaze stoneware' but a thicker, tougher stoneware was later developed by Josiah Wedgwood, dipped in a solution of slip and fired to produce the famous 'Queen's ware' which the Wedgwood potteries were making from 1759.

Piecrust ware   Developed in the 1790s when the Napoleonic Wars brought shortages of all kinds to Britain and a heavy flour tax was imposed, preventing pie and pastry-making because of the prohibitive cost of flour. Josiah Wedgwood produced a range of vitrified stoneware 'crock pies' as a substitute for the elaborate pastry cases of the period, in unglazed biscuit-coloured stoneware. This was later imitated, in the 1830s, in a cruder ironstone which, though less decorative, could withstand the heat of an oven.

Ovenware   Wedgwood improved on the original crock pie concept in the 1850s by producing a range of ovenproof glazed stoneware pie dishes designed to fit under the ornamental piecrust cover. This was the first ovenproof crockery produced for the kitchen, from which the full range of pie dishes evolved.

Bibliography

BRAUDEL, FERNAND *The Structures of Everyday Life* (Collins, 1981).

CHURCH, R.A. *Kenricks in Hardware* (David & Charles, 1968).

DE HAAN, DAVID *Antique Household Gadgets and Appliances* (Blandford, 1977).

FRANKLIN, LINDA CAMPBELL *From Hearth to Cookstove* (House of Collectibles, 1978).

GENTLE, RUPERT and FEILD, RACHAEL *English Domestic Brass* (Elek, 1975).

GOULD, MARY EARLE *Antique Tin and Tole Ware* (Tuttle, Rutland, Vermont, 1958).

HARRISON, MOLLY *The Kitchen in History* (Osprey, 1972).

HARTLEY, DOROTHY *Food in England* (Macdonald, 1975).

HARTLEY, DOROTHY *The Land of England* (Macdonald, 1979).

LAND, PETER *The Industrial Revolution* (Weidenfeld & Nicholson, 1978).

LINDSAY, SEYMOUR *Iron and Brass Implements of the English House* (Tiranti, 1970).

NORWAK, MARY *Kitchen Antiques* (Ward Lock, 1975).

PERRY, EVAN *Collecting Antique Metalware* (Country Life Books, 1974).

PULLAR, PHILIPPA *Consuming Passions* (Hamish Hamilton, 1970).

STERNER, GABRIELE *Pewter through 500 years* (Studio Vista, 1980).

TANNAHILL, REAY *Food in History* (Eyre Methuen, 1973).

WILLS, GEOFFREY *The Book of Copper and Brass* (Country Life Books, 1968).

WILSON, C. ANNE *Food and Drink in Britain* (Constable, 1973).

References

N.B. Publisher and date of publication are only given the first time a work is mentioned.

1	*The Industrial Revolution*, Peter Lane (Weidenfeld & Nicholson, 1978).
2	Christopher Bankes, unpublished MS.
3	*Festive Fare and Tableware in Early America*, Louis C. Belden (Colonial Williamsburg Museum MS).
4	*Food in History*, Reay Tannahill (Eyre Methuen, 1973).
5–8	Christopher Bankes, unpublished MS.
9	*Food in England*, Dorothy Hartley (Macdonald, 1975).
10	*The Land of England*, Dorothy Hartley (Macdonald, 1979).
11	*The Compleat Cook*, Rebecca Price. Introduced by Madeleine Masson. (Routledge & Kegan Paul, 1974).
12–13	*Food and Drink in Britain*, C. Anne Wilson (Constable, 1973).
14	Christopher Bankes, unpublished MS.
15	Courtesy of the Henry Francis du Pont Winterthur Museum Library, Winterthur, Delaware, USA.
16	*The Land of England*, Dorothy Hartley.
17	*A History of Everyday Things in England*, M. and C.H.B. Quennell (Sixth Edition, Batsford, 1961).
18	*English Social History*, G.M. Trevelyan (Longman, 1942; Penguin, 1967).
19	*The Land of England*, Dorothy Hartley.
20	*The Industrial Revolution*, Peter Lane.
21	*Food in England*, Dorothy Hartley.
22–23	Courtesy Winterthur Museum Library.
24	*A History of Everyday England*, M. and C.H.B. Quennell.
25	Courtesy Winterthur Museum Library.
26	*Food and Drink in Britain*, C. Anne Wilson.
27	*England and the Salt Trade*, Markham Bridbury, quoted in *Food and Drink in Britain*, C. Anne Wilson.
28	*A History of Everyday England*, M. and C.H.B. Quennell.
29	*English Social History*, G.M. Trevelyan.
30	*Food and Drink in Britain*, C. Anne Wilson.
31	*English Social History*, G.M. Trevelyan.
32	*Food and Drink in Britain*, C. Anne Wilson.
33	*The Compleat Cook*, Rebecca Price.
34	Pine Grove Accounts, Courtesy Winterthur Museum Library.
35	Courtesy Winterthur Museum Library.
36	*Kenricks in Hardware*, R.A. Church (David & Charles, 1968).
37	Christopher Bankes, unpublished MS.
38	*The Ladies New Book of Cookery*, Sarah Josepha Hale.
39	*Food and Drink in Britain*, C. Anne Wilson.
40	*Kenricks in Hardware*, R.A. Church.

41   M. Martin, 'A description of the Western Isles of Scotland *circa* 1695' and 'A Late Voyage to St Kilda' (ed. D.J. Macleod, Stirling, 1934), from *Food and Drink in Britain*, C. Anne Wilson.

42   H.E. Salter, 'The Assize of bread and ale 1309–1351' (Oxford Historical Society, 1919), from *Food and Drink in England*, C. Anne Wilson.

43–45 *Two Fifteenth Century Cookery Books* (Harlean MSS), from *Food and Drink in Britain*, C. Anne Wilson.

46   John Evelyn.

47–48 Christopher Bankes, unpublished MS.

49   Courtesy Winterthur Museum Library.

50   *The Land of England*, Dorothy Hartley.

51–53 *Food and Drink in Britain*, C. Anne Wilson.

54   *The Land of England*, Dorothy Hartley.

55–56 Christopher Bankes, unpublished MS.

57–58 J. Murrel, 'A new Boke of Cookerie' (1617), from *Food and Drink in Britain*, C. Anne Wilson.

59–60 Christopher Bankes, unpublished MS.

61   *The Last Bourbons of Naples*, Harold Acton (Methuen, 1961).

62   *Seven Centuries of English Cooking*, Maxine McKendry (Weidenfeld & Nicholson, 1973).

63   *English Social History*, G.M. Trevelyan.

64   *Food and Drink in Britain*, C. Anne Wilson.

65–66 Christopher Bankes, unpublished MS.

67   *Larousse Gastronomique*.

68   Henry Russell's 'Boke of Nurture', in *Early English Means and Manners* (ed. J. Furnivall, Early English Text Society, 1868), quoted in *A History of Everyday England*, M. and C.H.B. Quennell.

69   From *A Fifteenth Century Courtesy Book* (ed. R.W. Chambers, 1914), quoted in *Occupational Costume in England*, Phillis Cunnington and Catherine Lucas (A. & C. Black, 1967).

70   *Food in History*, Reay Tannahill.

71   *Seven Centuries of English Cooking*, Maxine McKendry.

72–73 From *A Fifteenth Century Courtesy Book* (ed. R.W. Chambers, 1914), quoted in *Occupational Costume in England*, Cunnington and Lucas.

74   Daniel Defoe, *Every Body's Business* (1725), quoted in *Occupational Costume in England*, Cunnington and Lucas.

75   *The China Trade*, Carl L. Crossman (The Pyne Press, Princeton, 1972).

76   *English Social History*, G.M. Trevelyan.

77   John Evelyn, *Acetaria* (1699).

78–84 Christopher Bankes, unpublished MS.

85   Samuel Timmins, quoted in *Kenricks in Hardware*, R.A. Church.

Index